高校英语选修课系列教材

许建平 编著

英汉互译入门教程（第二版）

An Introduction to English-Chinese
and Chinese-English Translation

(2ND EDITION)

清华大学出版社
北京

内容简介

本教程以句子翻译为讲解和训练单位，分门别类讲解了包括遣词用字、词类转换、句子成分转换增添、省略、结构调整、各类从句、语态转换、正反调换等翻译方法技巧，并就翻译的标准与直译意译问题、专有名词的翻译、翻译中的"陷阱"等问题做了探讨。为方便读者自学，教程各单元配有适当的英汉互译练习及参考答案和解析，帮助读者切实掌握各类常用技巧。另外，本书还结合教育部颁布的《大学英语课程教学要求》和最新的考试改革趋势，简要分析了四、六级考试中翻译部分的命题模式及解题技巧。

本书读者对象：大学低年级学生、高职类院校学生和具有高中以上英语水平的社会自学者。

版权所有，侵权必究。举报：010-62782989，beiqinquan@tup.tsinghua.edu.cn。

图书在版编目（CIP）数据

英汉互译入门教程 / 许建平编著. —2版. —北京：清华大学出版社，2015（2023.8重印）
（高校英语选修课系列教材）
ISBN 978-7-302-39784-7

Ⅰ. ①英… Ⅱ. ①许… Ⅲ. ①英语–翻译–高等学校–教材 Ⅳ. ①H315.9

中国版本图书馆CIP数据核字（2015）第077171号

责任编辑：刘细珍
封面设计：常雪影
责任校对：王凤芝
责任印制：杨 艳

出版发行：清华大学出版社
网　　址：http://www.tup.com.cn, http://www.wqbook.com
地　　址：北京清华大学学研大厦A座　　邮　编：100084
社 总 机：010-83470000　　邮　购：010-62786544
投稿与读者服务：010-62776969, c-service@tup.tsinghua.edu.cn
质量反馈：010-62772015, zhiliang@tup.tsinghua.edu.cn

印 装 者：三河市东方印刷有限公司
经　　销：全国新华书店
开　　本：170mm×230mm　　印　张：19.25　　字　数：310千字
版　　次：2009年7月第1版　　2015年5月第2版　　印　次：2023年8月第11次印刷
定　　价：66.00元

产品编号：061489-05

第二版前言

《英汉互译入门教程》自 2009 年出版发行以来,转眼间 5 年过去了。这期间,国内英语教学改革紧锣密鼓,力度加大,跨入了一个新的历史时期:高考英语有了新的改革方案,不再全国统考、一锤定音;大学英语加强了对翻译的重视,从 2013 年 12 月起,四、六级的翻译部分由原单句汉译英调整为段落汉译英,分值比重由以前的 5% 提高到 15%。

为了跟上并适应外语教学与考试的新形势,我们对《英汉互译入门教程》做了适当的调整和修订,形成了目前的《英汉互译入门教程(第二版)》,其主要修订内容如下。

1. 修订了各单元的讲解内容和方案,增添、更换、精简了其中的一些例句和练习,每单元后面的英译汉、汉译英翻译练习统一为 12 个例句;

2. 对原 13 个单元的内容做了适当的调整、补充、完善,将原第十二单元"避开翻译中的'陷阱'"替换为"谨防'假朋友'的陷阱",并增补了"英语中的常见'假朋友'";

3. 删除了原附录一、附录二;将附录一"《大学英语课程教学要求》与四、六级翻译考试"替换为第十四单元"《大学英语课程教学要求》与四、六级翻译考试",并为各单元翻译练习提供了详尽的参考译文及解析;

4. 配合大学英语四、六级翻译考试的变化,加大了第十四单元翻译练习的力度。按大学英语四、六级翻译考试大纲规定的"内容涉及中国的历史、文化、经济、社会发展"的思路,编写了配套的汉译英段落翻译练习 30 篇;在保留原

I

书翻译模拟题的基础上，新添加了 2014 年 6 月前四、六级统考的翻译考试内容，将其整合为单句翻译练习 120 题和段落翻译练习 30 篇。无论是段落翻译还是单句翻译，均为读者提供了详尽的参考译文及考点分析。

编著者
2015 年 1 月于清华大学荷清苑

第一版前言

翻译使中国融入世界，也使世界走近中国。随着北京奥运会和上海世博会的相继成功举办，中国与外界的交流日趋频繁，开放的中国需要越来越多的翻译专业人才，而外语院校的翻译专业远远不能满足社会的需要。因此，沟通不同语言文化、促进对外交流这一重任便历史性地落到了新世纪年轻一代的肩上。

然而翻译并不像很多人想象的那样，英语学好了，词汇量上去了，自然而然也就无师自通。只要亲手动动笔我们就不难发现，翻译并非简单的文字词汇互换，它所涉及的包括语言结构、思维模式、风俗习惯、社会文化、传播媒介等方方面面的知识，需要使用恰当的翻译技巧、方法才能准确通顺地将一种语言文字转换成另一种文字。正是出于上述考虑，我们配合业已出版的《英汉互译实践与技巧》，编写了这本《英汉互译入门教程》，旨在为读者提供必要的翻译入门知识和初步的英汉互译技巧训练。

《英汉互译入门教程》以句子翻译为讲解训练基本单位，英译汉、汉译英并行。英译汉译例多出自大家熟悉的统编高中教材、大学英语低年级阅读材料；汉译英则着眼于英汉句式结构对比与表达差异。通过英汉比较对照，对各种翻译方法技巧进行详细讲解。考虑到绝大多数院校在大学英语阶段没有条件开设翻译课，我们在内容编排上尽量浅显易懂，循序渐进，以利于读者自学。每一单元后面均配以与该单元主题密切相关的英汉互译练习，使学习者深入浅出，举一反三，潜移默化地将学到的翻译知识灵活地用于实践。

《英汉互译入门教程》全书安排为 13 个相互衔接的单元节。第一单元为引言，

英汉互译入门教程（第二版）
An Introduction to English-Chinese and Chinese-English Translation (Second Edition)

通过国内外若干翻译问题说明翻译的重要性，扼要介绍翻译知识的范畴和翻译方法技巧的分类；第二单元到第九单元就具体的翻译技巧方法做了详细的介绍和讲解，包括遣词用字、词类转换、句子成分转换、增添、省略、结构调整、各类从句、语态转换、正反调换等翻译方法技巧；第十单元到第十二单元就翻译的标准与直译、意译问题、专有名词的翻译、翻译中的"陷阱"等问题做了详细的探讨；第十三单元就如何培养与提高翻译能力做了综述，分别从语法词汇功底、分析判断能力、语言表达能力等方面提出作为一个合格的翻译工作者应具备的素质，旨在为翻译入门后的进一步深造指明方向。

十三单元之后是两个附录。附录一结合《大学英语课程教学要求》，介绍了大学英语四、六级考试中翻译题型命题模式及解题方法步骤，并对近几年四、六级考试中全部翻译试题内容逐一做了分析讲评，提供了翻译模拟试题；附录二为1—13单元的翻译练习参考译文及答案详解、分析，对每单元的英汉互译练习不但给出准确的参考译文，而且尽可能详尽地加以注释、分析、提示，以便读者自学。

《英汉互译入门教程》的读者对象为具有高中以上英语基础的高中毕业生、大学低年级学生，亦可供具有同等英语水平的社会读者学习使用。

编著者
2009 年 7 月

目 录

第一单元　翻译知识与翻译技巧
  一、从肯德基的一则海报谈起 1
  二、翻译的重要作用 3
  三、翻译知识与翻译方法技巧 7
  思考与练习 8

第二单元　遣词用字与词义判定
  一、遣词用字与词典的关系 11
  二、遣词用字与上下文语境 12
  三、英汉词字的对应关系 15
    1. 完全对等 15
    2. 部分对等 16
    3. 无对等词 17
  四、英译汉词义判定三依据 18
    1. 依据构词法确定词义 18
    2. 依据上下文语境或词语搭配确定词义 19
    3. 依据不同学科或专业类型确定词义 22
  五、汉译英的遣词用字 23
  思考与练习 28

第三单元　词类转换与句子成分转换
  一、英语的词类和句子成分 30
  二、汉语的词类和句子成分 32
  三、英译汉的词类转换 33
    1. 各种词类转换成动词 34
    2. 各种词类转换成名词 35

3. 各种词类转换成形容词 ·· 36
  4. 各种词类转换成副词 ·· 36
 四、英译汉的句子成分转换 ·· 37
 五、汉译英的词类转换 ·· 39
  1. 动词转换成名词、介词、形容词、副词等 ························· 40
  2. 其他一些词类之间的转换 ··· 40
 六、汉译英的句子成分转换 ·· 41
 思考与练习 ·· 42

第四单元　增添技巧的运用

 一、英译汉增添技巧的运用 ·· 44
  1. 增添原文所省略的词语 ·· 45
  2. 增添必要的连接词语 ·· 45
  3. 表达出原文的复数概念 ·· 46
  4. 把抽象概念表达清楚 ·· 46
  5. 逻辑性增词 ··· 46
  6. 修辞性增词 ··· 47
  7. 重复性增词 ··· 47
 二、汉译英增添技巧的运用 ·· 48
  1. 增添必要的代词 ·· 48
  2. 增添必要的冠词 ·· 49
  3. 增添必要的介词、连词 ·· 49
  4. 增添必要的动词 ·· 50
  5. 增添必要的解释性词语 ·· 50
 思考与练习 ·· 51

第五单元　省略技巧的运用

 一、英译汉省略技巧的运用 ·· 53
  1. 冗余词语的省略 ·· 53
  2. 代词的省略 ··· 54
  3. 冠词的省略 ··· 54
  4. 介词、连词的省略 ··· 55
  5. 动词的省略 ··· 56
  6. 非人称代词"it"的省略 ··· 56
 二、汉译英省略技巧的运用 ·· 57
  1. 省略宾语 ·· 57

		2. 省略不必要的赘言 58
		3. 省略概念范畴类词语 58
		4. 省略过详的细节描述 59
	思考与练习 60

第六单元　句式结构调整

	一、英译汉的结构调整 63
		1. 原序法 64
		2. 逆序法 65
		3. 时序法／逻辑序法 65
		4. 拆分法／拆解法 66
		5. 重组法 66
	二、汉译英的结构调整 67
		1. 定语的结构调整 68
		2. 状语的结构调整 69
	思考与练习 70

第七单元　各类从句的翻译技巧

	一、英语各类从句的翻译技巧 72
		1. 英语名词性从句的翻译方法 72
		2. 英语定语从句的翻译方法 74
		3. 英语状语从句的翻译方法 78
	二、汉语复句的翻译技巧 79
		1. 分清主次关系，添加连接词语 79
		2. 将汉语的复句简化为单句 80
		3. 合并零散短句 80
		4. 使用无生命的名词充当役使主语 81
	思考与练习 81

第八单元　被动语态的翻译技巧

	一、英语被动语态的一般处理方法 85
		1. 直接去掉"被"字 86
		2. 主语和宾语相互对调 86
		3. 将状语译为主语 86
		4. 译为系表结构 87
		5. 译为"由……+动词"结构 87

6. 增添适当主语 88
  7. 译为无主句 88
  8. 保持原文的被动结构 89
  9. 采用其他手段替换 89
 二、汉译英被动结构的翻译 90
  1. 带有被动标签的结构 90
  2. 不带被动标签的结构 92
  3. 汉语主动结构转为英语被动 93
  4. 汉语一些习惯用语的被动译法 95
思考与练习 96

第九单元 翻译中的正反调换

 一、英译汉的正反调换 99
  1. 英语肯定，汉语译作否定 99
  2. 英语否定，汉语译作肯定 101
  3. 同一词语，肯定否定均可 102
  4. 双重否定与委婉肯定 103
  5. 否定的陷阱 105
 二、汉译英的正反调换 108
  1. 汉译英正反调换的一般情况 108
  2. 汉语肯定，英语译作否定 109
  3. 汉语否定，英语译作肯定 110
  4. 汉语四字成语的反说正译 111
思考与练习 112

第十单元 翻译的标准与直译、意译问题

 一、"信、达、雅"翻译标准 114
 二、忠实与通顺的翻译标准 116
 三、翻译实例分析讲解 116
 四、直译与意译 119
思考与练习 122

第十一单元 专有名词的翻译问题

 一、英语专有名词的翻译方法 126
  1. 音译法 126

    2. 直 / 意译法 126
    3. 混合式 126
  二、汉语地名的翻译方法 127
    1. 一般专名加通名构成汉语地名的翻译方法 127
    2. 由单字专名加通名构成汉语地名 127
    3. 通名专名化的英译法 128
    4. 通名为同一个汉字的多种不同译法 128
    5. 通名为不同汉字的同一种译法 129
  三、中文地址的翻译方法 130
  四、汉语拼音与韦氏拼法 131
  思考与练习 132

第十二单元　谨防"假朋友"的陷阱

  一、切忌"望文生义" 134
  二、学会比较对照 137
  三、当心"异常"结构 140
    1. 冠词 140
    2. 介词 140
    3. 名词的单复数 141
    4. 名词的大小写 142
    5. 其他搭配 142
  四、语音歧义、词汇歧义和语法歧义 143
    1. 语音歧义 143
    2. 词汇歧义 143
    3. 语法歧义 144
  思考与练习 144

第十三单元　翻译能力的培养与提高

  一、扎实的词汇语法功底 148
    1. 把握词语的搭配意义 148
    2. 利用构词法扩大词汇量 150
  二、敏锐的分析判断能力 152
    1. 词类鉴别分析 152
    2. 时态语态分析 153
    3. 上下文语境分析 154
    4. 逻辑分析 157

三、通顺的语言表达能力 158
  1. 避免生硬晦涩 158
  2. 克服母语影响 160
四、不懈的翻译实践 163
思考与练习 164

第十四单元　《大学英语教学指南》与四、六级翻译考试

一、《大学英语教学指南》对翻译的要求 166
二、四、六级翻译考试真题详解 168
  1. 四级翻译考试真题详解 168
   2013 年 12 月英语四级翻译 168
   2014 年 6 月英语四级翻译 171
  2. 六级翻译考试真题详解 174
   2013 年 12 月英语六级翻译 174
   2014 年 6 月英语六级翻译 178
三、四、六级翻译考试备考思考题与训练 182
  1. 思考题 183
  2. 翻译备考训练 183
   单句翻译练习 120 句 183
   段落翻译练习 30 篇 188

附　录　各单元翻译练习参考译文及解析

第一单元　翻译知识与翻译技巧 196
第二单元　遣词用字与词义判定 198
第三单元　词类转换与句子成分转换 202
第四单元　增添技巧的运用 204
第五单元　省略技巧的运用 206
第六单元　句式结构调整 209
第七单元　各类从句的翻译技巧 212
第八单元　被动语态的翻译技巧 217
第九单元　翻译中的正反调换 220
第十单元　翻译的标准与直译、意译问题 223
第十一单元　专有名词的翻译问题 227
第十二单元　谨防"假朋友"的陷阱 231
第十三单元　翻译能力的培养与提高 234
第十四单元　《大学英语教学指南》与四、六级翻译考试 237

第一单元
翻译知识与翻译技巧

一、从肯德基的一则海报谈起

翻译是外语学习中一个不可或缺的重要技能。从中小学到大学，乃至研究生，只要学外语，就少不了会有翻译练习和考试。可是不少人学了数年甚至十几年外语，翻译也始终未能入门，一旦动手翻译就显得力不从心。也有人对此不以为然，认为翻译没什么大不了的：有什么不懂的地方，查一查字典不就行了？可实际问题往往并非想象的那么容易——词典所给出的释义未必就那么管用。请看这样一例：WE DO CHICKEN RIGHT！

这是肯德基炸鸡（KFC）店里挂的一则海报，这句话中的每一个单词连小学生都看得懂，但要翻译成恰当的汉语就比较棘手了。简简单单4个英语单词的一句话，据说竟然出现了十几种不同的汉语译文，例如：

1. 我们做鸡是对的。
2. 我们做鸡有理！
3. 我们可以做鸡，对吧！
4. 我们只做右边的鸡。
5. 我们从右边做鸡。
6. 我们做鸡做得很正确。
7. 我们用正确的方法做鸡。
8. 我们用的鸡才是正宗。
9. 我们行使了鸡的权利。
10. 我们有做鸡的权利。
11. 我们有做鸡肉的权利。
12. 我们要维护鸡的权利！
13. 我们公正地做鸡！
14. 我们知道鸡是对的。
15. 我们的材料是正宗的鸡肉！
……

不难看出，以上各译文中除了代词 WE（我们）和名词 CHICKEN（鸡）两个词的译法比较一致外，对 DO 和 RIGHT 的理解和表达都相差悬殊，因此译文不着边际，一塌糊涂。

为什么会造成上述各种荒唐可笑的翻译结果呢？显而易见，问题的关键在于译者对 DO 和 RIGHT 两个词的不同理解。查阅一下词典我们知道，DO 光是作及物动词的意义便有以下十余种：

做，实行，尽力，给予，忙于，制作，扮演，模仿，引起，产生，使出，表现，整理，算出，解答……

RIGHT 的意义就更可观了。作名词的意义有：正义，公正，正确，权利，右边，右派……；作形容词的意义有：正当的，正确的，对的，合适的，恰当的，健康的，健全的，正面的……；作副词的意义有：正当地，正确地，一直地，直接地，完全地，彻底地，在右边……；作动词的意义有：扶直，使端正，整理，整顿，纠正，补偿，修补，赔偿，弥补……

WE DO CHICKEN RIGHT 这句话究竟应当怎样翻译？我们可以结合肯德基炸鸡快餐连锁店的实际情况来考虑：既然与鸡的烹饪有关，DO 与 CHICKEN 的搭配意思必然是"炸鸡"无疑；而 RIGHT 一词根据语法分析，此处为副词，意思是"正好"、"恰当地"、"恰到好处地"，与"正义、公正、正确、权利、右边、对的、直立的、健全的"等意思都毫不沾边。因此这句话我们不妨译作：

我们的炸鸡棒极了！或：我们的鸡炸得恰到好处！

由此可见，翻译并不像很多人想象的那么简单。正如英国著名文艺批评家理查兹（I. A. Richards）所说的那样："翻译很可能是整个宇宙进化过程中迄今为止最复杂的一种活动。"鲁迅先生谈到翻译，也不无感慨地说："我向来总以为翻译比创作容易，因为至少是无需构思。但到真的一译，就会遇到难关，譬如一个名词或动词，写不出，创作时可以回避，翻译上可不成，也还得想，一直弄到头昏眼花，好像在脑子里面摸一个急于要开箱子的钥匙，却没有。"

二、翻译的重要作用

翻译作为一种语言文化交流手段，起着沟通世界各国人民思想，促进政治、经济、文化、教育、科技交流的重要作用。正如季羡林先生所指出的那样："在人类历史发展的长河中，在世界多元文化的交流、融会与碰撞中，在中华民族伟大复兴的进程中，翻译始终都起着不可或缺的先导作用。"

好的翻译准确精当、传神达意，对沟通思想、扫清语言障碍起着积极促进的作用，如：club（俱乐部）、humor（幽默）、Coca-Cola（可口可乐）、hacker（黑客）、blog（博客）等，这类翻译音意兼顾，朗朗上口，因而能深入人心，成为大家普遍认可的定译。另一方面，一些翻译从一开始就不到位，因而留下了原本可以避免的遗憾。最典型的两例便是英语中的 dragon 和 renaissance 的翻译问题。dragon 一词的英语解释是：a mythical monster traditionally represented as a gigantic reptile having a lion's claws, the tail of a serpent, wings, and a scaly skin（一种传说中的怪物，一般被描述成有狮爪、蛇尾、翅膀及鳞状外皮的巨型爬行动物）。在西方，dragon 通常被认为是邪恶的象征，是凶残肆虐的怪物。在一些描写圣徒和

Saint George and the Dragon

This painting by Italian Renaissance artist Paolo Uccello depicts the 4th-century Christian Saint George rescuing a princess as he killed a dragon that had been terrorizing a city. Painted about 1460, *Saint George and the Dragon* is in the National Gallery in London, England.

（《圣乔治与Dragon》由意大利文艺复兴时期的画家Paolo Uccello所画。画中描述的是基督徒圣乔治杀死Dragon，救出公主，解除了全城人民的长期恐怖。此画创作于约1460年，现收藏于英国伦敦国家美术馆。）

英雄的传说中讲到和dragon作斗争的事迹，多以这种怪物被杀为结局。而我们的翻译家却将这么狰狞可怖的一种怪物译作"龙"，与中国传统的"龙"的概念大相径庭。看看下面这幅油画及其文字说明我们就不难理解dragon在西方读者心目中的形象了。

再如renaissance一词，其英语解释是：The humanistic revival of classical art, architecture, literature, and learning that originated in Italy in the 14th century and later spread throughout Europe（古典艺术、建筑、文学和学识的人文主义复兴，起源于14世纪的意大利，后来蔓延到整个欧洲）。覆盖面如此之广、影响范围如此之大的 renaissance，却被轻描淡写地译作"文艺复兴"，大大缩小了其范围和影响。

翻译中的类似问题，轻者会造成误会，如：menu 菜单（容易误导），laser 镭射（名不副实），nylon 尼龙（读写不一）；重者则会酿成灾难性的严重后果。众所周知的两个国际政治事件，就与翻译的失当不无相关。一是"二战"期间日本政府对英美联军敦促投降的《波茨坦公告》的表态，日方的答复用了 mokasutu 一词，写成汉字为"默殺"，其含义有二：①"高明地不表态"（keep silent sophisticatedly）；②"不理睬，蔑视"（ignore, despise）。译员将其理解为后者，由此导致了广岛、长崎的灭顶之灾，遭受了原子弹轰炸。二是关于阿以争端的领土问题。联合国242号决议要求以色列 withdrawal from occupied territories（从所占阿拉伯领土撤出）；译成法语之后成了 le retrait des territoires occupés（法语 des territoires 近似英语的 the all territories，即"从所占领的一切领土撤出"）。以色列执行的是英语文件，而阿拉伯世界却坚持只接受法语文件，由此造成了长期的国际争端。

汉译英的种种问题也不容忽视。无论是日常生活、工作，还是人际往来、社交活动，都不时会听到由于翻译失误造成的种种笑话：将客套话"哪里，哪里"译作 where, where；将"白酒"译作 white wine（白葡萄酒）；将"教师休息室（lounge）"译作 Teacher's restroom（公用厕所，洗手间）；将"望子成龙"译作 Hope the son to be a dragon 等等。一些公示语翻译所暴露出的问题更是到了令人触目惊心的地步。

据报道，某市国际机场的紧急出口上"平时禁止入内"（No entry at ordinary times）的告示牌，英文却写成 No entry on peacetime（和平时期禁止入内）。某市的交通要道上，一块警告行人"注意安全，小心路滑"（Look out! Slippery Ground!）的牌子，被翻译成 To Take Notice of Safe; The Slippery are Very Crafty（要注意保险箱；滑动的东西非常狡猾）。北京的中华民族园（Ethnic Park），是介绍中国各少数民族文化习俗的公园，牌子上的英文却被写成 Racist Park（种族主义者公园）。其他一些诸如此类的问题更不胜枚举。譬如，"小心坠河"被译作

Carefully fall to the river（小心地往河里掉）；"残疾人专用厕所"被译成了有贬义色彩的 Deformed Man Toilet（变形人厕所）；某饭馆的"童子鸡"被译成了"没有性生活的鸡"（Chicken Without Sexual Life）；"夫妻肺片"被翻译成 Man and Wife Lung Slice；某超市的"干货"，英文被译成了 Fuck Goods；而餐盒等"一次性用品"（Disposable Articles），被翻译成 A Time Sex Thing（一次性交行为的东西）；等等。

上述种种不负责任的"翻译",人为地造成了语言文化沟通的障碍,轻者会闹出用洋文出洋相的国际笑话,重者会影响或损害政府机关的形象,甚至会对国家政治、经济造成无可挽回的重大损失。

三、翻译知识与翻译方法技巧

随着中国在经济、文化、科技等领域同国外交往的增多,特别是WTO实质化阶段的到来以及北京2008年奥运会的成功举办和上海2010年世界博览会的举办,为中国的翻译事业带来一个黄金发展期。翻译使中国融入世界,也使世界走近中国。科技文化、学术交流、国际贸易、时事政治等都离不开翻译,翻译在历史上的地位从未像现在这样不可或缺。另外,从全球角度审视,中国的翻译任重而道远。尽管我们在改革开放30余年翻译取得了举世瞩目的成就,但对于我们这样一个拥有13亿人口的泱泱大国来说,其翻译实力与大国的地位还很不相称。正如国务院新闻办公室主任赵启正在"中国翻译成就展"剪彩仪式上的讲话中指出的那样:世界上使用汉语的人最多,但使用汉语的国家却几乎最少,这是中国与世界交流的一大障碍。尽管中国人学习外语的人员中,在校大、中学生就有8 000万之多,但是由于传统文化、社会发展、政治体制的区别,和需求相比,能精当地翻译的专业人士真是凤毛麟角。我们今天的对外版权贸易:中国和外国的逆差是16∶1!原因是我们向外国传递中国文化的力量确实还比较弱,也包括我们的外语力量欠缺。

因此,要克服"交流障碍",减少乃至于避免种种翻译失误,我们就必须加强翻译知识的学习,掌握必要的翻译方法技巧。

翻译知识比较抽象,其涉及范围很广,从翻译的一般原则、标准到各类文体的识别,从语言文化差异到社会风俗习惯、时事政治、宗教文化、天文地理、风土人情……,翻译涉及包罗万象的百科知识,需要我们在平时的工作学习中点滴积累、逐步完善。

翻译技巧相对比较具体,是指人们通过翻译实践摸索出来的系统的翻译方法手段。由于着眼点的不同以及探索处理方法上的差异,英汉翻译技巧的分类也不尽一致。有人将其分为八大技巧，有人分为十大技巧，有人分得更多、更细。常用的翻译技巧有：1. 分清主从；2. 遣词用字；3. 词字的增添；4. 词字的省略；5. 词类及句子成分转换；6. 结构调整；7. 语态转换；8. 正反调换；9. 长句切分等。还有人将结构调整进一步细分为顺序法、逆序法、重组法等，也有人在词字的增添技巧之外再分出词字的重复，再加上各类从句的处理等等，各种方法技巧林林总总不下十几种。

　　需要指出的是，各种翻译技巧方法源于翻译实践。常言道：熟能生巧。离开了具体的翻译实践，再高明的技巧方法也难以培养出译者的翻译能力。因此，我们翻译学习的重点应放在翻译实践上，通过"实践—理论—实践"这样的反复循环来掌握各种翻译技巧方法，最终达到独立翻译得心应手的程度。从下一单元开始，我们将对各种主要翻译方法技巧逐一进行讲解探讨。

思考与练习

一、简要回答以下问题

1. 你认为翻译学习的主要困难是什么？
2. 翻译在语言文化交流中起到什么样的作用？哪些因素会造成翻译失误？
3. 翻译知识涉及哪些方面？最重要的是哪些方面？
4. 常用的翻译技巧有哪些？你自己常用哪些技巧方法？试举例说明。

二、英汉互译翻译练习

1. 英译汉。阅读下面两则笑话，试将其中的英语文字翻译成汉语。

   A

   > 一个在美国学习的外国学生坐在窗前看书。她听见有人喊 Look out！就把头伸到窗外去看。上面掉下一块板子，差点儿砸着她。她又生气，又害怕，往上一看，见一个人在修屋顶。那人问她：Didn't you hear me call 'look out'? 她回答说：Yes, and that's what I did.

B

　　一天，小明过马路不小心与一位外国人相撞，于是发生了下面这段莫名其妙的对话：

小明：I am sorry!

外宾：I am sorry too!

小明：I am sorry three!

外宾：What are you sorry for?

小明：I am sorry five!

外宾：!!??

2. 汉译英。指出下面译文的错误。

1）禁止拍照！

　　* Forbid photograph!

2）当心碰头！

　　* Carefully bump your head!

3）机房重地，非请莫入。

　　* Engine room is serious place. Don't enter without asking.

4）欢迎再来！

　　* Welcome again!

5）欢迎大家批评指正。

　　* Welcome all people's criticisms and comments.

6）请关闭计算机。

　　* Please close the computer.

7）请带好随身物品。

　　* Please carry your thing with you.

8）紧急情况请拨打110。

　　* Being urgent call 110 quickly.

9）下雨或雪天过桥慢行。

　　* Rain or snow day slow-driving on bridge.

10）下车请注意关好车窗门。

　　* When you get down car, please turn off door and window.

11）严禁吸烟，违者罚款。

　　* Smoking is prohibited if you do will be fined.

12）请文明游览，保持环境整洁！

　　* Visit in civilization, pay attention to environment hygiene!

第二单元
遣词用字与词义判定

　　遣词用字是翻译学习中的基本功,也是翻译的基本技巧方法之一。"遣词用字"用英语表达是 diction,也就是 the choice and use of words and phrases(对词语的使用或选择),大家所熟知的 dictionary(词典)一词便是由 diction 加后缀派生而成,"遣词用字"的重要性由此可见一斑。

　　无论是英译汉还是汉译英,遣词用字都是译者自始至终需要面对的情况,也是我们在翻译过程中随时出现、需要不断解决的问题——我们必须根据译文表达的需要,对词典所提供的词义做出取舍,翻译出原文的准确意思。

一、遣词用字与词典的关系

　　有人可能会说,查词典谁不会?问题的关键不是会不会查,而是会不会准确地定位。我们知道,由于英汉两种语言的差异很大,词与词、词与字之间往往没有相对固定的词义对应关系。以英语单词 set 一词为例,《新英汉词典》收入了及物动词 24 义,不及物动词 11 义,形容词 9 义,名词 17 义,总共 61 义;而《英汉大词典》收入了及物动词 45 义,不及物动词 20 义,形容词 16 义,名词 34 义,总共 115 义。如果再加上收入的数十个固定词组短语,其含义之广就更可观了。我们在第一单元中谈到的肯德基广告 WE DO CHICKEN RIGHT 就是一个典型的例子。这 4 个单词中除了代词 WE、名词 CHICKEN 在汉语中有比较固定的对应词之外，动词 DO 既可以作及物动词，又可以作不及物动词；还可以作代动词、情态动词等。各种词义，再加上各种固定短语、搭配，总共 100 多种词义。而 RIGHT 一词与汉语的词义对应关系就更复杂了，既可以作形容词、副词，又可以作名词、动词，甚至还可以用作感叹词！再加上各种固定短语、搭配，总共也有几十种词义。

这就为遣词用字留下了很大的回旋余地。同一句话，同一篇原文，经过不同译者的翻译，产生的译文意思可能会差不多，但措辞语气绝不会相同——由此可见，译者在遣词用字方面有很大的主观能动性。那么，遣词用字需要从哪几个方面入手呢？这就是本单元要解答的主要问题。

二、遣词用字与上下文语境

什么是语境？所谓语境，顾名思义，也就是产生语言活动的环境，包括时间、空间、语言交际参与者及语言活动目的等，在口语中叫做"前言后语"，反映在文字材料中亦称"上下文"。语境是一切言语活动存在的前提。离开了语境，就没有言语活动；没有一定的上下文，文字翻译也就无从谈起。请看下面这一简单句子：

I'll **finish** the book next week.

这句话中几乎每一个英语单词都能找到相应的汉语词语，但是在没有上下文的情况下，如果不知道 I 的身份到底是读者、还是作者或编审，我们就不能确定 finish 一词的具体措辞，究竟该译作"看完"、"写完"还是"审完"。如果上文有 I've been reading/writing/editing（我一直在看／写／审这本书）等信息，或是下文有 go to library/the press（去图书馆／出版社）等字样，finish 一词的翻译就很好确定了：我下周要**看／写／审**完这本书。

此外，并非所有的英语词语都有固定的汉语对应词。譬如"Linda's brother married Michael's sister."这句话就很难译成汉语。因为没有上下文，我们就不知道 brother 是指 Linda 的哥哥还是弟弟；sister 是指 Michael 的姐姐还是妹妹。而有了一定的上下文，问题也就迎刃而解了，如：

例 1. My brother is three years younger than me. 我弟弟比我小三岁。

英语中的 brother 既可以是"哥哥"，又可以是"弟弟"，但通过 three years younger（小三岁），我们便可很轻易地将 brother 定为"弟弟"。

不过，在有些情况下光凭句中的上下文还不够，还得借助其他一些相关背景，如下面几例：

例 2. My cousin is very tall.
例 3. My cousin is very pretty.
例 4. My little cousin is very pretty.

英语中的 cousin 一词根据不同的语境可分别译作"堂兄"、"堂弟"、"堂姐"、"堂妹"、"表兄"、"表弟"、"表姐"、"表妹"等 8 种不同的译法。即便忽略"姑表"、"姨表"之类表达法，略去"堂"、"姨"二字，例 2 的译文仍可能有 4 种不同的译法：

我的表兄／表弟／表姐／表妹个子很高。

例 3 中的 cousin 受 pretty（漂亮的）的制约，显然是指女性，因此可将歧义消除一半：

我的表姐／表妹很漂亮。

例 4 中的 cousin 受 little（幼小的）的制约，显然是指表妹无误，因此便有了准确的译文：

我的小表妹很漂亮。

语境所涉及的范围很广，光靠上下文不能解决遣词用字的问题，有时，还需要结合社会时代背景、时间、场合等情况加以综合考虑。请看下面一段话中的语境译例。

The Most Important Speech of the Century

We learned how far up he's come on New Year's Day when every Chinese newspaper heralded a 6,000-word speech in which Deng signaled the end of thousands of years of Chinese xenophobia. It may eventually come to be regarded the most important speech of the century. For in it, the Maximum Leader of the nation that comprises one-fourth of mankind served notice that China is joining the rest of the world (save Albania) in the 20th century.

例 5. The Most Important Speech of the Century

这是一篇英语新闻报道评述的标题,其中的 Speech 应当译为"演说"、"演讲",还是"发言"、"讲话"？ the Century 是译为"世纪"、"本世纪",还是"上世纪"？在查阅相关材料之后我们可知,这篇报道的时代背景为 20 世纪 80 年代,是邓小平在中央顾问委员会上的一次讲话,所以这一标题应当译作"20 世纪最重要的讲话"。

例 6. We learned how far up he's come on New Year's Day when every Chinese newspaper published Deng's 6,000-word speech.

翻译这句话也涉及外部语境问题。how far up he's come（直译：他已走了多远）传达出的是一种什么概念？必须通过了解当时的时代背景,分析各语句的上下文关系,才能确定此处的 come up 是什么含义：改革开放已进展到了什么程度。由此可翻译出如下的文字：

元旦这天,中国各家报纸纷纷发表了邓小平的一篇 6 000 字的讲话,我们由此了解到他在改革开放上已迈出了多大的步子。

例 7. China is joining the rest of the world (save Albania) in the 20th century.

这句话中的 the rest of the world 和 save Albania 同样也涉及外部语境问题。the rest of the world 指的是（除自身以外的）世界上的其他所有国家,因为在改革开放之前,中国的社会主义建设提倡的是"独立自主,自力更生"方针,基本上是关着门搞自己的社会主义建设。而 save Albania 指的是"除阿尔巴尼亚外"的所有国家——阿尔巴尼亚是欧洲巴尔干半岛西南部的一个国家,长期与世隔绝,同世界各国交往很少,这种闭关自守的状况一直持续到 20 世纪 90 年代。有了这样一些背景知识，这句话的遣词用字也就比较容易了：

20 世纪的中国行将加入整个世界（除阿尔巴尼亚外）的阵营。

三、英汉词字的对应关系

不少同学在学习英语的过程中养成了这样一种习惯：喜欢将英语单词与汉语某个固定词语画等号，如 school= 学校、student= 学生、table= 桌子、chair= 椅子，等等。这种方法显然不利于英语学习，因为如前所述，英语单词往往没有固定的单一词义，在没有上下文的情况下，哪怕是一个十分简单的词，也可能会有若干不同的意思。

譬如 school，除了通常的"学校"的意思之外，还有"上学、受教育、求学、授课时间、（大学的）院系、研究所、学派"等含义，与鱼类相关时是指"鱼群、鲸群"；student 除了通常的"学生"的意思之外，还有"学者、研究者、新手"等含义；table 除了通常的"桌子"的意思之外，还有"餐桌、菜肴、工作台、石板、表格、目录"等含义；chair 除了通常的"椅子"的意思之外，还有"（会议的）主席、主席座位、主席职位、教授职位"等含义。

同理，汉语中的词语在英语中也很少有固定的对等词。以最简单的"人"字为例，除了最常见的 man 之外，在很多情况下都需要根据不同的语境译为 human, human being, people, person, fellow, individual, soul，等等。明白了这个道理，遣词用字我们便可以灵活处理，摈弃死记硬背的坏习惯。

当然，英汉词字的对应关系也有画等号的情况，但这类情况毕竟只占极少数。一般来说，英汉词字对应关系有以下几种。

1. 完全对等

这种情况多见于专有名词（如人名、地名、专门机构名称等），以及专业科技词汇、术语等，如：

Norman Bethune ＝诺曼·白求恩

Saudi Arabia ＝沙特阿拉伯

the United Nations ＝联合国

计算机＝ computer

白血病＝ leukemia

这类词语的翻译往往采用词字一对一的固定译法，一般不会造成什么翻译问题。不过，有时候为了达到某种特殊效果，不一定非按常规翻译不可。如电影 *Waterloo Bridge* 就没有直译为《滑铁卢桥》，而是意译为《魂断蓝桥》；小说 *Oliver Twist* 音译为《奥列弗·退斯特》，拍成电影则成了《雾都孤儿》；而小说 *Uncle Tom's Cabin* 既有直译的书名《汤姆叔叔的小屋》，又有意译的《黑人吁天录》。

2. 部分对等

这种情况最为普遍，即一种语言中的词同另一种语言中的词只有部分意义对等。如 book 不能总是译为"书"：

a **book** of matches　　一盒火柴

a **book**-keeper　　簿记员

to cook the **books**　　做假账

"书"也不能总是译为 book：

结婚证**书**　　marriage lines

说**书**　　storytelling

挑战**书**　　a letter of challenge

翻译这一类词语需要把握英汉两种词语部分意义对应方面有哪些，不对应的方面有哪些，以便能在翻译时做出正确的取舍。如上述的 book 一词，作名词除了有"书"的意思之外，还有"卷、篇、账簿、名册、工作簿、一包"等含义；而汉语的"书"除了"书籍、书本"的意思之外，还有"信件、信函、文书、文件、书法、文字"等含义。由此可见，book 与"书"只有很小一部分的意义完全对等。再以汉语的"笔"与英语的 pen 为例。

钢笔、铅笔、圆珠笔、蜡笔、粉笔、毛笔、画笔、电笔……，其英语对应词语分别为：

pen, pencil, ballpoint pen, wax crayon, chalk, writing brush, painting brush, electroprobe...

通过比较不难看出，汉语的"笔"不论什么性质，只要能写、能画，或有笔的形状的东西都可称之为"笔"；而英语却没有汉语这种抽象的"笔"的概念：除了 pen, pencil, ballpoint pen 中还能见到"笔"的影子之外，其他一些在汉语看来是"笔"的东西均与英语的 pen 无关。

3. 无对等词

一些词语在某种语言中有，而在另一种语言中却没有，语言学家称之为"语义空白"。在这种情况下，便产生了无对等词现象。翻译中的这种情况并不常见，偶有发生，一般采用解释、音译或两者结合的方法来解决英汉对应词语空缺问题，如：

teenager　13 至 19 岁的青少年（解释）

cyberslacker　利用工作时间在公司上网、做与工作无关的事情的雇员（解释）

阴　yin（in Chinese thought) the soft inactive female principle or force in the world（音译加解释）

阳　yang（in Chinese thought) the strong active male principle or force in the world（音译加解释）

随着时代的发展，一些过去被认为没有对应词的情况逐渐有了公认的译法，如英语中的 hacker（黑客）、blog（博客）等。同样，汉语的一些传统的东西，也通过音译为英语界所广泛接受、采纳，如豆腐（tofu）、功夫（Kong Fu）等便属此类。

四、英译汉词义判定三依据

词义辨析是遣词用字的前提，少不了借助各类词典。但词典给出的词义解释罗列繁杂，需要我们一一甄别，适当取舍。一般来说，大致可以从三个方面来确定一个词的具体含义。

1. 依据构词法确定词义

熟悉英语构词法对词义辨析非常重要。在很多情况下，我们可以根据词的前缀、后缀、词根、词干来辨析词义。请看下面两例。

miniultrasonicprober = mini（微型的）+ ultra（超）+ sonic（声音的）+ prober（探测器）；即：微型超声波金属探测仪

macrospacetransship = macro（巨型的）+ space（太空）+ trans（转运）+ ship（船）；即：巨型空间转运飞船

例 1. Until such time as mankind has the sense to lower its population to the point where the planet can provide a comfortable support for all, people will have to accept more "unnatural food".

本句的主体框架是：
Until such time as..., people have to... 除非……时候，否则人们将不得不……
句末的 unnatural food 需要通过构词法来确定词义。所谓 unnatural，是与 natural 相对应的"不自然的,非天然的"之意,此处可根据上下文译作"人造食品"。

译文：除非人类最终意识到应该减少人口，以便使地球能为所有的人提供充分的饮食，否则人们将不得不接受更多的"人造食品"。

例 2. Social science is that branch of intellectual enquiry which seeks to study humans and their endeavors in the same reasoned, orderly, systematic, and dispassioned manner that natural scientists use for the study of natural phenomena.

这是一个带定语从句的复合句，句中的 intellectual enquiry 和 dispassioned manner 翻译起来都比较棘手，intellectual 由 intellect（智力）+ ual 构成形容词"智力的"，与 enquiry 合在一起，其字面意思为"智力的探索"，可意译为"知识探索"；dispassioned 可根据构词法将其一分为三：dis-（除掉，去掉）+ passion（激情，热情）+ ed（过去分词后缀）。将三部分的意思合在一起，也就是"被除掉激情的"，即"冷静的"。经过这一分析，我们可以用"分译法"逐一翻译出这一带有两个定语从句的复合句。

译文：社会科学是知识探索的一个分支，它力图像自然科学家研究自然现象那样，用理性的、有序的、系统的和冷静的方式研究人类及其行为。

2. 依据上下文语境或词语搭配确定词义

语境分析是翻译的重要手段，没有一定的上下文，翻译就无从着手。譬如下面这一句：

Tension is building up.

这句话中的主语 tension 和谓语 build up 都有各种不同的上下文意思。

tension *n.* 紧张（局势／状态），不安，拉紧，压力，张力，牵力，电压，拉力；拉伸度，绷紧度；焦虑；悬念，精神紧张；（人与人或国与国之间）关系紧张，互相猜忌……

build up 树立，增进，增大，堵塞；增进；加强，形成……，如：

1）At sea the wind can **build up** giant, powerful waves.
   在海上，风能**形成**巨大强劲的波浪。

2）Hard working conditions **build up** character.
   艰苦的工作条件能**磨炼**人的性格。

3）Promote physical culture and **build up** the people's health.
   发展体育运动，**增强**人民体质。

4）I'm very glad to see that your vocabulary is gradually **building up**.
   看到你的词汇量在逐渐**增长**，我很高兴。

5）We are **building up** a good business.

我们的生意**兴隆**。

由此可见，根据不同的上下文语境，这句话可以形成以下各种不同译文：

1）形势紧张起来。
2）张力在增大。
3）电压在增加。
4）压力在增强。
5）血压在增高。
6）紧张情绪在加剧。
……

例3. The supply of oil can be shut off unexpectedly at any time, and in any case, the oil wells will all run dry in thirty years or so at the present rate of use.

此句中的 shut off 有"关掉,切断,停止……的流动或通道,中断（供水、供气）、与……隔绝"等意，与主语 supply of oil 连在一起，可译作"切断"或"中断"。后半句中的 run 一词在不同的上下文中有不同的含义。光是作动词就有"跑,奔,逃跑,竞选,跑步,蔓延,进行,行驶,（机器）转动,运转,流淌,融化"等含义。请看下面各例。

1) He **ran** across the road. 他**跑**过马路。
2) I'll **run** the car into town. 我会把汽车迅速**开**进城里。
3) He **ran** his eyes down the list. 他的眼睛迅速地在名单上**扫**了一下。
4) The car **ran** down the hill. 汽车迅速**驶下**山岗。
5) The engine **runs** well. 发动机**运转**良好。
6) The story **runs** like this... 故事是这样**说**的……
7) He **ran** for president. 他**参加**总统**竞选**。
8) The buses **run** every ten minutes. 公共汽车每10分钟（**开**）**一班**。

9) Most of motor vehicles **run** on petrol. 大部分机动车的行驶**以汽油作燃料**。

10) Your nose is **running**. 你在**流**鼻涕。

11) The river has **run** dry. 这条河已经**干涸**了。

12) The butter will **run** if you put it near the fire. 如果你把黄油放近火旁，就会**融化**。

13) The road **runs** beside the river. 这条路沿着河边**延伸**。

14) The insurance **runs** for another month. 保险有效期**还有**一个月。

15) The coal industry is being **run** down. 煤矿工业正逐步**停产**。

16) Is everything **running** well in your office? 你们办公室一切都**进行**得顺利吗？

很明显，此句与11）类似，run 与 the oil wells 和 dry 搭配，就形成了"油井会完全干涸"的意思。

译文：石油供应可能随时被切断；不管怎样，以目前这种石油消费速度，只需30年左右，所有的油井都会枯竭。

例 4. Children will play with dolls equipped with personality chips, computers with in-built personalities will be regarded as workmates rather than tools, relaxation will be in front of smell-television, and digital age will have arrived.

这是由4个单句组合而成的并列句，句子的主要框架为：
Children will play with... 儿童将与……玩耍
computers...will be regarded as...rather than... 计算机……将被视为……而不是……
relaxation will be... 休闲将会是……
and digital age will have arrived 数字化时代就到来了

此句中比较棘手的是 play with 翻译，按一般搭配，play with 有以下4种含义：

1) 拿……玩；如：The children were playing with a ball. 孩子们在玩球。

2) 与……一起玩；如：The teacher were playing with their children. 老师正在和孩子们玩。

3) 摆弄，玩弄；如：play with fire 玩火，冒险

4) 戏弄，嘲弄；如：Don't play with me. 别耍我了。

此处的 play with 显然是第一种意思。此外，句中的 dolls equipped with personality chips（装有个性化芯片的玩具娃娃），computers with in-built personalities（具有内置人格的计算机），smell-television（能发出气味的电视机），digital age（数字化时代）等词语都需要根据上下文才能准确译出原文的含义。

译文：儿童玩的将是装有个性化芯片的玩具娃娃；具有内置人格的计算机将被视为工作伙伴而不是工具；人们将在能发出气味的电视机前休闲。人类已进入了数字化时代。

3. 依据不同学科或专业类型确定词义

同一单词在不同的学科专业里有不同的含义，翻译时应视不同的情况而选用恰当的词语。请看下面一例。

例 5. Whether Arab oil flows freely or not, it is clear to everyone that world industry cannot be allowed to depend on so fragile a base.

此句中的 base 一词在不同的学科或专业中有不同的译法，我们应当在充分理解原文的基础上，根据不同的学科专业特点，将其用准确的术语翻译出来。请看下面各例。

1) The lathe should be set on a firm **base**. 车床应安装在坚实的**底座**上。（机械）

2) As we all know, a **base** reacts with an acid to form a salt. 众所周知，**碱**与酸反应生成盐。（化学）

3) A transistor has three electrodes, the emitter, the **base** and the collector. 晶体管有三个电极，即发射极，**基极**和集电极。（电子）

4) Line AB is the **base** of the triangle ABC. AB 线是三角形 ABC 的**底边**。

（数学）

5) The weary troops marched back to the **base**. 疲惫不堪的士兵行军返回**基地**。（军事）

6) He is on the second **base**. 他在二**垒**。（体育）

7) It is a skyscraper built on a **base** of solid rock. 这是一座建在坚实岩石**地基**上的摩天高楼。（建筑）

8) The **base** of the thumb is where it joins the hand. 拇指的**起点**是在与手掌接合处。（解剖学）

9) That company has offices all over the world, but their **base** is in Paris. 这个公司的办事处遍布全世界，但**本部**在巴黎。（商务）

10) Ordinary numbers use **base** 10, but many computers work to **base** 2. 普通数字用 10 **进位制**，但许多计算机用 2 **进位制**。（计算机）

此外，base 一词还有其他一些各种各样的译法：在测绘学中译为"基线"，商务中为"本金"，词汇学中为"词根"，对数的"底"，油漆工艺的"底层"，金融证券的"基价"，等等。例 5 中的 base，根据与 depend on（依靠）一词所形成的上下文语义，可译作"能源基础"。

译文：无论阿拉伯石油是否会源源流出，现在人人都清楚这一点：世界工业不能依赖于如此脆弱的能源基础了。

五、汉译英的遣词用字

汉译英的遣词用字问题与英译汉的情况有所不同。英译汉时译者输出的是自己所熟悉的汉语词汇、语法结构，很多表达法早就在头脑里形成了概念，只需译者一一甄别，做出正确取舍即可；而汉译英则需从一大堆我们不那么熟悉的词语中去寻找答案——这也解释了为什么人们普遍认为，在同一档次的翻译上，汉译英的难度要大大超过英译汉。

以汉语中最简单的"人"字为例。汉语以"人"为中心词的构词非常简单，只要在"人"字前加一个修饰语就行了：男人、女人、夫人、个人、工人、猎人、行人、证人、盲人、主持人、法人、仇人、成人、他人、本人、爱人、情人、好人、坏人、恩人、报人……

而英语却没有这样的便利，上述汉语词语的英语表达形式分别是：man, woman, lady/Mrs. individual, worker, hunter, pedestrian, witness, blind, host, legal person, personal enemy, adult/grown-up, others, oneself, wife/husband, lover, good man/woman, bad person, benefactor, journalist... 我们不难发现，除了少数词语可以加后缀 -er, -ian, -or, -ist（如 worker, pedestrian, benefactor, journalist）之外，大都不能像汉语那样将两部分随意相加，自由组合成新词。此外，英语在很多情况下有阴性、阳性的区别，而汉语则没有。"爱人"是指"妻子"还是"丈夫"，"好人"是男是女？稍不小心，就会闹出将"我妈妈是一个好人"译成 My mother is a good man 之类的笑话。

再以汉语以"人"为修饰语的词语为例，汉语的构词只需将"人"字往被修饰的词语前一放就构成一个新词，而英语的表达却非常复杂，与汉语形成了截然不同的对照：

1）人才 talent/man of ability
2）人潮 stream of people
3）人称 person/be called
4）人道 humanity/humanism/humane
5）人格 character/personality
6）人工 man-made/artificial
7）人海 a huge crowd
8）人家 household other people
9）人间 the world
10）人杰 an outstanding personality
11）人口 population
12）人类 mankind/humanity
13）人力 manpower/labor power

14）人马 forces/troops

15）人们 / 人民 people

16）人命 human life

17）人品 character/looks

18）人情 reason/human relationship/worldly wisdom

19）人权 human rights

20）人群 crowd/throng

21）人人 everybody/everyone

22）人身 / 人体 human body

23）人生 life

24）人士 personage/public figure

25）人事 personnel matters/occurrences in human life

26）人手 manpower/hand

27）人寿 human longevity/life insurance

28）人头 head/the number of people

29）人望 prestige/popularity

30）人文 human culture/human studies

31）人物 character/figure

32）人像 image/figure

33）人心 the will of the people/conscience

34）人性 humanity/normal human feeling nature

35）人选 person selected/candidate

36）人烟 signs of human habitation

37）人言 people's words

38）人员 personnel/stuff

39）人缘 relations with people

40）人证 testimony of a witness

41）人质 hostage

42）人种 ethnic group/race

……

下面我们再分别以汉语形容词"老"字、动词（名词／量词／介词）"把"字为例，看看汉译英的遣词用字问题。先看有关"老"的一些译法：

1）老百姓 civilian/common folk/the people
2）老板 boss/manager
3）老表 cousin
4）老本 last stake/capital
5）老兵 veteran
6）老大 the eldest child
7）老大娘 aunty/granny
8）老儿子 the youngest son
9）老皇历 ancient history/last year's calendar
10）老黄牛 a willing ox
11）老家 hometown/native place
12）老毛病 chronic ailment/old weakness
13）老前辈 one's senior
14）老芹菜 overgrown celery
15）老生常谈 cliché/commonplace/platitude
16）老师傅 a master craftsman
17）老乡 fellow-villager/fellow townsman
18）老早 very early
19）老账 old debts/long-standing debt
20）老祖宗 ancestor/forefather

一见到汉语的"老"字，我们就自然而然地对应到英语的 old。在很多情况下这样译当然没错。不过，英语的 old 一词，一般来说只有两层意思，一是年龄上的"衰老"、"年迈"，如：old man；二是"历时长久的"、"旧的"，如：old friend, old debts；而汉语的"老"字，除了这两层意思之外，还有下面这样一些含义：

1）娴熟的，富有经验、有阅历深的，如：老师傅、老兵、老手
2）对先辈、年长者的尊称，如：老大娘、老先生、老前辈、老祖宗
3）加在姓氏和某些称谓的前面，如：老师、老板、老表、老弟、老李；加在某些动植物名词前面，如：老虎、老鼠、老玉米
4）加在兄弟姐妹排行次序上，如：老大、老二、老儿子、老闺女
5）用在形容词前面，表示程度深，相当于"很"、"极"；如：老早、老长、老大不愿意
6）用在动词前面，表示某种动作、行为或状态在一段较长时间里一直持续不断发生或时常重复出现，有"经常"、"时常"的意思；如：老是、老说、老爱动等

因此，汉语的"老"除了表示"年长"、"旧"的概念可以译作 old 之外，在一般情况下应根据上下文进行变通处理，将其理解为"老练"、"老手"、"老资格"、"排行"、"很"、"经常"等含义。将上述译例的英语表达回译成汉语，便不难理解汉语中的"老"字在不同语境中的真实含义了。

再看看汉语的"把"字在各种不同情况下的译法。

不少同学不了解英汉遣词用字的差异，试图一劳永逸地找一个与汉语的"把"字相对应的英语词语，其结果往往会大失所望——因为英语中压根儿就没有这样一种可以兼作动词、名词、量词、形容词、介词的词语。

汉语"把"字的用法大致如下。

1）作动词：把握 hold，把持 control，把门 guard the entrance，把风 keep watch，把玩 appreciate，把脉 feel sb's pulse，把揽 monopolize
2）作名词：把、小捆儿 bundle，车把、门把手 handle/grip，把戏 acrobatics/game/cheap trick
3）作量词：一把刀 a knife，一把椅子 a chair，一把米 a handful of rice，一把子强盗 a gang of bandits
4）作形容词：个把月 about a month/a month or so，百把块钱 some hundred dollars；把兄弟 sworn brothers

5）作介词：用在直接宾语之前，宾语之后跟着及物动词。如：把门关上 close the door，把头一扭 toss one's head，把他乐坏了 he is overwhelmed with joy，等等

由此可见，同一个"把"字，由于不同的语境及上下文搭配，需要用各种不同的词性，其遣词用字很不好掌握。因此，汉译英遣词用字没有什么捷径可走，关键在于平时词汇的日积月累，翻译时多比较，勤练习，巧模仿，抓规律。

思考与练习

一、简要回答以下问题

1. 什么是"遣词用字"？
2. 遣词用字与上下文语境之间是什么关系？
3. 英汉词字的对应关系一般有哪几种？
4. 英译汉确定词义的依据是什么？
5. 汉译英遣词用字有哪些常见问题？你觉得最困难的是什么？

二、英汉互译翻译练习

1. 英译汉。翻译下列各句，注意遣词用字。

    1) She had the surprise of her life.
    2) He was supposed to be a doctor.
    3) This trifle is beneath our notice.
    4) The old man is very rigid in his ideas.
    5) Her grandson is the apple of her eye.
    6) The sailor has a rich stock of tales of adventure.
    7) She told me she was moving to Europe for good.
    8) Dr. Manette had been put in prison for no good reason.
    9) Worse still, the lion could even carry off the baby in its mouth.
    10) It is enough to dip into the book and read bits here and there.

11) But it will be more than 100 years before the country begins once again to look as it did before.

12) The best things in life were free: sunshine, laughing, walks in the beauty of the country, friends and music.

2. 汉译英。注意"有"字的不同译法。

1) 这里没有这本书。

2) 这家伙很有胆量。

3) 全部损失有多少?

4) 这个村子有3家商店。

5) 我的旧汽车对我很有用。

6) 吸烟有害健康。

7) 这门课程有3个学分。

8) 可能在大部分地区还有雪。

9) 如果有错的话,我会改正的。

10) 你有选举资格吗?

11) 院子四周都围有篱笆。

12) 这个队本星期有没有获胜的机会?

第三单元
词类转换与句子成分转换

在学习词类转换与句子成分转换技巧之前，我们有必要先了解英汉两种语言关于词类和句子成分的一些基本知识。

一、英语的词类和句子成分

词类（parts of speech）是根据词的语法意义和语法功能划分出来的词的类别。英语的词类划分为 10 种：名词（noun）、代词（pronoun）、数词（numeral）、动词（verb）、形容词（adjective）、副词（adverb）、介词（preposition）、连词（conjunction）、感叹词（interjection）和冠词（article）。

名词用以表示人或事物的名称，分为可数名词（countable noun），如：a pen 一支钢笔，two apples 两个苹果，three boys 三个男孩；不可数名词（uncountable noun），如：news 新闻，air 空气，grain 粮食。

形容词表示人或事物的特征（如：good, bad, beautiful, ugly）。

副词用以修饰动词、形容词或其他副词（如：very, quickly, slowly）。

动词表示动作或状态（如：study, be），分为可以带宾语的及物动词（如：advise, agree, ask, beg, decide, demand, determine, dictate）和不可以带宾语的不及物动词（如：come, go, live, rise, sleep, stand, stay）。

代词用以代替名词、数词等（如：we, you, they, one）。

数词表示数量或顺序（如：one, five, tenth）。

介词用以表示名词、代词和其他词的关系（如：in, for, of）。

连词用以连接词与词或句与句（如：and, but, because）。

感叹词表示说话时的感情或口气（如：oh, hey, well）。

冠词用以限制名词的意义，分为定冠词 the（主要用来表示指定的人或事物）和不定冠词 a/an（用来表示不肯定的"某一个"或"任何一个"）。

以上 10 大类词前 6 类都有实际意义，在句子中能独立担任一定的句子成分，称为实词；后 4 类没有实义，不能在句中独立担任任何成分，称为虚词。

组成句子的各个部分叫句子成分。英语句子成分有主语（subject）、谓语（predicate）、宾语（object）、表语（predicative）、定语（attribute）、状语（adverbial）、宾语补足语（object complement）、同位语（appositive）等。

主语表示句子主要说明的人或事物，一般由名词、代词、数词、不定式等充当。如：

● **He** likes watching TV. **他**喜欢看电视。

谓语说明主语的动作、状态或特征，可以有不同的时态、语态和语气。如：

● I **can speak** a little English. 我**可以说**一点英语。

表语是谓语的一部分，它位于系动词之后，说明主语身份，特征，属性或状态，一般由名词、代词、形容词、副词、不定式、介词短语等充当。如：

● My sister is **a nurse**. 我姐姐是**护士**。

宾语表示动作行为的对象，跟在及物动词之后，能作宾语的有名词、代词、数词、动词不定式等；有些及物动词可以带两个宾语，往往一个指人，一个指物，指人的叫间接宾语，指物的叫直接宾语。如：

● He gave **me some ink**. 他给了**我一点墨水**。

有些及物动词的宾语后面还需要有一个补足语，意思才完整，宾语和它的补足语构成复合宾语。如：

● We make him **our monitor**. 我们选他**当班长**。

在句中修饰名词或代词的成分叫定语。用作定语的主要是形容词、代词、数词、名词、副词、动词不定式、介词短语等。形容词、代词、数词、名词等作定语时，通常放在被修饰的词前面；但副词、动词不定式、介词短语等作定语时，则放在被修饰的词之后。如：

- The bike **in the room** is mine. **房间里的**自行车是我的。

修饰动词、形容词、副词以及全句的句子成分叫状语。用作状语的通常是副词、介词短语、不定式和从句等。状语一般放在被修饰的词之后或放在句尾。如：

- He lived **in London last year**. 他**去年**住**在伦敦**。

二、汉语的词类和句子成分

现代汉语的词类主要是根据语法，在参照词的意义和词的形态的基础上，将词类划分为 12 大类：名词、数词、量词、代词、动词、形容词、副词、介词、连词、感叹词、拟声词和助词，其中，前 6 类属于实词，后 6 类属于虚词。

名词用以表示人或事物，如：学生、人民、书、树木；同时也用以表示时间、方位、处所，如：早晨、下午、现在、春天、上、下、左、右、学校、北京、欧洲等。

数词分为基数词（一、二、五、一百……）、序数词（第一、第三、第二十四……）。

量词分为名量词（如：尺、斤、辆、个、本）、动量词（次、趟、回、阵、场、番）和时量词（天、年、日、季、周）。

动词分为及物动词（如：写、爱、想、支持、扩大）和不及物动词（如：休息、咳嗽、病、睡觉）；趋向动词（如：来、去、进、退）；助动词（又称能愿动词）（如：能、会、要、愿、可以）和判断动词（如：是、就是）。

形容词包括表示性质的形容词（如：好、香、高、老实）、表示状态形容词（雪白、笔直、水灵灵、冷清清），带区别性质的词（如：正、副、雌、雄、急性、慢性）。

副词用以表示程度（如：极、顶、最、非常、更、多么）、范围（如：都、总、共、凡、只、仅仅、才）、时间频率（如：立刻、已经、刚刚、时常、曾经）、肯定否定（如：一定、当然、没、莫、的确）、情状（如：明明、猛然、互相、赶紧、怪不得）、语气（如：难道、毕竟、简直、也许、何必）等。

代词包括指示代词（如：这、那、另外、别的、某、各）、人称代词（如：你、我、他、它、您、咱们、他们）、疑问代词（如：谁、哪儿、怎么、多少）。

介词用以表示时间（如：从、在、由、到、于、趁)，处所和方向（如：在、从、打、向、朝、冲、沿着、顺着），表示对象和范围（如：对、跟、同、和、给、为、至于、关于），表示依据和方式（如：按照、依据、以、本、通过、经过），表示原因和目的（如：由于、因为、为了、为着），表示比较（如：比、同、和、与），表示排除（如：除了、除开）。

连词常用来连接词或短语（如：和、跟、同、与、或、及、而且），也常用来连接分句或句子（如：于是、不但……而且、或者、就是、因为……所以）。

助词包括结构助词（的、地、得）、时态助词（着、了、过）、其他助词（所、似的、被、给）、语气词（呢、啦、嘛、吧、啊）。

叹词表示强烈感情以及应答、招呼等语气（如：唉、哼、哦、嗯、哎哟）。

拟声词即模拟各种声音的词（如：轰、嘀嗒、叮当、稀里哗啦）等等。

汉语句子成分的划分不像英语那样有一个统一标准。传统汉语语法学一方面根据词的意义划分词类；另一方面按照印欧语的词类划分方法，简单地将汉语的词类与句子成分对应起来，认为汉语中作主语、宾语的是名词，作定语的是形容词，作谓语的是动词，作状语的是副词。如果动词和形容词出现在主语和宾语的位置上，就认为这些动词和形容词"名物化"了。汉语实词一般都能充当句子成分，虚词不能作句子成分。词类与句法成分没有对应关系，这与英语很不相同。英语中词类的功能比较单纯，词类与句法成分之间存在简单的对应关系：名词只能作主语和宾语，动词只能作谓语，形容词只能作定语和表语，副词只能作状语。

通过以上对照我们不难发现，英汉无论是词类划分还是句子成分结构都不完全一致。英语中没有汉语的量词、助词、拟声词，汉语没有英语的冠词。尽管其他 9 类在名称上完全一致，但使用方法和范围却不尽相同。尤其是在句子成分结构的划分上更是相差悬殊，翻译时我们对此现象应当予以足够的重视，视情况的不同而区别对待。

三、英译汉的词类转换

在翻译过程中，由于英汉两种语言在语法和表达习惯上的差异，有时必须改变原文某些词语的词类才能有效地传达出原文的准确意思。请看下面两例：

- This watch never **varies** more than a second in a month.

这句英语中的 vary（改变，不同）为动词，汉语没有这样的表达习惯，所以只能将其转换为"误差"才能形成准确的译文：这块表一个月的**误差**从不超过一秒。（动词转换为名词）

- The **emphasis** on data gathered first-hand, **combined with** a cross-cultural perspective brought to the analysis of cultures past and present, makes this study a unique and distinctly important social science.

强调收集第一手资料，**加上**在分析过去和现在文化形态时**采用**跨文化视角，使得这一研究成为一门独特并且非常重要的社会科学。（名词 emphasis、过去分词短语 combined with 均转换为动词）

英译汉的词类转换包括各种词类转换成汉语动词、名词、形容词、副词等，常见于以下各类情况。

1. 各种词类转换成动词

英语的每个句子只能有一个谓语动词，而汉语一句话中动词的数量不受语法限制，动词的使用频率比英语高得多。所以将英语各种词类转换成汉语动词是最常见的词类转换。

- He made such rapid progress that before long he began to write articles **in** English **for** an American newspaper.

他取得了如此迅速的进步，以至于没多久就开始**用**英语**为**一家美国报纸撰稿。（介词 in 和 for 转换为动词"用"和"为"）

- It is now **against** the law to throw anything into the sea within five kilometers of land.

现在将任何东西弃入距海岸 5 千米之内的海域属**违**法行为。（介词 against 转换为动词"违"）

- I hope there will be a **change** in the weather.

我希望天气**变一变**。（名词 a change 转换为动词"变一变"）

- He gave my words a **misleading twist**.

他**曲解**了我的话。（名词 twist 转换为动词"曲解"）

- I am **suspicious** of that woman—I think she may have stolen something from our shop.

  我**很怀疑**那位妇女，我想她可能偷了我们商店的东西。（形容词 suspicious 转换为动词"很怀疑"）

- You should have left a note. It was very **inconsiderate** of you to do so.

  你本应该留下便条。你这样做实在是**考虑不周**。（形容词 inconsiderate 转换为动词"考虑不周"）

- When the switch is **off**, the circuit is open and electricity doesn't go **through**.

  当开关**断开**时，电路就形成开路，电流不能**通过**。（副词 off, through 转换为动词"断开"和"通过"）

2. 各种词类转换成名词

这种情况同样适用于英语的各种词类。在很多情况下，英语句中的动词、形容词、副词、代词等需要转换成名词。一般来说，动词、形容词转换成名词主要是受习惯表达法的影响；副词、代词转换成名词主要是为了表达清楚，减少不必要的指代混乱。

- The design **aims** at automatic operation, easy regulation, simple maintenance and high productivity.

  设计的**目的**在于自动操作，调节方便，维护简单，生产效率高。（动词 aim 转换为名词"目的"）

- The new contract would be **good** for ten years.

  新的合同**有效期**为 10 年。（形容词 good 转换为名词"有效期"）

- In the fission processes the fission fragments are very **radioactive**.

  在裂变过程中，裂变碎片具有强烈的**放射性**。（形容词 radioactive 转换为名词"放射性"）

- He is **physically** weak but **mentally** sound.

  他**身体**虽弱，但**心智**健全。（副词 physically, mentally 转换为名词"身体"、"心智"）

- The specific resistance of iron is not so small as **that** of copper.

  铁的电阻率不像铜的**电阻率**那样小。（代词 that 转换为名词"电阻率"）

- A good book may be **among** the best of friends.

  一本好书可以成为你最要好的朋友中的**一员**。（介词 among 转换为名词"一员"）

3. 各种词类转换成形容词

这种转化主要也是出于汉语行文表达的需要考虑，没有什么固定的模式，只要译文通顺达意就行。

- I agree with you about its being a **mistake**.

  我同意你的看法，这事儿**错了**。（名词 mistake 转换为形容词"错了"）

- This letter made me certain of his **innocence**.

  这封信使我相信他是**无罪的**。（名词 innocence 转换为形容词"无罪的"）

- It is demonstrated that gases are **perfectly** elastic.

  已经证实，气体具有**理想的**弹性。（副词 perfectly 转换为形容词"理想的"）

- The pressure **inside** equals the pressure **outside**.

  内部的压力和**外部的**压力相等。（副词 inside, outside 转换为形容词"内部的、外部的"）

- Tom is **above** average in his lessons.

  汤姆的成绩**高于**平均水平。（介词 above 转换为形容词"高于"）

- These two reports of the accident **disagree**.

  关于那次事故的两份报告说法**不同**。（动词 disagree 转换为形容词"不同"）

- Good reading **elevates** the mind.

  阅读好书可使思想**高尚**。（动词 elevate 转换为形容词"[使]……高尚"）

4. 各种词类转换成副词

这种转换情况主要是受其他词类转换的影响以及汉语的表达习惯的限制。有时候，根据表达的需要，英语的各种词类（包括形容词、名词、动词、介词等）需要转为汉语副词才符合汉语的表达习惯。在通常情况下，英语的名词被转换成汉语动词之后，其修饰形容词也就地转换成相应副词。

- I took the **wrong** way.

  我走**错**了路。（形容词 wrong 转换为副词"[走]错"）

- I had a **long** discussion with my friends about the matter.

  这件事我跟朋友们商讨了**很久**。（形容词 long 转换为副词"很久"）

- Things are going **from** bad **to** worse.

  事态**越来越**糟糕了。（介词 from...to... 转换为副词"越来越"）

- Rapid evaporation at the heating-surface **tends** to make the steam wet.

  加热面上的迅速蒸发，**往往使**蒸汽的湿度变大。（动词 tends 转换为副词"往往使"）

- Below 4℃, water is in **continuous** expansion instead of **continuous** contraction.

  水在 4 摄氏度以下就**不断地**膨胀，而不是**不断地**收缩。（形容词 continuous 转换为副词"不断地"）

- Only when we study their properties can we make **better** use of the materials.

  只有研究这些材料的特性我们才能**更好地**利用它们。（形容词 better 转换为副词"更好地"）

- I have the **honor** to inform you that your request is granted.

  我**荣幸地**通知您，您的请求已得到批准。（名词 honor 转换为副词"荣幸地"）

- The new mayor earned some appreciation by the **courtesy** of coming to visit the city poor.

  新市长**礼节性地**看望城市贫民，获得了他们的一些好感。（名词 courtesy 转换为副词"礼节性地"）

四、英译汉的句子成分转换

句子成分的转换主要也是为了便于汉语的表达需要。在很多情况下，英语中的句子成分可以灵活地进行互相转换调整，将主语转为宾语、宾语转为主语、主语转为谓语、主语转为定语、状语转为主语，等等。句子成分的转换没有固定的模式，只要是按照原文的结构翻译出来显得生硬，就需要考虑将句子成分进行转换。请看下例：

- As the match burns, **heat** and **light** are given off.

这句话的主、谓、宾结构是 heat and light are given off（热和光被释放出来），如果照字面直译，会令人费解。进行必要的句子成分转换，方可译成通顺的汉语句子。

火柴燃烧时发出**光和热**。（主语转换为宾语）

下面是一些常见的英译汉句子成分转换的例句。

- I am **no drinker**, **nor smoker**.

  我既**不饮酒**，也**不抽烟**。（系表结构转为动宾结构）

- She **behaves** as if she were a child.

  她的**举止**像是个孩子。（谓语动词转换为主语）

- **Care** must be taken at all times to protect the instrument from dust and damp.

  应当始终**注意**保护仪器，以免其沾染灰尘和受潮。（主语转换为谓语）

- Careful **comparison** of them will show **you** the difference.

  只要仔细把它们**比较**一下，**你**就会发现不同之处。（主语转换为谓语，宾语转换为主语）

- **The baby** doubled its weight in a year.

  这婴儿的体重一年中长了一倍。（主语转换为定语）

- There's been some change **in the rule**.

  这条规则已有一些改动。（状语转换为主语）

- **Mathematics** is well taught **at that school**.

  那个学校的数学教得好。（主语转换为宾语，状语转换为主语）

- Tipping is a subject that has long **interested and irritated me**.

  长期以来，付小费一直是**让我既感兴趣又十分恼火**的事。（动宾结构转换为主谓结构）

- **The ocean** was filled with **turtles and fish**, ready for the net.

  海洋里鱼鳖成群，张网可得。（主语转换为状语，宾语转换为主语）

五、汉译英的词类转换

汉语的词类与句法成分之间的关系比较复杂，除了副词主要用作状语（少数副词可以作补语）外，其他词类都可以充当多种句法成分。例如名词主要作主语、宾语和定语，还可以作谓语和状语；动词主要作谓语，还可以作定语、主语、宾语和状语。

此外，汉语词语的兼类词在整个词库中占有很大的比重，这给句子成分划分也造成很大的困难。汉语的许多名词同时可兼作量词，如：年、日、月、岁、日、分、秒等；许多名词也可兼作动词，如：工作、学习、建议、主张、希望等，许多形容词同时也可兼作名词，在特定的语言条件下，动词、形容词的词性很容易朝着名词转移，从而出现"名物化"现象。如：

- **游泳**是一项非常有益的体育活动。（动词作主语）

  Swimming is a very wholesome sport.（动名词作主语）

应该注意的是，汉语中名词作谓语、状语，动词作主语、宾语时，本身的词性并没有改变，名词还是名词，动词还是动词。与英语相比，汉语的语法不严谨。英语是一种"形合"的语言，句子严格地遵守语法规则，句中主、谓、宾、定、状、补，井然有序，句子成分可通过语法结构进行层层分析。而汉语则是一种"意合"的语言，不受严格的语法约束，也没有固定的句式结构。譬如"我完成了作业"（I have finished my homework）这样一句话，亦可表达为"我完成作业了"、"我作业完成了"、"作业我完成了"——怎么说都可以，只要达意就行，而英语句子却没有这样随意的自由组合。

另外，汉语由于不受严格的语法约束，句式中动词的使用频率很高。因此，汉译英的词类转换需要解决的一个重要问题就是如何将汉语中的动词转换成英语的其他词类。譬如这样一例：

- **住**在楼上的人家**得提**着水桶**去**楼下的水龙头**打**水。

  Families upstairs **have to carry** pails to the taps downstairs for water.

汉语句子里一连5个动词：**住、得、提、去、打**，翻译成英语之后，转换了其中的 4 个。由此可见，汉译英的一个重要任务就是将汉语中的大量动词转换为名词、形容词、介词、副词、不定式、动名词、分词等各种非谓语动词形式。只有这样，才能使译文符合英语的习惯表达法。

1. 动词转换成名词、介词、形容词、副词等

- 校长鞠躬**致谢**。

  The headmaster bowed his **thanks**.（动词"致谢"转换为名词 thanks）

- 她**看**电视**看**得厌倦了。

  She was tired of **watching** television.（动词"看"转换为动名词 watching）

- 偷窃是**犯**法行为。

  It is **against** the law to steal.（动词"犯"转换为介词 against）

- 博士摇头**表示拒绝**。

  The doctor shook his head **in refusal**.（动词短语"表示拒绝"转换为介词短语 in refusal）

- 这列火车**开往**上海。

  This train is **bound for** Shanghai.（动词"开往"转换为介词短语 bound for）

- 他们没有**意识到**这场突如其来的暴风雪的严重性。

  They were not **aware of** the graveness of the unexpected snow-storm.（动词"意识到"转换为形容词 aware of）

- 她叫我**帮**她**绕**毛线。

  She asked me **to wind** the wool **for** her.（动词"绕、帮"转换为不定式 to wind 和介词 for）

- 病人已经**脱离**了危险。

  The patient was **out of** danger.（动词"脱离"转换为介词 out of）

2. 其他一些词类之间的转换

- 这种举止是罪犯的心理**特征**。

  This kind of behavior **characterizes** the criminal mind.（名词"特征"转

换为动词 characterize）
- 各国的风俗**不同**。
  Customs **differ** in different countries.（形容词"不同"转换为动词 differ）
- 她总是干得很**出色**。
  She always does **a competent job**.（形容词"出色"转换为名词 a competent job）
- 他过得很**舒服**。
  He lived **in comfort**.（形容词"舒服"转换为介词短语 in comfort）
- 这房子是**最近**买的。
  The house is a **recent** purchase.（副词"最近"转换为形容词 recent）
- 这个城镇的外观**变化**颇大。
  The appearance of the town is **quite changed**.（动词"变化"转换为系表结构 quite changed）
- 我们的教育方针，应该使受教育者在**德育、智育、体育**几方面都得到发展。
  Our educational policy must enable everyone who receives an education to develop **morally, intellectually and physically**.（名词"德育、智育、体育"转换为副词 morally, intellectually and physically）

六、汉译英的句子成分转换

汉译英句子成分的转换包括主语转换为状语、宾语转换为主语、定语转换为主语等，翻译时应根据英语的表达习惯进行必要的转换。

- **北京**欢迎你。
  You are welcome to **Beijing**.（主语转换为状语，宾语转换为主语）
- **我国**盛产**煤**。
  Coal abounds **in our country**.（主语转换为状语，宾语转换为主语）
- 我的车**引擎**出了问题。
  My car has got **engine** trouble.（主语转换为定语）

- 他们的**婚姻**很美满。

  They have a happy **marriage**.（主语转换为宾语）
- 这儿在初夏季节常**下雨**。

  Rains are frequent here in early summer.（谓语转换为主语）
- **在这个湖里**游泳危险。

  This lake is dangerous for swimmers.（状语转换为主语）
- 数码相机的**成像质量好**，且售价低。

  Digital cameras **take better pictures** for less money.（系表结构转换为动宾结构）
- 在餐馆吃的食物所含的**脂肪、糖和盐的成分**都很高。

  The foods that you take in restaurants are high **in fat, sugar and salt**.（主语转换为状语）

思考与练习

一、简要回答以下问题

1. 英语的词类和句子成分是怎样划分的？
2. 汉语的词类和句子成分是怎样划分的？
3. 英、汉词类和句子成分划分有什么异同？
4. 英译汉的词类转换、句子成分转换有哪几种？
5. 汉译英的词类转换、句子成分转换有哪几种？

二、英汉互译翻译练习

1. 英译汉。翻译下列各句，注意使用转换技巧。

   1) The shoes adapt me well.

   2) His opinion accorded with mine.

   3) Lights will go off if no one is in the room.

   4) The villagers rose against the aggressors.

5) She felt sick at the sight of the dead rat.

6) I acknowledge the truth of his statement.

7) It'll take time for her to recover from the illness.

8) Some students followed Prof. Jones on a field trip.

9) We differ from them on that question.

10) The house came to him on his mother's death.

11) French people kiss each other hello and goodbye more often than British people.

12) Gratifying achievements have been made in physical culture and sports in the past 60-odd years in China.

2. 汉译英。翻译下列各句，注意使用转换技巧。

1）工人师傅带我参观工厂。

2）他气得声音都发抖了。

3）苏珊去年和约翰离了婚。

4）这台电脑好像有点毛病。

5）孩子昨天晚上表现挺好。

6）我们所有的工作都白费了。

7）校长的日程表排得满满的。

8）公司登广告招聘一名新秘书。

9）这些鱼的重量从3磅到5磅不等。

10）我父亲把诚实看得比什么都重要。

11）喝下这杯冰茶你会感到清凉。

12）经过了35年的改革开放，中国的现代化建设已经发展到一个新阶段。

第四单元
增添技巧的运用

作为翻译的一个普遍准则，译者不应对原文的内容随意增减。不过，在实际翻译过程中往往很难做到不增减词字。要准确地传达出原文的信息，译者难免要对译文作一些增添或删减。

按美国翻译家奈达（E. A. Nida）的观点，好的译文一般略长于原文。因为原作对于原文读者来说很少有语言文化上的障碍，而译文读者却没有这样的便利，因此译者往往需要把原文中隐含的一些东西增补清楚，以便于读者理解。譬如下面几句关于 wash 一词的翻译：

- Mary **washes** before meals. 玛丽饭前洗**手**。
- Mary **washes** before going to bed. 玛丽睡前洗**漱**。
- Mary **washes** after getting up. 玛丽起床后洗**脸**。
- Mary **washes** for a living. 玛丽靠洗**衣**度日。
- Mary **washes** in a restaurant. 玛丽在饭店洗**碗碟**。

根据不同的语境，以上各例译文分别增添了"手"、"漱"、"脸"、"衣"、"碗碟"等字眼。

一、英译汉增添技巧的运用

英译汉的增词法一般用于以下几方面。

1. 增添原文所省略的词语

这种情况较为隐蔽，需要增添原文中所省略的词语，如：动词的省略、词性的改变、以及英语的一些特殊表达法（如 so do/be 结构，neither...nor 之类的否定结构）。

- **She looks younger than she is**.

  她看起来比**她的实际岁数**显得要年轻。（将 she is 增译为"她的实际岁数"）

- **I haven't read this book and my brother hasn't either**.

  我没有看过这本书，我兄弟**也没看过**。（将 either 增译为"也没看过"）

- **A warm bath** will calm you.

  洗个热水澡会使你平静下来。（将 a warm bath 增译为"洗个热水澡"）

此外，在英语的某些及物动词用作不及物动词时，译成汉语时应作适当的增添，以确保句子的整体语义完整。如：

- **One boy was reading; another was writing**.

  一个男孩在**读书**，另一个在**写字**。（将 reading, writing 增译为"读书、写字"）

2. 增添必要的连接词语

英语中的并列连词和从属连词大都是以单个单词形式出现，而汉语中的联合连词和偏正连词大都成双成对使用。因此，在将英语译成汉语时，应将汉语的连词补充完整。如：if..., 如果……那么……；because... 因为……，所以……；although..., 虽然……，但是……；unless... 除非……否则……；等等。掌握了这一点，就容易克服英语写作中经常犯的 although...but 的错误了。

- **Though** he is rich, his life is not happy.

  他**虽然**很有钱，**但**生活并不幸福。

- The baby never cries **unless** he is hungry.

  这婴儿**除非**饿了，**否则**是绝不会哭的。

- Rashly **as** he had behaved, he didn't deserve the punishment he received.

  尽管他行为鲁莽，**但**是不应受到那样的处罚。

- **Since** air has weight, it exerts force on any object immersed in it.

因为空气具有重量，**所以**其作用力遍布于空气中的任何物体。

3. 表达出原文的复数概念

英语中没有量词，往往用一个复数形式就代表了若干数量。而汉语量词却不可缺少，如：a horse 一**匹**马，an orange 一**个**橘子，first thing 第一**件**事，the first oil well 第一**口**油井，等等。在有些情况下，英语的复数概念比较模糊，翻译时应视上下文灵活使用量词。

- They live among the **mountains**.
  他们住在**群山**之中。
- John showed me the **scars** on his arms.
  约翰让我看他**双**臂上的**道道**伤痕。
- When she came to, Susan saw smiling **faces** around her.
  苏珊苏醒过来，看见周围的一**张张**笑脸。

4. 把抽象概念表达清楚

英语靠词类（part of speech）的划分将主、谓、宾、定、状语区分开来。汉语没有这种优势，不通过上下文就不能辨清词性（如：学习、劳动），有时候需要用增词法把抽象概念表达清楚。

- The classroom was full of **activity**.
  教室里充满了**活跃的气氛**。（将 activity 增译为"活跃的气氛"）
- **Traffic** decreases on holidays.
  节假日**行人车辆**减少了。（将 Traffic 增译为"行人车辆"）
- The artist looked at her with **scorn**.
  艺术家以**蔑视的眼光**看着她。（将 scorn 增译为"蔑视的眼光"）
- Everywhere are scenes of **prosperity**.
  到处都是**一片繁荣昌盛**的景象。（将 prosperity 增译为"一片繁荣昌盛"）

5. 逻辑性增词

在很多情况下，英语字面上没有的意思而实际上已包括在句中，翻译时需要作逻辑性增词。譬如一些科技常识、英语所特有的时态语态等。以时态为例,英语可以通过不同时态来表达事情发生的先后顺序。汉语则不然,只能靠增添助词"着"、"了"、"过"、"现在"、"过去"、"将来"之类的时间状语来表达清楚。

- Air pressure decreases **with altitude**.
  气压随海拔高度的**增加**而下降。
- I **was taught** that two sides of a triangle were greater than the third.
  我学**过**,三角形的两边之和大于第三边。
- If it **hadn't been** for your help, I really don't know what I'd have done.
  要**不是当初**得到你的帮助,我真不知道自己现在会做出什么样的结果。
- We won't retreat; we never have and never will.
  我们不会后退,我们从来没有**后退过**,**将来**也决不**后退**。

6. 修辞性增词

这主要是从译文的行文措辞或语气连贯考虑,适当使用汉语习语、成语、四字结构,可以使译文朗朗上口,富有文采。

- His life is one long **round of meetings**.
  他的生活就是**一个会议接着一个会议**。
- They **build** roads, houses, bridges, ships, pipelines, and canals.
  他们**修**路、**盖**房、**架**桥、**造**船、**铺**管道、**挖**运河。
- One of the articles is **interesting, informative, and easy to read**.
  其中一篇文章**趣味盎然、内容丰富、通俗易读**。
- While in Europe, the tourists enjoyed to their heart's content **the weather, the food** and **the theatre**.
  这些旅游者在欧洲尽情地**沐浴**阳光,**品味**佳肴,**观赏**演出。

7. 重复性增词

英语的修饰语可以一词修饰若干名词,而汉语往往需要分别表述,否则会造成费解或歧义。在这种情况下,往往需要进行重复性增词。有时候,为了准确地表达原文的意思,或是为了突出原文的要点,需要对个别措辞进行必要的重复。

- There are three types of **tiger** living in China: the South China, the Northeastern, and the Bengal.

  目前中国有三种**虎**,即华南**虎**、东北**虎**和孟加拉**虎**。(重复翻译原文中省略的 tiger)

- Avoid using this computer in **extreme** cold, heat, dust or humidity.

  不要在**过**冷、**过**热、灰尘**过**重、湿度**过**大的情况下使用此电脑。(重复翻译形容词 extreme)

- You must **change** with the times.

  你必须随着时势的**转变而改变**。(重复翻译动词 change)

- He passed the test, whether **by** skill or luck.

  他通过了考试,**要么是靠**技术,**要么是靠**运气。(重复翻译介词 by)

二、汉译英增添技巧的运用

汉译英的增词法其主要目的是使译文符合英语的语法结构和表达习惯。汉译英的增词法往往用于这样一些情况:1. 增添必要的代词;2. 增添必要的冠词;3. 增添必要的介词、连词;4. 增添必要的动词;5. 增添必要的背景解释性词语。

1. 增添必要的代词

英语代词的使用率、复现率均大大高于汉语。因为英语重"形合",代词的指代意义往往通过词汇、语法的表现形式而得到固定;而汉语重"意合",其指代关系不言而喻,在很大程度上取决于话题的内容,其表现手段正如王力先生所言,要么省略,要么重复使用前面已出现过的名词,很少像英语那样大量地重复使用代词,而省略掉的成分往往需读者自己通过上下文去把握。

- 大作收到,十分高兴。

  I am very glad to have received **your** writing.(增添代词 I, your)

- 三思而后行!

  Think before **you** act!(增添代词 you)

- 这小男孩言行不一。

  This boy's conduct disagrees with **his** words.（增添代词 his，介词 with）
- 老人的儿子为国捐躯。

  The son of the old man gave **his** life as a sacrifice for **his** country.（增添两处代词 his）

2. 增添必要的冠词

汉语没有冠词，而英语的冠词总是与名词相伴，因此汉译英要时时注意增添必要的冠词。

- 石油供不应求。

  The supply of oil is inadequate to meet **the** demand.
- 天空碧蓝，海上风平浪静。

  The sky is blue, and **the** sea is calm.
- 正方形有四条边。

  A square has four sides.
- 我们对问题必须做全面的分析，才能妥善地加以解决。

  We must make **a** comprehensive analysis of **a** problem before it can be properly solved.

3. 增添必要的介词、连词

汉语比英语简洁，词语之间的许多连接成分往往可以省略，形成一种固定的表达套路。汉语不太喜欢使用介词、连词，而英语的词与词、句与句之间介词、连词却不可或缺。所以在很多情况下，汉译英需要增添必要的介词、连词。

- 你是白天工作还是夜间工作？

  Do you work **in** the daytime or **at** night?（增添介词 in, at）
- 该地区已没什么城乡差别。

  There is little difference **between** town **and** country **in** this region.（增添介词 between, and, in）
- 她不老实，我不能信任她。

Since she is not honest, I cannot trust her.（增添连词 since）
- 虚心使人进步，骄傲使人落后。

  Modesty helps one to go forward, **whereas** conceit makes one lag behind.（增添连词 whereas）

4. 增添必要的动词

如第三单元所示，汉语的句子成分的划分不像英语那样有一个统一的标准。汉语句子可以没有主语、没有谓语动词。汉语的名词除了作主语、宾语和定语之外，还可以作谓语和状语；形容词除了作定语和表语之外，还可以作谓语。而英语句子有严格的主、谓、宾结构。所以在有些情况下，需要增添必要的动词。

- 天高云淡。

  The sky **is** high and the clouds **are** pale.（增添动词 is, are）
- 小姑娘脸红了。

  The face of the little girl **turned** red.（增添动词 turned）
- 小伙子十八岁，朝气勃勃。

  The young man **is** eighteen, full of vitality.（增添动词 is）
- 这孩子大眼睛，高鼻梁。

  The boy **has** a pair of big eyes and a Roman nose.（增添动词 has）

5. 增添必要的解释性词语

这种增添主要是为译文的读者考虑，将一些时代背景、历史政治事件、语言文化习惯等做补充说明。譬如"解放前"、"改革开放以来"之类的词语，对中国人来说耳熟能详，外国读者就不一定清楚，增添 in 1949, since 1978 等字眼，表达也就清楚了。

- **解放**以后，劳动人民当家做主。

  After **Liberation in 1949**, laboring people have become the masters of the country.
- **改革开放**以来，我们从海外引进了大量的人才、资金和技术。

  Since **the reform and opening up in 1978**, a large number of talents, vast amount of capitals and technologies have been imported from abroad.

- 这真是俗话说的,"旁观者**清**"。

  It is just as the proverb goes, "The onlooker sees **most of the game**."

- 我们提倡"**五讲四美**"。

  We advocate **the culture of** "five stresses and four points of beauty", i.e. **stress on decorum, manner, hygiene, discipline and morals; beauty of the mind, language, behavior and the environment**. ("五讲"即讲文明、讲礼貌、讲卫生、讲秩序、讲道德,"四美"指心灵美、语言美、行为美、环境美。)

思考与练习

一、简要回答以下问题

1. 在实际翻译过程中我们能否做到译文和原文完全一致,不增一词,不减一字?为什么?
2. 英译汉常用增词技巧有哪几种?试举例说明。
3. 汉译英常用增词技巧有哪几种?试举例说明。

二、英汉互译翻译练习

1. 英译汉。翻译下列各句,注意使用增词技巧。

   1) The two boys fought.
   2) That's where we differ.
   3) Music can enrich your whole life.
   4) The city streets are full of traffic.
   5) He was a little man with thick glasses.
   6) Born a free man, he was now in chains.
   7) Cook was the first to map the east coast.

8) It is often thought that disabilities are total.

9) Two thirds of the country is dry or desert.

10) She could not make a decision about the dress.

11) He fell into a thorn bush and was covered with scratches.

12) Not only do disabled people read, write, draw pictures, paint and cook, but they also study, go to university, take exams and have jobs.

2. 汉译英。翻译下列各句，注意使用增词技巧。

1）去伪存真。

2）她演得最糟。

3）果园的苹果熟了。

4）有困难，找民警。

5）他数学差，但英语好。

6）俗话说，后来居上。

7）驾驶员突然向左转。

8）这事别怪他，该怪我。

9）我们经理 60 岁时退休了。

10）一个乞丐骗了他 100 元。

11）飞行员在事故中险些丧命。

12）这项政策关系到国计民生的大问题。

第五单元
省略技巧的运用

省略法是与增词法相对的翻译方法。在同一个译例，要是英译汉用的是增词法，那么将汉语回译成英语，就得用省略法了。一般来说，汉语比英语简练，因此英译汉时，许多在原文中必不可少的词语要是原原本本地译成汉语，就会成为不必要的冗词，译文会显得拖泥带水。请看下面这样一例：

The time-keeping devices of electronic watches are much more accurate than those of mechanical ones. 电子表比机械表准确得多。

原文中的主语 The time-keeping devices of、谓语动词 are 和代词 those of 在译文中都省略了。要是按字面直译为"电子表这种计时器是比那些机械类的表准确得多"，会显得十分啰唆，不堪卒读。

一、英译汉省略技巧的运用

省略法在英汉翻译中的使用十分广泛，主要旨在删去一些可有可无、不符合译文习惯表达法的词语。英译汉常见的省略情况有以下几种。

1. 冗余词语的省略

英语的一些习惯表达法文句啰嗦累赘，直译出来不符合汉语的表达习惯，翻译时可考虑将其省略（请注意比较对照，以下各译例的黑体字部分为省略词语）。

- Our great motherland is flourishing **with each passing day**.

  我们伟大的祖国蒸蒸日上。

- He appropriated public funds **for his own private use**.

  他私自挪用公款。

- The true joy **of joys** is **the joy that joys in the** joy of others.

  与人同乐才是真乐。

- They used to travel around **from place to place** with teams of dogs which pulled their baggage.

  他们过去常常用一群群的狗拉着行李，居无定所，四处迁徙。

2. 代词的省略

英语代词有主格、宾格、所有格之分，功能齐全，各司其职。以第三人称单数代词为例：he, him, his, she, her, it, its 一清二楚，怎么也乱不了套。汉语虽然也有"他、她、它"之分，但不分主格宾格，不分青红皂白，统统读作一个音：tā，一不小心就会造成指代上的混乱。因此汉语中代词的使用频率比英语要低得多。因此在翻译时英语的代词不可照搬，必须做出省略，以符合汉语的表达习惯。

- After getting up, I wash **my** face, brush **my** teeth, and comb **my** hair.

  起床后，我洗脸、刷牙、梳头。

- You should adapt **yourself** to the new environment.

  你应该适应新环境。

- They robbed the people **of their** liberty.

  他们剥夺了人民的自由。

- The professor put a finger in **his** mouth, tasted **it** and smiled, looking rather pleased.

  教授把一个指头放到嘴里尝了尝，微笑着露出一副很满意的样子。

3. 冠词的省略

汉语没有冠词，英译汉时可视情况省略冠词。有人由此断定，英译汉凡是遇到冠词便统统应当省略。这种说法十分片面。因为在很多情况下，英语中的冠词有其特定的含义，不能省略。

一般来说，有两种情况不能省略冠词。一是不定冠词 a, an 具有数词 one 的含义，如：

- **An** apple **a** day keeps the doctor away.

　　［谚］**一**天**一**个苹果，医生没有事做（意即不生病）。

二是定冠词 the 具有指示代词 this, that, these, those 的含义，如：

- This is **the** book you wanted.

　　这就是你要的**那本**书。

除此两点之外，都可以考虑省略冠词，如以下各例：

- **The** moon was slowly rising above **the** sea.

　　月亮慢慢从海上升起。

- Any substance is made of atoms whether it is **a** solid, **a** liquid, or **a** gas.

　　任何物质，不论是固体、液体或气体，都由原子组成。

- The direction of **a** force can be represented by **an** arrow.

　　力的方向可以用箭头表示。

- In **the** north, **the** winters are long and hard, with snow for six months of **the** year.

　　北方的冬季漫长寒冷，一年有 6 个月积雪。

4. 介词、连词的省略

王力先生曾指出："西洋语的结构好像连环，虽则环与环都联络起来，毕竟有联络的痕迹；中国语的结构好像无缝天衣，只是一块一块的硬凑，凑起来还不让它有痕迹。西洋语法是硬的，没有弹性的；中国语法是软的，富于弹性的。因为是硬的，所以西洋语法有许多呆板的要求，如每一个 clause 里必须有一个主语；因为是软的，所以中国语法只以达意为主，如初系的目的位可兼次系的主语，又如相关的两件事可以硬凑在一起，不用任何的 connective word。"由此可见，英语中的大量连词、介词在翻译成汉语时可考虑省略。

- Hydrogen is the lightest element **with** an atomic weight **of** 1.008.

  氢是最轻的元素，其原子量为 1.008。（省略介词 with, of）

- Some people like fat meat, **whereas** others hate it.

  有些人喜欢肥肉，有些人讨厌肥肉。（省略连词 whereas）

- **In** 1756 the Seven Years War **between** Britain and France broke out **and** Cook joined the navy.

  1756 年英法七年战争爆发，库克参加了海军。（省略介词 In, between，连词 and）

- Only **after** I had heard his explanation did I understand what it was all **about**.

  听了他的解释，我才知道究竟是怎么回事。（省略连词 after，介词 about）

5. 动词的省略

英语句子严格遵循主谓结构，而汉语句子可以没有主语，也可以没有谓语动词。在不少情况下，英语动词在翻译成汉语时要作必要的省略，以符合汉语的表达习惯。尤其是汉语的系表结构，一般情况都不用动词，如：他今年 18 岁；今天星期五；桌子一尺二；等等。

- It **is** very quiet in the classroom.

  教室里静悄悄。（省略动词 is）

- When the pressure **gets** low, the boiling point **becomes** low.

  气压低，沸点就低。（省略动词 get, becomes）

- The house **has** a very fine situation.

  这房子的位置很好。（省略动词 has）

- For this reason television signals **have** a short range.

  因此，电视信号的传播距离很短。（省略动词 have）

6. 非人称代词"it"的省略

英语中的代词 it 十分灵活，使用率很高。除人称代词之外，也常常用作无人称主语，表示天气、时间、距离等，还普遍用作先行主语、先行宾语、强调句等。

在翻译在这类句型结构时，it 往往略去不译。

- **It** is very cold and often snows here in winter.（it 表示天气）

  此地冬天很冷，常常下雪。

- Outside **it** was pitch-dark and **it** was raining cats and dogs.（it 表示时间、天气）

  外面一团漆黑，大雨倾盆。

- **It** is about two miles from here to the petrol station.（it 表示距离）

  这儿离加油站大约两英里。

- **It** seems that the result of this test will be very important to the oil industry.（it 用作先行主语）

  看来，这个试验的结果对石油工业非常重要。

- This formula makes **it** easy to determine the wavelength of sounds.（it 用作先行宾语）

  这一公式使得测定声音的波长变容易了。

- **It** is to reduce friction that roller bearings are used.（it 用于强调句）

  正是为了减少摩擦，才使用滚珠轴承。

二、汉译英省略技巧的运用

省略法也同样适用于汉译英。常见的汉译英的省略情况包括省略宾语、省略不必要的重复、冗词之类的赘言、省略概念范畴类词语等。

1. 省略宾语

在很多情况下，汉语动词必须加上宾语才能确保句子意义完整，而英语有些不及物动词在一定的上下文中本身就具有完整的意义，将宾语按字面翻译出来反而会造成译文不通顺。

- 他 5 岁便开始读**书**写**字**。

  He started reading and writing at five.（省略宾语"书"、"字"）

- 他们**你一句**，**我一句**，说个没完。
  They talked on and on. （省略赘言"你一句，我一句"）
- 我给她写了**信**，但她没有回**信**。
  I wrote to her, but she did not reply. （省略两处宾语"信"）
- 匪军所至，杀戮**人民**，奸淫**妇女**，焚毁**村庄**，掠夺**财物**，无所不用其极。
  Where the bandit troops went, they massacred and raped, burned and looted, and stopped at nothing. （省略宾语"人民"、"妇女"、"村庄"、"财物"）

2. 省略不必要的赘言

汉语的一些赘言、动宾重复结构，英语不宜套用。此外，汉语句子中的主语可以反复出现，翻译成英语必须做出适当省略或简化，否则会造成画蛇添足。

- 这些新型汽车**速度**快，**效率**高，**行动**灵活。
  These new cars are **fast**, **efficient and handy**. （省略"速度"、"效率"、"行动"）
- 我已经提前完成了交给我的工作，他也**提前完成了交给他的工作**。
  I have fulfilled my assigned work ahead of schedule, **so has** he. （简化"提前完成了交给他的工作"）
- 质子带正电荷，电子带负电荷，而中子**既不带正电荷，也不带负电荷**。
  A proton has a positive charge and an electron a negative charge, but a neutron has **neither**. （简化"既不带正电荷，也不带负电荷"）
- 我们说，**长征**是历史记录上的第一次，**长征**是宣言书，**长征**是宣传队，**长征**是播种机。
  We answer that **the Long March** is the first of its kind in the annals of history, **and it** is a manifesto, a propaganda force, a seeding-machine. （省略三次重复主语"长征"）

3. 省略概念范畴类词语

汉语喜欢用一些概念范畴类词语，提及工作，往往会将其归入任务范畴，于是便有了"工作任务";说到困难,就归入某种情况,于是便有了"困难情况";谈到就业,觉得这是一个问题,于是便有了"就业问题"。而在英语中,工作是工作,任务是任务;困难是困难,情况是情况。尤其是"问题"一词,在很多情况下,其实并非什么 problem,而是某一话题(topic)罢了。因此,在翻译这类词语时,应从英语的思维角度出发,才能准确地传达出原文的意思。

- 这些都是人民内部矛盾**问题**。
  All these are **contradictions** among the people.(省略"问题"二字)
- 他一直处在极度紧张**状态**之中。
  He has been under a severe **strain**.(省略"状态"二字)
- 我们党结束了那个时期的社会动荡和纷扰不安的**局面**。
  Our Party has put an end to the social **unrest and upheaval** of that time.(省略"局面"二字)
- 她的朋友们听到她家中的困难**情况**后,都主动伸出援助之手。
  After her friends heard about her family **difficulties**, they offered her a helping hand.(省略"情况"二字)

4. 省略过详的细节描述

汉语有些表达法约定俗成,带有强烈的民族文化色彩,或汉语特有的措辞语气,如照字面翻译成英语,会令读者费解,必要时可考虑使用省略或简化。此外,汉语的一些过详的细节描述也不宜照字面译成英语。

- 生**也好**,死**也好**,我们要**忠于**党,**忠于**人民,**忠于**祖国。
  Live or die, we should be loyal to our Party, to our people and to our motherland.(省略两处语气词"也好"、两处动词"忠于")
- 这个国家的 2/3 的地方**气候**干燥或者是沙漠**地区**。
  Two thirds of the country is dry or desert.(省略"气候"、"地区")
- 50 年**风起云涌**,50 年**花开花谢**,他科研的脚步从没停息片刻。
  In the past fifty springs and falls, he has never stopped his steps in scientific research.(简化"风起云涌"、"花开花谢")
- 花园里面是人间的乐园,有的是吃不了的**大米白面**,穿不完的**绫罗绸缎**,

花不完的**金银财宝**。

The garden was a paradise on earth, with more food and clothes than could be consumed and more money than could be spent.（简化"大米白面"、"绫罗绸缎"、"金银财宝"）

思考与练习

一、简要回答以下问题

1. 翻译中的省略法一般用于什么情况下？
2. 英译汉常用省略技巧有哪几种？试举例说明。
3. 汉译英常用省略技巧有哪几种？试举例说明。

二、英汉互译翻译练习

1. 英译汉。翻译下列各句，注意使用省略技巧。

   1) When in Rome do as the Romans do.
   2) He was timid about investing money.
   3) Lao Wang began to earn his living when he was 16 years old.
   4) Professor Zhang has a good command of the French language.
   5) This strange animal lays eggs, yet feeds its young on its milk.
   6) Xiao Li busied himself with answering letters all day long.
   7) The speaker switched the conversation from one subject to another.
   8) The population in and around San Francisco is now ten times more than it was in 1906.
   9) In size New Zealand is bigger than Guangdong Province, yet has a much smaller population.
   10) These developing countries cover vast territories, encompass a large population and abound in natural resources.

11) If individuals are awakened each time they begin a dream phase of sleep, they are likely to become irritable even though their total amount of sleep has been sufficient.

12) They went in to dinner. It was excellent, and the wine was good. Its influence presently had its effect on them. They talked not only without acrimony, but even with friendliness.

2. 汉译英。翻译下列各句，注意使用省略技巧。

1）同一个世界，同一个梦想。

2）园丁正在花园里挖地。

3）盖子啪的一声弹开了。

4）这件大衣真是买得便宜。

5）老师叫他干什么，他就干什么。

6）食物对于维持生命不可或缺。

7）他从一个极端走到另一极端。

8）姐姐买了一件礼物给她的朋友。

9）她一个人坐在教室的角落里动也不动。

10）孩子们在公园里唱歌、跳舞、做游戏。

11）人们利用科学了解自然，改造自然。

12）如同液体和气体一样，固体也能膨胀和收缩。

第六单元
句式结构调整

结构调整是英汉互译中的一种常用翻译技巧。由于英汉不同的造句结构和表达习惯，翻译中有时需要打破原文的句式结构，对译文进行结构调整，以符合汉语的表达习惯。

英汉语言属于不同的语系，因此在思维模式、句式表达上的差异甚大。如语言学家所示，英语的思维模式是由点及面的外展螺旋式，其表达方式是**由小到大，由近及远，由轻到重，由弱到强**；而汉语恰恰相反，**由面到点，由大到小，由远及近，由重到轻，由强到弱**。以家庭住址为例，英语先是门牌号码，然后街道、城市、州、国家；汉语正好相反，例如：

- His address is **3612 Market Street, Philadelphia, PA 19104, USA**.
  他的地址是**美国宾夕法尼亚州费城市场街 3612 号。邮政编码 19104**。

再以日常生活中的常见情况为例，同事或朋友之间请求帮助，英美人士脱口就说 **Can you help me?** 然后再说明需要帮助的具体方面，解释其原因等。而汉语则不然，同样的情况首先要寒暄一番，然后问对方有没有空，能否抽出时间帮忙解决具体问题，最后再提出请求。谁也不会唐突地一见面就问"你能帮我一下吗？"不少同学喜欢将汉语的这种思维方式套入英语。譬如某同学因故上课迟到，向外教解释迟到的原因。按英语表达习惯应当先说 **"I'm sorry to be late for class. I..."** 可他却不得要领，按汉语的"因为……所以"的表达习惯解释了很久，最后才对自己的迟到感到抱歉——用这种方式道歉其效果自然会大打折扣。由此可见，英汉表达的语序差异会对语言交流造成负面影响。

一、英译汉的结构调整

英语倒装结构较多，翻译时应按汉语习惯处理。请看下面几种常见的英语倒装结构：

1）疑问倒装，用于英语疑问句，询问相关信息。
- **What did you** do yesterday?

你昨天干**什么**来着？

2）命令倒装，用于英语祈使句，表示命令或恳求。
- "**Speak you**," said Mr. Black, "Speak you, good fellow!"

布莱克先生叫道："**说**，说吧！伙计！"

3）惊叹倒装，用于英语感叹句，表示惊呼、感叹等强烈语气。
- **How** dreadful this place **is**!

这地方**好**可怕啊！

4）假设倒装，用于英语条件句，表示假设条件。
- **Had you** come yesterday, you could have seen him here.

要是你昨天来了，你就会在这里看到他的。

5）平衡倒装，这种倒装主要是为了避免句子结构的头重脚轻。
- **Through a gap came** an elaborately described ray.

从一条**缝隙**透出一束精心描绘的光线。（这句话的正常语序为：An elaborately described ray came through a gap. 主语及修饰部分太长，利用平衡倒装使句子显得平稳。）

6）衔接倒装，这种倒装主要是为了与上文紧密衔接。
- **On this depends** the whole argument.

整个争论都**以此**为论据。（这句话的正常语序为：The whole argument depends on this.）

7）点题倒装，这种倒装主要是为了突出话题。

- **By strategy is** meant something wider.

    战略的意义比较广。（这句话的正常语序为：Strategy means something wider.）

8）否定倒装，这种倒装主要是为了加强否定语气。

- **Not a word did** he say.

    他**一言不发**。（这句话的正常语序为：He didn't say a word.）

汉语倒装结构的使用并不像英语那样频繁。这也是为什么上述所有英语倒装结构，翻译成汉语之后基本上都没有保持倒装结构的原因。以上各句，我们分别采用问号、感叹号、感叹词、或调整状语的位置加以处理。

鉴于英汉两种语言有着不同的行文造句特点和表达习惯，翻译时我们常常需要打破原文的句式结构，对译文进行结构调整，以符合汉语的表达习惯。常见的英译汉结构调整有原序法、逆序法、时序/逻辑序法、拆分法/拆解法、重组法等5种情况。

1. 原序法

即大致保持原文的句子顺序，按句子的意群逐一翻译成汉语，仅对其中的个别词语作微调处理。一般情况下，在英汉语言结构语序比较一致的情况下可采用此法。

- One should always live in the best company, whether it be of books or of men.

    一个人应该经常生活在最佳友伴之中，不管这友伴是书还是人。

- Written English is more or less the same in both Britain and the United States, though there are some spelling differences.

    英国和美国的书面英语差不多完全一样，尽管在拼法上有些差异。

- Today, Abraham Lincoln is considered as one of the greatest of all American presidents.

    今天，亚伯拉罕·林肯仍被认为是美国历届总统中最伟大的总统之一。

- In order to survive, to feed, clothe and shelter himself and his children, man is engaged in a constant struggle with nature.

为了生存，为了自己和子孙后代的衣食住行，人类同大自然不断进行斗争。

2. 逆序法

即颠倒原文的顺序，将句首的内容放到句尾，句尾的内容放到句首。这种情况尤其适用于翻译以 it 作形式主语、形式宾语的情况，以及时间状语、原因状语、条件状语、让步状语等。英语状语可以随意置前置后，而汉语的这种情况通常只能前置。

- The sea was calm **after the storm**.
  风暴后，大海平静下来了。
- **I am sorry** to hear that your brother passed away.
  听到你兄弟去世的消息，**我很难过**。
- **It is much cheaper** to post or e-mail a long report than to fax it.
  通过邮寄或电子邮件的方式发一篇长报告比用传真**便宜得多**。
- Gandhi was thrown off a train and later a mail bus **for insisting on travelling in the whites-only section**.
  旅行时，甘地由于坚持要坐入白人专用区座位，曾先后被人从一列火车和一辆邮车中扔出。

3. 时序法／逻辑序法

这种方法不考虑原文语序，只按事件发生的时间先后顺序或逻辑顺序安排译文结构。英语语法严谨，一般将重要信息放在句子的主谓结构；而汉语却不受严格的语法约束，也没有固定的句式结构，其表达方式一般按时间或逻辑顺序展开。先发生的事先说，后发生的事后讲。先因后果；先假设，后结论；先条件，后结果。

- She closed her speech **with a funny joke**.
  她**用一个有趣的笑话**结束了发言。
- **I was angered** by Xiao Li's refusal to come to the party.
  小李拒绝来参加晚会，**我很生气**。
- The athlete **smiled in satisfaction** when he won the race.
  运动员赢得比赛后**满意地笑了**。

- **It was a keen disappointment that** I had to postpone the visit I had intended to pay to China in January.

  我原打算在 1 月份访问中国，但后来又不得不推迟行程，**这使我深感失望**。

4. 拆分法／拆解法

这种方法是将原文中的某一部分（如单词、短语或从句）拆分出来单独处理，放在译文句首或句末。这种拆分主要用于表达作者对某一观点、行为或事件的看法和见解，或是根据汉语习惯表达的需要，将英语的短语、从句拆分出来单独翻译，作为全句的补充或说明。

- The candidate **had the good sense** to withdraw from the election contest.

  这位候选人退出了竞选，**很明智**。（将 had the good sense 拆分出来单独译作"很明智"）

- They, **not unexpectedly**, did not respond.

  他们没有答复，**这完全是意料之中的事**。（将 not unexpectedly 拆分出来单独译作"这完全是意料之中的事"）

- This jacket is **a real bargain** at such a low price.

  这件夹克衫这么便宜，**真划算**。（将 a real bargain 拆分出来单独译作"真划算"）

- **Illogically**, she had expected some kind of miracle solution.

  她满以为会有某种奇迹般的解决办法，**这显然不合逻辑**。（将 Illogically 拆分出来，另起一句）

- **It is not surprising that**, when humidity is low, the water evaporates rapidly from the fruit.

  在大气湿度低的情况下，水果里的水分蒸发就快，**这是不足为奇的**。（将 It is not surprising that 后置，另起一句译作"这是不足为奇的"。）

5. 重组法

重组法也叫做综合法，在准确地领会、把握了原文的基础上，彻底改造原文的结构，用译者自己的话恰如其分地表达出原文的信息、含义和精神风貌。

- Also present will be a person who thinks up an idea for an advertisement, and a person who will buy space in newspapers or time on TV.

  与会人员中还将有一位广告策划者以及一位想在报纸或电视上打广告的客户。

- The whole country was very sad at the news of his death; the people had considered him to be a great leader, and a wise, kind and honest man.

  噩耗传来，举国悲恸，人们已把他看作一位伟大的领袖，公认他是一位英明、慈祥而正直的人。

- As a boy, Mr. Huang recycled bottles after school to supplement the income of his farming family.

  黄先生生于农家，早在孩童时代就为生计奔波，常常在放学以后回收废弃瓶子，以此贴补家用。

- Interest in historical methods has arisen less through external to the validity of history as an intellectual discipline and more from internal quarrels among historians themselves.

  人们关注历史研究的方法，主要是因为史学界内部意见不统一，其次是因为外界怀疑历史是不是一门学科。

- In practice, the selected interval thickness is usually a compromise between the need for a thin interval to maximize the resolution and a thick interval to minimize the error.

  为保证最大分辨率必须选用薄层，为使误差最小却须选用厚层，实际上通常选择介于两者之间的最佳厚度。

二、汉译英的结构调整

与英语相比，汉语的倒装结构很少，偶见于主谓倒装句式。汉语的这类倒装句翻译成英语时可根据译文表达的需要适当地采用主谓倒装、条件状语或祈使句等表达手段。如：

- 来了一人。

  Here comes a man.（译作倒装句）

- 不愿干就走人。

  You may go away if you don't like this job.（译作条件状语）

- 安息吧，亲爱的战友！

  May you rest in peace, comrade-in-arms!（译作祈使倒装句）

一般情况下，英译汉的结构调整法同样也适用于汉译英，主要用于定语、状语的安排调整以及一些否定结构的处理。此外，如前所述，英汉表达的轻重顺序也不一样。汉语习惯上把重的、强的词语放在前面，而英语恰恰相反，按轻、重顺序排放。比如一些习惯用语，汉语先说重的、厉害的。"钢铁工业"，"钢"在先，"铁"在后；"分清敌我"，"敌"在先，"我"在后；"救死扶伤"，"死"在前，"伤"在后。而英语却恰恰相反，先说"iron"，后说"steel"：the iron and steel industry；先说"ourselves"，后说"enemy"：distinction between ourselves and the enemy. 此外，英语的代词可以提前放到所指代的名词之前，形成代词的"预指"，如：Young as he is, the little boy has learned a lot.（尽管这小男孩尚年幼，可已学了不少知识。）如果不了解英语的这种表达方式，照英语的句子结构去生搬硬套，就会闹出"尽管他年纪轻轻，可孩子已学了不少知识"之类的翻译笑话。

1. 定语的结构调整

汉语作修饰成分的定语往往将最重要的性质放在首位，而英语则放在紧靠被修饰的中心词的位置；汉语的定语无论多长，总是放在被修饰词语的前面，而英语除了单个词语之外，词组、短语都放在被修饰词语的后面；汉语先分散，后集中，英语先集中，后分散。

- **社会主义的现代化强**国

  a modern, powerful socialist country

- **一位美国当代优秀**作家

  an outstanding contemporary American writer

- **各条战线上的**先进工作者们

  advanced workers **from various fronts**

- **只有他一人**知道这个秘密。

  He alone knows the secret.

- 这是能**想象得出的**最好解决办法。

  This is the best solution **imaginable**.

- 假如少种一些经济作物,就可能生成更多的粮食,就会**杜绝或减少**饥饿现象。

  If fewer cash crops were grown, more food could be produced and there would be **less or no** starvation.

- 这所大学现有**计算机科学、高能物理、激光、地球物理、遥感技术、遗传工程6个新建的**专业。

  This university has **6 newly established** faculties, **namely, Computer Science, High Energy Physics, Laser, Geophysics, Remote Sensing, and Genetic Engineering.**

2. 状语的结构调整

在很多情况下,汉语和英语状语的结构顺序不尽相同。汉语的"水陆并进"、"左顾右盼",翻译成英语应先说"陆",后说"水",先是"右",后是"左",译为:advance by both land and water, look right and left。汉语的"必须或者应当",翻译成英语应先轻后重,译为:should or must。从时间地点状语上看,汉语先说时间,后说地点,英语则先说地点,后说时间,如:

- 我的伯父于**2007年9月12日凌晨2时30分在医院**逝世。

  My uncle passed away **in hospital at 2∶30 a.m. on September 12, 2007**.

- 我们**活捉**了敌哨兵。

  We captured the enemy sentry **alive**.

- **救死扶伤**,实行革命的人道主义。

  Heal the wounded, rescue the dying, practice revolutionary humanitarianism.

- 他们的部队**水陆并进**,及时抵达前线。

  Their troops **advanced by both land and water**, and arrived at the front in time.

- 他过马路时，**左顾右盼**，害怕撞到过路的车子上。

  While crossing the street, he **looked right and left**, afraid that he might run into some passing car.

- 因此，我们并不认为，他们**必须或者应当**采取中国的做法。

  Therefore, we do not maintain that they **should or must** adopt the Chinese way.

- 许多代表激动地说，"我们**从来没有**看见过这样光明的前途！"

  A great number of deputies said excitedly, "**Never have we seen** so bright a future before us!"

- 中国人民正**在中国共产党的领导下**，**团结一致**地进行着伟大的社会主义建设。

  Led by the Chinese Communist Party, the Chinese people, **united as one**, are engaged in the great task of building socialism.

思考与练习

一、简要回答以下问题

1. 翻译中为什么要进行结构调整？试举例说明。
2. 英语常见的倒装结构有哪些？翻译成汉语都有什么变化？
3. 常见的英译汉结构调整主要有哪些方面？
4. 汉语句式结构与英语有什么差异？汉译英的结构调整应注意哪两方面？

二、英汉互译翻译练习

1. 英译汉。翻译下列各句，注意结构调整。

   1) He was wet to the skin.
   2) The weather here alters almost daily.
   3) It was silly of me to say such a thing.
   4) It's too early to evaluate its success.

5) SARS highlighted all the events of 2003.

6) Altogether there were eight people in the bus.

7) I was astonished to see he got up so early.

8) The old lady never had any visitors.

9) The enemy seized the town after a violent attack.

10) At this moment his footsteps sounded on the stairs.

11) It's restful to sit on the beach, watching the gentle lapping of the waves.

12) Scientists are afraid that one day an even bigger earthquake will hit the area around San Francisco.

2. 汉译英。翻译下列各句，注意结构调整。

1）他一推，门就开了。

2）公元476年罗马帝国灭亡。

3）海运最大的缺点是速度慢。

4）要掌握英语必须经常不断地练习。

5）我们已决定提前完成这项工作。

6）患病的孩子痛得叫了起来。

7）空气中散发着水仙花的香味。

8）你走了这么远的路，一定很累。

9）父亲乘坐的是开往北京的5次特快列车。

10）警察搜查了在犯罪现场的每一个人。

11）这位学者正在研究东西方的政治理论。

12）除了继续前进，我们没有别的选择余地。

第七单元
各类从句的翻译技巧

翻译中我们往往会遇到各式各样的句型，如简单句、并列句、复合句等。其中复合句的结构比较复杂，也是翻译的一大难点。英语复合句由主句、从句两部分组成；主句结构简单，从句类别繁杂。本单元着重对各类从句的翻译方法进行分析讲解。

英语的从句可分为3大类：名词性从句、形容词性从句及副词性从句。名词性从句是指在完整的句子中以名词性质出现的从句成分，包括主语从句、宾语从句、表语从句和同位语从句。形容词性从句用于修饰主句中某一名词或代词（有时也可说明整个主句或主句中一部分），起定语作用，所以叫作定语从句。副词性从句包括各类状语从句，主要用于修饰主句或主句的谓语。

一、英语各类从句的翻译技巧

1. 英语名词性从句的翻译方法

名词性从句在句子中的作用相当于名词，或是作主语，或是作宾语、表语、同位语，因此习惯上称之为名词性从句。相对而言，主语从句、宾语从句、表语从句的翻译比较容易，大致按照原文的结构顺序翻译就行了，只是在以"it"为形式主语、形式宾语的情况下，语序往往需要前后颠倒。在必要时也可视其上下文作灵活处理。

- **What he told me** was only half-truth.（主语从句）

  他告诉我的只是半真半假的东西而已。（保持原文结构顺序）

- It doesn't make much difference **whether he attends the meeting or not**.（It 作形式主语）

  他参不参加会议都没多大关系。（颠倒原文前后顺序）

- Computers can only do **what men have them do**.（宾语从句）

  电脑只能做**人让它们做的事**。（保持原文结构顺序）

- I regard it as an honor that **I am chosen to attend the meeting**.（it 作形式宾语）

  能被选中参加这个会议，我感到十分荣幸。（颠倒原文结构顺序）

  我感到十分荣幸**能被选中参加这个会议**。（保持原文结构顺序）

- This is **where the shoe pinches**.（表语从句）

  这就是**问题的症结所在**。（保持原文结构顺序）

  问题的症结就在这里。（颠倒原文结构顺序）

- Things are **not always as they seem to be**.（表语从句）

  事物并**不总是如其表象**。（保持原文结构顺序）

相对而言，英语同位语从句的翻译比较麻烦，一般可按这样 **4 种方法来处理**：

1）保持原本的语序，用类似宾语从句的方法来翻译；

2）将同位语从句前置，用翻译定语从句的类似结构来翻译，或单独翻译成一句；

3）加入冒号、破折号或"这样"、"这一"、"即"等字眼；

4）改变原文的同位语结构，用汉语的无主句或其他方式译出。

请看下面同位语从句的处理方法。

- He expressed **the hope that he would come over to visit China again**.

  他表示**希望能再来中国访问**。（保持原本的语序）

- Yet, from the beginning, **the fact that I was alive** was ignored.

  然而，从一开始，**我仍活着这一事实**却偏偏被忽视了。（加入"这一"字眼）

- But considering realistically, we had to face **the fact that our prospects** were less than good.

但是现实地考虑一下，我们不得不正视**这样一个事实：我们的前景并不妙**。（加入冒号）

- An order has been given **that the researchers who are now in the skylab should be sent back**.

已下命令要求**将现在在航天实验室里的研究人员送回来**。（译成汉语无主句）

2. 英语定语从句的翻译方法

定语从句是英语各类从句中较常见的一种。引导定语从句的关系代词包括 that, which, who, whose, whom 等，关系副词包括 when, where, why。英语定语从句句子可长可短，结构繁简不一，在翻译时需根据不同情况采用不同的方法。

汉语没有定语从句之说，作为修饰成分的定语习惯上放在被修饰词之前（左边），呈左封闭状。而英语的定语从句呈右开放状，可以向右无限扩展。请看下面这组英汉定语结构比较：

- This is the hunter.

  这就是那个猎人。

- This is the hunter who shot the wolf.

  这就是那个击毙了狼的猎人。

- This is the hunter who shot the wolf that killed the sheep.

  * 这就是那个击毙了咬死了羊的狼的猎人。

- This is the hunter who shot the wolf that killed the sheep that were shut in the pen.

  ** 这就是那个击毙了咬死了关在羊圈里的羊的狼的猎人。

- This is the hunter who shot the wolf that killed the sheep that were kept in the pen that was newly built last month.

  *** 这就是那个击毙了咬死了关在上个月新修的羊圈里的羊的狼的猎人。

不难发现，汉语译文从第 3 句起便读不通了。要使译文通顺，就得将其切分开来处理：

* 这就是那个猎人。他击毙了咬死了羊的狼。

** 这就是那个击毙了狼的猎人。狼咬死了关在羊圈里的羊。

*** 这就是那个击毙了狼的猎人。狼咬死了关在羊圈里的羊。羊圈是上个月新修的。

由此可知，翻译复杂的英语定语长句最有效的方法就是将其切分，逐一处理。英语定语从句的翻译方法一般有以下 4 种。

A．合并法

即在定语从句的句式较短的情况下（一般在 10 个词之内），将定语从句并入主句，用"……的"结构译出。

- It was the first time **when I spoke in public**.

  这是我第一次**在公共场合发言**。

- **The girl who spoke** is my best friend.

  那个讲话的女孩是我最好的朋友。

- **In the room where the electronic computer is kept**, there must be no dust at all.

  在存放电子计算机的房间里，不能有一点灰尘。

- The sun, **which had hidden all day**, now came out in all its splendor.

  整天躲在云层里的太阳，现在光芒四射地露面了。

B．分译法

即化整为零，分别翻译；对于长而复杂的定语从句，可以采取此法。

- They are striving for **the ideal which is close** to the heart of every Chinese and **for which**, in the past, many Chinese have laid down their lives.

  他们正在为实现一个**理想而努力**，**这个理想是**每个中国人所珍爱的，在过去，许多中国人**为了这个理想**而牺牲了自己的生命。

- In 1898 she discovered the first of these new radioactive minerals, **which she named "polonium" in honor of her motherland**.

  1898 年，她发现了这批新放射性矿物中的第一种元素。**出于对自己祖国波兰的敬意，她将这一元素命名为"钋"**。

- Between these two tiny particles, the proton and the electron, there is a powerful attraction **that is always present between negative and positive electric charges**.

  在质子和电子这两个微粒之间有一个很大的吸引力，**而这个吸引力总是存在于正、负电荷之间**。

C．替换法

即打破原文的定语结构，在准确理解原文的基础上，用自己的话译出原文的意思，用不带定语成分的句式替换原文的定语结构。这种方法尤其适用于英汉表达差异较大、译作定语结构容易造成误解的情况。

- There were men in that crowd **who had stood there every day for a month**.

  在那群人中，有些人**每天站在那里，站了足足一个月**。

- There are some metals **which possess the power to conduct electricity and the ability to be magnetized**.

  某些金属**既能导电，又能被磁化**。

- Good clocks have pendulums **which are automatically compensated for temperature changes**.

  好的钟表可以自动补偿温度变化造成的误差。

D．兼有状语功能的定语从句

在有些情况下，英语定语从句兼有状语的功能，在翻译这类定语从句时，可视情况将其译作相应的表示原因、结果、目的、时间、条件、让步等汉语分句。

a．表示原因

- A solid fuel, like coal or wood, can only burn at the surface, **where it comes into contact with the air**.

  固体燃料，如煤和木材，只能在表面燃烧，**因为表面接触空气**。

- You must grasp the concept of "work" **which is very important in physics**.

  你必须掌握"功"这个概念，**因为它在物理学中很重要**。

b．表示结果

- There was something original, independent, and heroic about the plan **that pleased all of them**.

  这个方案富于原创性，独具一格，很有魄力，**因此他们都很喜欢**。

- Copper, **which is used so widely for carrying electricity**, offers very little resistance.

  铜的电阻很小，**所以广泛地用来传输电力**。

c. 表示让步

- He insisted on building another house, **which he had no use for**.

  他坚持要再造一幢房子，**尽管他并无此需要**。

- Electronic computers, **which have many advantages**, cannot carry out creative work and replace man.

  尽管电子计算机有许多优点，但是它们不能进行创造性工作，也不能代替人。

d. 表示条件

- Nowadays it is understood that a diet **which contains nothing harmful** may result in serious disease if certain important elements are missing.

  现在人们已经懂得，**如果饮食中缺少了某些重要成分**，即使其中不含有任何有害物质，也会引起严重疾病。

- For any machine **whose input and output forces are known, its mechanical advantage can be calculated**.

  对于任何机器来说，**如果知其输入力和输出力**，就能求出其机械效率。

e. 表示目的

- They have built up a new college here, **where students will be trained to be engineers and scientists**.

  他们在这里建了一所学院，**以培养工程师和科学家**。

- I'll try to get an illustrated dictionary dealing with technical glossary, **which will enable me to translate scientific literature more exactly**.

  我要设法弄一本有插图的技术名词词典，**以便把科学文献译得更准确**。

77

3. 英语状语从句的翻译方法

英语状语从句主要用来修饰主句或主句的谓语。一般可分为 9 大类，分别表示时间、地点、原因、目的、结果、条件、让步、比较和方式。尽管种类较多，但由于状语从句与汉语结构和用法相似，所以理解和掌握起来并不难，通常按主从关系译作相应的汉语状语分句即可。在个别情况下，也可译作汉语的并列句或平行结构。

- Please turn off the light **when you leave the room**.（时间状语从句）
  离屋时请关电灯。（译作汉语时间状语分句）

- **Where water resources are plentiful**, hydroelectric power stations are being built in large numbers.（地点状语从句）
  哪里水资源充足，就在哪里修建大批的水电站。（译作汉语条件分句）

- The crops failed **because the season was dry**.（原因状语从句）
  因为气候干燥，农作物歉收。（译作汉语原因分句）

- Steel parts are usually covered with grease **for fear that they should rust**.（目的状语从句）
  钢制零件通常涂上润滑脂，**以防生锈**。（译作汉语目的分句）

- To such a degree was he excited **that he couldn't sleep last night**.（结果状语从句）
  他**昨夜**激动得**睡不着觉**。（译作汉语结果分句）

- **If something has the ability to adjust itself to the environment**, we say it has intelligence.（条件状语从句）
  如果某物具有适应环境的能力，我们就说它具有智力。（译作汉语条件句）

- The old man always enjoys swimming **even though the weather is rough**.（让步状语从句）
  即便天气很恶劣，那老人也总是喜爱游泳。（译作汉语让步分句）

- **The more** you exercise, the **healthier** you will be.（比较状语从句）
  你**越锻炼**，身体就**越健康**。（译作汉语比较结构）

- She behaved **as if she were the boss**.（方式状语从句）
  她的举止**仿佛是个老板**。（译作汉语简单句）

二、汉语复句的翻译技巧

汉语不存在类似英语的各类从句。汉语的复句主要分为联合复句和偏正复句两类。与英语相比，汉语句子较为简短、零散，词序也较为固定，翻译时应注意句子的合并以及语序的调整。此外，句式重心也是一个需要考虑的因素，同样一个句子，根据不同的侧重会有不同的译文。譬如这样一例：

- 他站在窗口向外看。

翻译这句话首先要分清侧重点是"站"还是"看"。根据不同语境，此句可分别译作：

He stood at the window, looking outside.（着重于"站"）

或：Standing at the window he looked outside.（着重于"看"）

如果不强调某一动作，则可译作并列结构：

He stood at the window, looked outside, (and then walked away).（无侧重，仅表达动作的先后顺序）

翻译汉语复句的关键在于抓住句子的重心，将主要信息译作英语的主句，其余部分视情况可分别用分词、动名词、不定式、介词短语等来翻译。

汉语复合句的翻译技巧需把握这样几点：一是分清主次关系，添加连接词语；二是简化为单句，避免不必要的啰唆；三是注意合并零散短句，使译文句式结构规范；四是用无生命的名词充当役使主语，使译文表达符合英语习惯。

1. 分清主次关系，添加连接词语

汉语贵在"不言而喻"，句与句之间往往没有明显的连接词，仅仅靠一种"意合"的机制衔接而成，翻译时需要细心把握。

- 老师在等我，我得走了。

The teacher is expecting me, **so** I must be off now.（添加连词 so）

- 人不犯我，我不犯人。

We **won't** attack others **unless** we are attacked.（添加连词 won't... unless）

- 种瓜得瓜，种豆得豆。

  As you sow, **so will** you reap.（跳出字面意义采用意译，添加连词 as..., so）

- 打肿脸充胖子，吃亏的是自己。

  If you get beyond your depth, **you'll** suffer.（跳出字面意义采用意译，添加连词 if）

2. 将汉语的复句简化为单句

为了便于连贯表达，汉语的有些复句可以通过使用英语介词、介词短语、分词、不定式等简化为单句。

- 我们还是把这搁一搁，以后**再说吧**。

  Let's put this off **till** some other time.（使用介词 till）

- 他十分孤独，**急需**找到一位朋友。

  He was lonesome **for** a friend.（使用介词 for）

- 他**生来本是**个自由人，现在却戴上了镣铐。

  Born a free man, he was now in chains.（使用过去分词 born）

- **坐在**这张椅子里，我感到非常舒服。

  I feel very comfortable **to sit** in this chair.（使用不定式 to sit）

3. 合并零散短句

与英语相比，汉语句子较为简短、零散，词序也较为固定，翻译时应注意将短句合并，做必要的语序调整。

- 我有一个问题弄不懂，想请教你，你能回答吗？

  Can you answer a question which I want to ask and which is puzzling me?

- 学问，学问，要学要问；边学边问，才有学问。

  Acquisition of knowledge entails learning and seeking for explanation.

- 门口放着一堆雨伞，少说也有 12 把，五颜六色，大小不一。

  In the doorway lay at least twelve umbrellas of all sizes and colors.

- 我访问了一些地方，遇到了不少人，要谈起来，奇妙的事儿可多着呢。

  There are many wonderful stories to tell about the places I visited and the people I met.

4. 使用无生命的名词充当役使主语

英语的一大特点是用无生命的名词（如：时间、地点、事件、抽象名词等）充当役使主语发出动作，而汉语却没有这样的造句法。

- **一看到**那棵大树，我便会想起童年的情景。

  The sight of the big tree always reminds me of my childhood.

- **风向突然一转**，森林大火就被遏制了。

  A sudden change of wind checked the forest fire.

- **恕我孤陋寡闻**，对此关系一无所知。

  My total ignorance of the connection must plead my apology.

- 我走在厚厚的**地毯上**，一点脚步声也没有。

  The thick carpet killed the sound of my footsteps.

思考与练习

一、简要回答以下问题

1. 英语名词性从句主要包括哪几类？主要采取什么翻译手段？
2. 英语定语从句与汉语定语修饰成分有什么差异？主要采取哪些翻译手段？
3. 兼有状语功能的英语定语从句应当怎样翻译？
4. 英语状语从句主要分哪几类？一般采取什么翻译手段？
5. 汉语复句与英语复合句有什么差异？翻译时应注意哪些问题？

二、英汉互译翻译练习

1. 英译汉。翻译下列各句，注意各类从句的翻译。

   1) The chance is that one smoker in four will die from smoking.

2) The potato is another plant that was taken back by early travelers.

3) The problem with electrical signals is that they get weaker and weaker as they travel along metal wires.

4) It is believed that before writing was developed, people in China used to keep records by putting a number of stones together.

5) Many parts of the world, which once had large populations and produced plenty of crops, have become deserts.

6) About a third of the people who had been chained up below at the beginning of the journey were missing.

7) In the European Union (EU), where 81% of the land is farmed, there is plenty of food, in fact often too much.

8) Once the satellite goes into its orbit round the earth, the panels are unfolded in order to catch the sunshine.

9) If they managed to sell lots of copies, then the money from the record sales could be spent on food and other things for Africa.

10) It is a far, far better thing that I do, than I have ever done; it is a far, far better rest that I go to than I have ever known.

11) All through his life Einstein was content to spend most of his time alone, although he married twice and had lots of close friends.

12) In fact, radium not only damaged the Curies' health but also made the laboratory equipment with which they were working radioactive.

2. 汉译英。翻译下列各句，注意适当调整语序。

1）恐怕这台旧收音机没法修了。

2）假设那是真的，我们该怎么办呢？

3）这儿就是两辆卡车相撞的地点。

4）他把旅途中发生的每件事都记录下来。

5）他一说话，我们就能辨出他的声音。

6）这是一项既耗时又耗精力的计划。

第七单元
各类从句的翻译技巧

7）我不在家时请你把房间收拾干净好吗?

8）委员会选取了那个似乎最切实可行的方案。

9）众所周知,火药是中国古代的四大发明之一。

10）因为没法把狗带回地球,所以狗死了。

11）大火也烧毁了大楼工作人员的汽车。

12）地方晚报刊登大量广告,这有助于降低报纸生产的成本。

第八单元
被动语态的翻译技巧

英语中的被动语态使用极广，尤其以科技英语为甚。为了突出话题，或保持文章的客观中立性，作者往往不用人称代词作主语，这就为被动语态创造了条件。以现行高中课本中的一个段落为例：

原文：It **is believed** that before writing **was developed**, people in China used to keep records by putting a number of stones together. As soon as writing **was developed**, people carved words on animal bones. Later, words **were carved** on metal pots; examples of these **have been found** from the 16th to the third century BC. Between the second and the fifth centuries AD people wrote on pieces of bamboo or wood and these **were tied** together to form a book. At the same time another kind of paper **was developed**, made from silk. Some silk books that **have been found** are over 2,140 years old.

译文：人们相信，在发明书面文字之前，中国人常常将若干石块放到一起记事。一发明了书面文字，人们便在动物骨头上刻字。稍后，又将字篆刻在金属器皿上，这方面的例证可以从16世纪追溯到公元前3世纪。在公元2世纪到5世纪之间，人们将字写在竹木片上，然后将它们穿在一起构成书。与此同时，用丝绸制作出了另一种纸。现已发现的有些帛书已有2 140多年的历史。

一个短短百余词的段落，竟出现了8处被动语态！同一段文字，翻译成汉语却一处也没有。由此可见汉语中的被动结构不那么常用。因为根据汉语的表达习

第八单元
被动语态的翻译技巧

惯，"被"、"遭"、"受"、"挨"等字眼一般总是给人不那么舒服的感觉，因此在英汉翻译时，我们应尽量将被动语态转换成主动结构。

英语被动语态主要用于以下 4 种情况。

1）用在不知道或不清楚动作的执行者是谁，如：

- We are kept strong and well by clean air.

  洁净的空气使我们身体健康。

2）出于礼貌委婉的考虑不愿说出动作的执行者是谁，如：

- Visitors are requested not to touch the exhibits.

  观众请勿触摸展览品。

3）动作的承受者是话题的中心，如：

- The three machines can be controlled by a single operator.

  这三台机器可以由一人单独操纵。

这句话的中心话题是 three machines，说明机器容易操纵，要是换一个说法：他一人可以单独操纵三台机器，话题的中心便转移到了"他"，说明他很能干。

4）便于句子结构的衔接连贯，如：

- John was a lawyer's son and was destined to the bar.

  约翰是律师的儿子，所以注定要当律师。

这句话中"约翰"是主语，为了便于与下一句的及物动词 destine（注定）衔接，使用了被动语态。the bar 原本指围栏：法庭上围住法官和律师所坐的位置，此处引申为律师业。这种修辞法叫作"借代"，同"红领巾"代表少先队，"三尺讲台"代表教师岗位一样。

一、英语被动语态的一般处理方法

英语被动语态的一般处理方法是将英语被动语态转为主动。具体可分为：1. 直接去掉"被"字；2. 将主语和宾语相互对调；3. 将状语译为主语；4. 译为系表结构；5. "由……"结构；6. 增添适当主语；7. 译为无主句；8. 保持原文被动结构等。

1. 直接去掉"被"字

这种方法保持英语原文的主谓结构顺序，只是不译出"被"字。主要是从译文的效果考虑，消除不必要的误解。要是硬译出"被"字，难免会给人一种"被迫、不舒服"的感觉，而原文并无此意。

- All his efforts **were wasted**.

  他的努力全都**白费了**。

- The meeting **has been postponed** to Friday.

  会议**已推迟**到星期五举行。

- Their dictionary **was published** last month.

  他们编的字典已于上月**出版发行**。

- Crude oil **can be refined** into various petroleum products.

  原油**可炼制成**各种石油产品。

2. 主语和宾语相互对调

这种方法是将主语和宾语相互对调，从而避开"被"字，使译文保持流畅自然。

- A new way of displaying time has been given **by electronics**.

  电子技术提供了一种新的显示时间的方法。

- He was astonished at **what he found**.

  他发现的情况使他大吃一惊。

- Travelers and business people both at home and abroad have been greatly helped **by this new computer**.

  这种新计算机给国内外旅行和经商的人提供了很大的帮助。

- **Fifteen million trees** had been blown down by the high winds, blocking roads, paths and railway lines.

  狂风刮倒了 **1 500 万棵树**，阻塞了大小通道和铁路线。

3. 将状语译为主语

在很多情况下，英语句中的状语可以译作汉语的主语，这主要是因为英汉句法结构差异所致。

- Mathematics is well taught **at that school**.

  那个学校的数学教得好。

- English is spoken **in many countries** in the world.

  世界上**很多国家**都讲英语。

- All kinds of precision machine tools are made **in this factory**.

  这家工厂制造各种精密机床。

- Communications satellites are used for international live transmission **throughout the world**.

  全世界都将通信卫星用于国际间的实况转播。

4. 译为系表结构

即将英语的被动语态转换成汉语"是……的"、"是……用"、"是以……"之类的系表结构。

- His poems **were directed** at the enemy.

  他的诗歌**是**针对敌人**的**。

- The shield **is used** to protect body during fighting.

  盾**是**打仗的时候用来保护身体**的**。

- This book **is intended** for the general reader, not for the specialist.

  这本书**是**为一般读者写**的**，不是为专家写**的**。

- People will not **be judged** by the color of their skin but by the content of their character.

  将**不是**以人们的肤色，**而是**以他们的品格优劣作为评价人的标准。

5. 译为"由……＋动词"结构

这种翻译方法与前面的系表结构类似，在翻译被动语态时很常见，有时候可以带一个"是"字。

- Everything **is made up** of matter.

  所有事物都**由**物质**组成**。

- The movie **was adapted** from a novel.

这部电影是**由**小说**改编**的。

- Houses will **be controlled** by a central computer.

  住宅将**由**一台中央计算机来**管理控制**。

- This merchant ship **was convoyed** by a destroyer.

  这艘商船**由**一驱逐舰**护航**。

6. 增添适当主语

在很多情况下，可以通过增添适当主语的方法来翻译英语的被动语态，尤其是英语的一些常用固定表达方式。

- It is well known that smoking is harmful to the health.

  众所周知，吸烟有害健康。

- Salt is known to have a very strong corroding effect on metals.

  大家知道，盐对金属有很强的腐蚀作用。

- To explore the moon's surface, rockets were launched again and again.

  为了探测月球的表面，**人们**一次又一次地发射火箭。

- Both Maori and Pacific Islanders **are encouraged** to use their own languages.

  当地政府鼓励毛利人和太平洋岛上的居民使用他们自己的语言。

7. 译为无主句

汉语表达比较灵活，不像英语那样受严格的主、谓、宾结构限制。汉语句子可以不要主语，因此在很多情况下，可采用汉语的无主句来翻译英语的被动语态。这往往有助于提高译文的表达效果。

- Your idea will **be incorporated** in the plan.

  将把你的意见**编入**计划。

- Some 300 papers were presented **at the conference**.

  会上提交了大约300篇论文。

- **Attention has been paid to** the new measures to prevent corrosion.

  已经注意到要采取防腐新措施。

- Children should **be made** to understand the importance of saving water.

  应该让孩子们明白节约用水的重要性。

8. 保持原文的被动结构

在有些情况下，原文的主语确实处于某种不利的境地，可以按汉语表达习惯分别用"被……"、"给……"、"遭……"等字眼。而"受……"、"为……所"等字比较中性，如：受表扬／批评，为大家所仰慕／蔑视／接受等等，翻译时可以忽略其负面含义。

- The scout **was hurt** but still conscious.

  侦察员**受**了伤，但神志还清醒。
- All the buildings **were destroyed** in a big fire.

  所有的建筑物均**为**一场大火**所焚毁**。
- He might **be attacked** and have his case **stolen** from him.

  他可能会**遭到**攻击，他的箱子可能会**被人偷**走。
- Dr Manette, **having been kept** a prisoner in the Bastille for many years, had recently **been set** free.

  被投入巴士底监狱许多年后，曼纳特医生最近**获释**。

9. 采用其他手段替换

在个别情况下，英汉语言的结构差异实在太大，英语的一些语句，汉语没有类似的表达法，很难套用原文的结构。这就需要我们跳出原文的圈子，另辟蹊径，用意译来表达出原文的含义。

- I **am attached** to my family.

  我对家人**依依不舍**。
- The news was **passed on** by word of mouth.

  众口相传，消息**不胫而走**。
- He has been **wedded** to translation.

  他与翻译**结下不解之缘**。
- The new land **was** quickly **populated** by the new settlers.

这块处女地很快**住上**了新来的移民。

二、汉译英被动结构的翻译

汉语中的被动结构不像英语那么常用。不过，通过仔细分析，我们不难发现，不少汉语句式看似主动，实际上却带有被动的含义，如："问题已解决了"，"路修好了"，"作业做完了"，"任务完成了"……其被动的含义不言而喻，只是不见"被"字罢了。

汉译英时所面临的被动结构一般有 3 种情况，一是带有"被"、"遭"、"受"、"挨"等被动标签的句子；二是看似主动，实为被动的不带被动标签的句子，而后者更为常见；第三类是完全主动意义的含义，考虑句子主次关系的衔接连贯，根据英语表达习惯，需要将其处理为被动结构。因此，汉译英被动结构的翻译关键是如何将汉语的某些看似"主动"的结构翻译成英语的被动语态，在主动和被动结构中进行自然流畅的转换。

1. 带有被动标签的结构

汉语这类结构中常见的被动词语标签有"被、受、给、让、由、叫、遭、挨、为……所、加以、予以、授予"等等。

- 他**被指控**偷了一辆汽车。

  He **was charged** with stealing a car.

- 班长深**受**大家的**尊敬**。

  The monitor **is greatly respected** by everyone.

- 老人差点儿**给**自行车**撞倒**。

  The old man **was** almost **knocked down** by the bike.

- 庄稼**让**大水**冲走**了。

  The crops **were washed away** by the flood.

- 他**叫**雨**淋**了。

  He **was caught** in the rain.

> 第八单元
> 被动语态的翻译技巧

- 这笔钱**由**他们两人**均分**。

  The money **was shared out** between them.

- 这家工厂在地震中**遭**严重**破坏**。

  The factory **was** severely **damaged** during the earthquake.

- 那个孩子由于表现不好而经常**挨骂**。

  The child **is** often **scolded** because of his bad behavior.

- 社会主义思想体系已**为**全国人民**所接受**。

  Socialist ideology **has been accepted** by the people of the whole country.

- 该计划将**由**一个特别委员会**加以**审查。

  The plan will **be examined** by a special committee.

- 应当对这种浪费现象**予以批评**。

  This waste phenomenon should **be criticized**.

- 马丁·路德·金**被授予** 1964 年诺贝尔和平奖。

  Martin Ruther King **was awarded** the Nobel Peace Prize for 1964.

需要注意的是,并非所有带有被动标签的结构都应译成被动语态,有些汉语的"被",翻译成英语需要用不及物动词,因此没有被动语态。如:

- 老太太**被**风**吹病了**。

  The old lady **fell ill** because of the draught.

- 她的帽子**被吹掉**了。

  Her hat **blew away**.

- 天气真冷,河面都**给冻住**了。

  It was so cold that the river **froze**.

以上 3 例中,fall、blow 和 freeze 均为不及物动词,不能用被动语态;其中 blow 为"刮风,吹,被吹走"之意,要是用作及物动词"吹动",便可译作被动,如:The telephone wires were blown down by the rainstorm. 电话线**被**暴风雨**刮落**了。同理,此处的 freeze 为"冷冻,结冰"之意,要是用作及物动词,便可译作被动。如:Wages have been frozen and workers laid off. 工资已**被冻结**,工人也下岗了。

在个别情况下,一些汉语句式里看似毫不含糊的被动句子,但翻译成英语可能却是主动结构，这主要与我们对词语的领悟及英汉表达习惯的不同有关。如：

- 他们控告他**受贿**。

    They accused him of **taking bribes**.

- 市长的演讲**受到**冷遇。

    The mayor's speech **met with** a cold acceptance.

以上两例中，"受贿"看似被动，实为主动：接受贿赂，所以应当译为主动结构。"受冷遇"，英语有 meet with（偶遇，遭受）这样一个固定短语搭配，所以不一定非照字面译作被动语态 be coldly treated 不可。

2. 不带被动标签的结构

汉语这类结构中见不到被动词语，但却明显地带有被动的含义，所以翻译成英语时需要使用被动语态。

- 办公楼内**禁止**抽烟。

    Smoking **is prohibited** (**No smoking**) in the office building.

- 这项工作还**未完成**。

    The work **is not completed** yet.

- 关于这个题目已**说得**够多了。

    Enough **has been said** on this topic.

- 这趟火车抵达**晚点了**。

    The arrival of the train **was delayed**.

- 付款已**延期**到下星期。

    Payment **has been deferred** until next week.

- 该故事可以用一句话来**概括**。

    The story may **be summed up** in one sentence.

- 这个价位范围内的房子**已售完**。

    The houses **are sold out** within this price range.

- 这堵围栏用金属丝**加固**了。

    The fence **was strengthened** with wire.

- 这座桥将在今年年底**建成**。

The construction of the bridge will **be completed** by the end of this year.

- 环保问题就是在这样的基础上**提出来**的。

The question of environmental protection **was raised** on such a basis.

对于不带被动标签的这类结构，翻译时需要我们利用逻辑思维进行分析：主语究竟能不能自行完成某一动作。譬如：前面在修路。根据逻辑分析我们知道"路"不能自行修建，而需要由人来完成，这与"张三在修路"显然是两码事，所以这句话应当译成被动语态：The road **is being built** in the front. 再譬如：这个问题正在研究。显然"问题"不能自行研究，一定是由人来完成，所以应当译成被动语态：The problem **is being studied**. 换一种情况，要是说"问题正在显露出来"，"问题"可以自行"显露"，所以理所当然要译成主动语态：The problem **is emerging**.

3. 汉语主动结构转为英语被动

在有些情况下，汉语的一些句子完全没有被动的含义，但翻译成英语却需要转换成被动语态。这样做主要是为了突出句子的某一成分，或是便于上下文的衔接。请看下面这些译例。

- 那个男孩**受了重伤**，医院立即把他收下了。

The boy who **was seriously injured was** immediately **admitted** into the hospital.

这句话如果照字面直译为 The boy was seriously injured, and the hospital immediately admitted him. 会造成一句话两个主谓结构，主题不清楚，也不合英语表达习惯。而用定语从句和被动语态就有效地解决了这一问题。

- 刚才有人在这里讲了一些不该讲的话。

Some things were said here just now which should not have been said.

这句话要是照字面直译为 "Just now someone said some things which he should not have said" 会造成话语的不连贯。根据上下文，这句话的重心是"讲的话"，因此话题的内容应当围绕 some things 展开，而不是以某人为话题中心，否则会显得不委婉礼貌，也不符合英语的表达习惯。

- 到 1979 年，中美已经**建立**了外交关系。

译文 A：By 1979, China and the United States **had established** diplomatic relations.

译文 B：By 1979，Diplomatic relations **had been established** between China and the United States.

译文 A 以 China and the United States 为主语，后面可以衔接与"中美"相关的很多话题：譬如说，中美不但建立了外交关系，而且建立了经贸关系、军事关系，等等。如果是这样，那么完全可以译作主动语态。如果要突出的话题是"外交关系"而不是"中美"，那么就得用译文 B 这样的被动语态了。

- 我国各族人民每年都要热烈**庆祝**"十一"国庆节。

译文 A：The Chinese people of all nationalities enthusiastically celebrate National Day on Oct.1 every year.

译文 B：National Day **is** enthusiastically **celebrated** on Oct.1 by the Chinese people of all nationalities every year.

译文 A 以 Chinese people 为主语，要是下文紧接着以"各族人民"为谈论话题，这一译文应当非常妥帖。反之，要是这句话围绕"国庆节"展开话题，下文紧接着谈国庆节怎样怎样，那就要用译文 B 这样的被动语态了。

- 一群人立刻**把他围住**了，向他**提出**一个又一个的**问题**。

译文 A：Very soon a crowd surrounded him and asked him one question after another.

译文 B：Very soon he **was surrounded** by a crowd and **was snowed** under with questions.

很明显，原文的视点是"他"而不是"一群人"，所以用译文 B 这样的被动语态能够恰当地译出原文的意思。换一个视角，如果以"一群人"为全句的视点，后面紧接着是"然后他们又围住了另一个人"之类的话，显然就要用译文 A 这样的主动结构了。

- 他出现在舞台上，观众**给予热烈鼓掌**。

译文 A：When he appeared on the stage the audience applauded him warmly.

译文 B：He appeared on the stage and **was warmly applauded** by the audience.

很多同学都喜欢译文 A 这种译法，觉得这样用主动语态翻译起来很顺手。实际上译文 A 在此处并不十分恰当，因为这句话的聚焦点在"他"，而不是"观众"。这种译法冲淡了主题，将关注的焦点转移到观众身上去了。

4. 汉语一些习惯用语的被动译法

汉语的一些习惯用语或固定句型，看似主动结构，由于英汉对同一事物的着眼点不同，翻译成英语时可能会用被动语态。在主语的指代不明或不清楚动作的执行者是谁，或出于礼貌委婉的考虑不愿说出动作的执行者是谁的情况下，我们也往往采用被动语态进行翻译。事实上，很多这类表达法是在借鉴英语一些句型的基础上形成的现代汉语套话。将这些套话回译成英语，套用英语的现存句型模式就行了。如：据说（据调查／报告／谣传……）(It is said/investigated/reported/rumored...)，等等。

- 小女孩 10 岁时就**失学**了。

    The little girl **was deprived of** schooling at ten.

    将主动结构"失学"译作被动语态 was deprived of（被剥夺）。

- 李教授因病而**闭门不出**。

    Professor Li **is confined** to the house by illness.

    将主动结构"闭门不出"译作被动语态 is confined to（被限制在……）。

- 科学家**面临**很多困难。

    The scientist **is confronted** with many difficulties.

    将主动结构"面临"译作被动语态 is confronted（使面对）。

- 这地方因生产乳品而**出名**。

    The place **is known** for its dairy produce.

    将主动结构"出名"译作被动语态 is known for（以……而著名）。

- 这一工程**估计**耗去资金 900 万美元。

    The project **was estimated** to have cost $9,000,000.

    将主动结构"估计"译作被动语态 was estimated（据估计）。

- 这次火车事故使这封信**耽搁**了 3 天。

    The letter **was delayed** three days by the train accident.

将主动结构"耽搁"译作被动语态 was delayed（被耽搁）。

- 1989年**通过**了一项国际法，禁止人们把废物倒入大海。

  In 1989 an international law **was passed** to stop people putting waste into the sea.

将主动结构"通过"译作被动语态 was passed（获得通过）。

- **应该说**，情况基本上是不错的。

  It should be said that the situation is basically sound.

将主动结构"应该说"译作被动语态 It should be said that...。

- **据谣传**，那场事故是由于玩忽职守而造成的。

  It is rumored that the accident was due to negligence.

将主动结构"据谣传"译作被动语态 It is rumored that...。

- **必须指出**，有些问题还需要澄清。

  It must be pointed out that some questions have yet to be clarified.

将主动结构"必须指出"译作被动语态 It must be pointed out that...。

思考与练习

一、简要回答以下问题

1. 翻译中为什么要进行语态转换？试举例说明。
2. 常用的英语被动语态的处理方法主要有哪些？
3. 汉语被动结构一般用于什么情况？试举例说明。
4. 汉译英的被动结构主要有哪些类型？翻译时应注意哪几点？

二、英汉互译翻译练习

1. 英译汉。翻译下列各句，注意被动语态的处理。

   1) He was blinded by the smoke.
   2) The road is all covered with snow.
   3) The children were led to a place of safety.

4) Polonium is used to set off a nuclear bomb.

5) The school is staffed entirely by graduates.

6) In this way stories were passed on from one person to another.

7) Students should be made to understand the importance of working hard.

8) In the following spring, the seeds should be knocked out of the seed-heads and sown.

9) The employment outlook for the next year is based in part on contracts signed this year.

10) Centuries ago, the word "beeline" was made to describe this thin line of bees flying through the air.

11) The volume is not measured in square millimeters. It is measured in cubic millimeters.

12) In 1898 a law was passed which meant that all people above a certain age were paid a weekly "old-age pension".

2. 汉译英。翻译下列各句，注意被动结构的处理。

1) 设计必须改动。

2) 这幅油画备受称颂。

3) 该国禁止出口黄金。

4) 敌人被迫放下武器。

5) 这一问题正在研究。

6) 请来宾出示入场券。

7) 超速驾车者应受严惩。

8) 没有查到他的死亡记录。

9) 她和丈夫应邀赴宴去了。

10) 天黑后士兵不准离开营房。

11) 他们为学生的爱国热情所激励。

12) 客户被这新颖的广告吸引住了。

第九单元
翻译中的正反调换

每种语言都少不了肯定与否定这一语言现象。按语言学家们的划分，英语的否定大致上有4类：完全否定（带 no 的词语，如 nothing, none 等）、半否定（hardly, scarcely 等）、部分否定（not all, not every 等）及带否定意义的词语（fail, without 等）。汉语的肯定和否定与英语大致相似，所以在一般情况下，翻译可以直接对号入座。不过，有时候英汉翻译中的肯定与否定并不完全对应，我们不能一看见 yes 便译作"是"。请看下面几例，都不宜简单地译作"是"字。

- "Li Xiaoli!" "**Yes**."
  "李晓莉！" "**到**。"
- Oh, **yes**; a very great success.
  啊，**不错**，了不起的成就。
- "Just one moment." "**Yes**, sir."
  "请稍等。" "**好的**，先生。"
- "Send it at once, will you?" "**Yes**, sir."
  "请你马上送来好吗？" "**行**，先生。"
- He covered himself quickly and got in, saying: "**Yes, yes**."
  他迅速走过来进入房间，一面说道："**来了，来了**。"
- "**Yes**?" The man standing at the door asked.
  "**有事吗**？"站在门边的人问。
- A: **Aren't** you going tomorrow?

B: **Yes**, I **am**./**No**, I'm **not**.

甲：你明天**不**去吗？

乙：**不**，我明天**去**。/**对**，我明天**不**去。

No 也不一定都可以简单地译作"不"字，请看下面几例。

- **No** farther!

  别再向前走啦 / **别再**说啦！

- **No** admission.

  非请**莫**入 / **禁止**入内。

- **No**! You're kidding!

  决**不可能**！你在开玩笑吧！（我才不信你呢！）

- Oh, **no**! My computer has been attacked by hackers.

  啊，**糟啦**，我的电脑遭到黑客破坏。

- A: I bought the camera for 50 yuan.

  B: **No**! Could it really have been so cheap?

  甲：我 50 元买了这部相机。

  乙：**不会吧**？有这么便宜吗？

由上可知，英语中的 yes, no 并不完全能和汉语的"是"、"不"打等号。在很多情况下，需要根据上下文语境或语气进行调整、转换。一般来说，完全肯定、完全否定和半否定比较直截了当，部分否定和带否定意义的词语则比较隐晦，稍不小心，就会造成翻译失误。

一、英译汉的正反调换

英译汉的正反调换包括正说反译、反说正译、正反两可、双重否定、委婉式肯定、否定的转移等翻译技巧和方法。

1. 英语肯定，汉语译作否定

有时候，照字面译出来会造成文句不通顺，因此需要正说反译。譬如 Please

keep the fire burning. 我们一般不说"请保持火燃烧",而是译作"别让火灭了"。这种方法可广泛用于各种词类、短语,甚至整个句子的翻译。

- He is **new** to this game.(形容词)

  这种游戏他**从来没有玩过**。

将形容词 new(新的)译作否定式"**从来没有玩过**"。

- One **careless** move loses the whole game.(形容词)

  一着**不慎**,满盘皆输。

将形容词 careless(粗心的,疏忽的)译作"不慎",整个句子由肯定式转为否定式。

- We have simply reached the **limit** of our patience.(名词)

  我们简直已到了**忍无可忍**的地步。

将句中的 reach the limit(达到极限)译作否定式"忍无可忍的地步"。

- It **pays** to be honest.(动词)

  老实人**不吃亏**。

句中动词 pay(支付,回报)译作否定式"**不吃亏**"。

- Cheap shoes soon **wear out**.(动词短语)

  便宜的鞋子**不耐穿**。

将动词短语 wear out(穿破,用坏)译作否定式"不耐穿"。

- He appealed **against** the judge's decision.(介词)

  他**不服**法官判决而上诉。

将句中的介词 against(反对)译作否定式"不服"。

- The guerrillas would rather fight to death **before** they surrendered.(连词)

  游击队员们宁愿战斗到死也**绝不**投降。

将句中的连词 before(在……之前)译作否定式"绝不"。

- Time is what we want most, but what, alas, many use **worst**.(副词)

  时间是我们最缺少的,但可叹之至,偏偏许多人**最不善于**利用时间。

将句中的副词 worst(最糟)译作否定式"最不善于"。

- My father went grey when he was **in his late thirties**.(名词短语)

  我父亲**不到 40 岁**就两鬓斑白了。

将句中的 in his late thirties（30 多岁后期）译作否定式"不到 40 岁"。

- This car may go 600 miles **on a thimble of** gas.（介词短语）

  这辆小汽车行驶 600 英里**费不了几滴**汽油。

将句中的介词短语 on a thimble of 译作否定式"费不了几滴"。

- Gandhi was **much more than** a clever lawyer, a fine speaker, a determined fighter for human rights and a political leader.（形容词短语）

  甘地**远不只**是一位聪明的律师、优秀的演说家、坚定的人权战士和政治领袖。

将句中的副词短语 much more than 译作否定式"远不只"。

2. 英语否定，汉语译作肯定

英语中的否定有时候需要译成汉语的肯定，而且在许多情况下，经过"反说正译"处理的译文读起来更自然，更能传达出原文的意义。"反说正译"这种方法可以广泛用于各种词类、短语，甚至整个句子的翻译，尤其适用于某些特殊句式结构，如：not...until, no sooner than, hardly (scarcely)...when (before), rather than, nothing but, cannot...too, cannot help, cannot but，以及双重否定等。

- Words **cannot describe** the beauty of the scene.（动词）

  用言词**很难形容**这景色的优美。

将句中的否定式 cannot（不能）译作肯定式"很难"。

- All the articles are **untouchable** in the museum.（形容词）

  博物馆内一切展品**禁止触摸**。

将句中的否定式 untouchable（不可接触的）译作肯定式"禁止触摸"。

- You **can't see** through the telescope **until** it is adjusted to your eyes.（固定搭配）

  只有把望远镜调节到适合你的目光，你**才**看得见东西。

将句中的否定式 not...until 译作肯定式"只有……才"。

- **Don't lose time** in posting this letter.（动词短语）

  赶快把这封信寄出去。

将祈使句 Don't lose time（不要丧失时间）译作肯定式"赶快"。

- **Hardly** a month goes by **without** traffic accidents occurred in that city.（双重否定）

那个城市**几乎**月月**都有**交通事故。

将句中的双重否定 Hardly...without 译作肯定式"几乎都有"。

- You **couldn't** turn on the TV **without** seeing advertisements.（双重否定）

一打开电视，**你就总会**看到广告。

将句中的双重否定 couldn't...without 译作肯定式"一……就总会……"。

- In some parts of Britain, one person in ten, by the age of thirty, **has no teeth** left!（名词）

在英国有些地方，1/10 的人年方 30，**牙齿就掉光**了。

句中的名词带否定 has no teeth（没有牙），中文译作肯定式"牙齿就掉光了"。

- Help will come from the UN, but the aid will be **nowhere near what's needed**.（从句）

联合国的救助就要到了，但只是**杯水车薪**。

将句中的否定式 nowhere near... 译作肯定式成语"杯水车薪"。

- Such flight **couldn't long escape notice**.（句子）

这类飞行**迟早总会被人发觉的**。

将否定结构 couldn't long escape（不能长期逃脱）译作"迟早总会被"，整个句子由否定式转为肯定式。

3. 同一词语，肯定否定均可

根据上下文的需要，这类情况可译作肯定式或否定式。在很多情况下，出于个人看问题的着眼点不同，使用的措辞和褒贬语气可能会有所不同，我们在进行肯定否定取舍时，需要对这方面的情况加以适当考虑。譬如：He is *free* with his money. 这句话既可翻译为"他花钱大手大脚"，也可翻译成"他花钱从不吝啬"。前者为贬义，用在花钱大吃大喝、玩乐等；后者为褒义，用在用钱帮助他人，助人为乐等。再如：The criminal is still at large. 从执法的角度可译作"罪犯还未捉拿归案"，从罪犯本人角度可译作"罪犯仍旧逍遥法外／逍遥自在"。

- The place is **strange** to me.

这地方我很**陌生**。（这地方我**不熟悉**。）

- Make haste, or you'll **be late**.

  快点，要不然就**迟到**了。（快点，否则就**来不及**了。）

- The station is **no distance** at all.

  车站**近在咫尺**。（车站**一点儿也不远**。）

- It's **no less** than a fraud.

  这**简直**是一场骗局。（这**无异于**一场骗局。）

- He realized that he was **in trouble**.

  他意识到**遇到麻烦了**。（他感到自己的**处境不妙**。）

- The post office is at the next corner, you **can't miss** it.

  邮局就在下个路口，你**会找到的**。（你**错不了**。）

- The works of art were left **intact**, the money gone.

  艺术品**还在**，钱却**没**了。（艺术品**原封未动**，钱却**不翼而飞**。）

- I **dropped** medicine and took up physics.

  我**放弃**学医，改学物理了。（我**不再**学医，改学物理。）

4. 双重否定与委婉肯定

双重否定一般来说可译作肯定，其道理如"负负为正"一样，可视为一种特殊强调句式。以 have to（不得不）为例，两个"不"字去掉之后意思不变，但语气强度就差多了。请看这样一例：

You **don't have to do** all the exercises.

照字面翻译：你**不不得不**做所有这些练习作业。

去掉两个"不"字，便成了：你不得做所有这些练习作业。

显然原文不是这个意思，而是"你不一定非做完这些作业不可"。所以在翻译双重否定时，不能简单地套用某一固定句型，最重要的是把握原文的真实含义。下面是一些较为典型的双重否定的不同译法。

- There is **no** rule that has **no** exception.

  没有不例外的规则。（反说正译：任何规则**都有**例外。）

- It is **impossible but** that a man will make some mistakes.

人**不会不**犯错误。(反说正译:人**总会**犯错误。)

- I am **not reluctant** to accept your proposal.

  你的建议我**并非不**愿接受。(反说正译:你的建议我**可以**接受。)

- Children **do not have to** cross busy streets to go to school.

  孩子们上学**不一定非**穿越繁忙的街道**不可**。(适当简化:孩子们上学**不用**穿过拥挤的马路。)

- There is **not any** advantage **without** disadvantage.

  有一利**必有**一弊。(译作汉语成语:祸兮福所倚,福兮祸所伏。)

英语中还有一类否定结构,字面看似否定,实为委婉迂回的肯定。这类迂回的表达肯定的方式切不可照字面理解、翻译。

- He **didn't half like** the girl.

  他**非常喜欢**那姑娘。(不可译作:他半点也不喜欢那姑娘。)

- I **couldn't** feel better.

  我觉得身体**棒极了**。(不可译作:我不能感到更好了。)

- I **couldn't agree** with you **more**.

  我**太赞成**你的看法了。(不可译作:我不能同意你太多。)

- If that **isn't what I want**!

  我所要的**就是这个呀**!(不可译作:如果那不是我所要的!)

- He **can't** see you **quick enough**.

  他会**尽快**和你见面。(不可译作:他不能尽快和你见面。)

对上述各译例有些同学可能会感到费解,其实我们在遇到类似的情况时,思路上不妨多转一个弯,吃透原文字里行间的弦外之音,原文的真实含义就不难把握了。下面是以上5个译例的理解思路。

He didn't half like the girl. 其原文意思是:他不是半心半意地喜欢那姑娘,所以意译为"他非常喜欢那姑娘"。

I couldn't feel better. 其原文意思是:我觉得身体好得不能更好了,所以译意为"我觉得身体棒极了"。

I couldn't agree with you more. 其原文意思是:我百分之百地同意你,完全同意,再没有任何保留的余地了,所以译意为"我太赞成你的看法了"。

If that isn't what I want! 其原文意思是：要是它不是我所要的（才怪呢），所以译意为"我所要的就是这个呀！"

He can't see you quick enough. 其原文意思是：他和你的见面已快得不能再快了，所以译意为"他会尽快和你见面"。

5. 否定的陷阱

英语中的一些否定结构如果按字面意义理解很容易出错，这些结构我们称之为"否定的陷阱"。下面就是一些有代表性结构。

A．not...because（并非因为……而）

- The engine **didn't stop because** the fuel was finished.

  引擎并**不是因为**燃料耗尽**而停止运转**。（暗示引擎本身出了问题）

- **Don't scamp** your work **because** you are pressed for time.

  不要因为时间紧**而敷衍塞责**。

- This scheme **is not placed** first **because** it is simple.

  这一方案**并不因为**其简易**而被放在首位**。

- In that city, we had **never suffered** discrimination **because** we were Jews.

  我们在那个城市**从未因为**是犹太人而遭受歧视。

- Gates **didn't drop out** because he wanted to avoid work but to start his company.

  盖茨辍学**不是想**逃避学业，而是为了开办自己的公司。

这类结构称之为"否定的转移"，即看似否定前面的内容，而实际上否定的却是后面。这类情况我们平时也见过，只不过没那么留心罢了。如：

- I don't suppose he'll come. 我看他不会来了。（看似否定前面的 suppose，实际上否定的是后面 he'll come）

有同学可能会问:在什么情况下需要进行否定转移，什么时候不需要转移呢?

答案很简单：凭借逻辑、常识来解决问题。

譬如：The engine didn't stop because the fuel was finished 和 Don't scamp your work because you are pressed for time 要是分别照字面译作"引擎因为燃料耗尽而

不停止运转""因为时间紧,所以不要而敷衍塞责",就违反了逻辑和常识,采用"否定的转移",这一问题自然就解决了。

此外,做否定转移这类翻译还必须准确把握事实依据。譬如:This scheme is not placed first because it is simple. 翻译这句话首先应弄清楚这一方案是不是被放在首位,如果答案是否定的,那么就应当按传统的方法译作"这一方案因为太简易所以没有被放在首位。"再如:In that city, we had never suffered discrimination because we were Jews. 如果事情发生在以色列,受歧视的应该是阿拉伯人,而不是犹太人,所以这句话也可以照常规情况译作:在那个城市我们因为是犹太人所以**从未**遭受歧视。

除 not...because 之外,否定的转移也常用于其他一些句型,请看下面这条出自奥巴马总统演讲的译例:

We **didn't start with** much money or many endorsements.

竞选伊始,我们的**资金并不充裕**,获得的**支持也不多**。

B. cannot...too(怎么……也不)

这是一种带有强调性的双重否定,此结构通常由情态动词 can 或 shall 加否定副词 not 或 never 等词语构成,如 cannot...too, cannot... enough, shall never...too, cannot be overestimated 等都属此类,看似否定,实为强烈的肯定语气。这类结构很容易对汉语思维造成干扰,不知不觉之中就将其按字面误译成"不能太……",而实际上这种表达法也是一种"负负为正"的强调式肯定,通常译作"无论怎么……也不过分",也可视不同情况灵活处理,适当调整语气措辞。

- You **cannot** be cautious **enough** in a new neighborhood.

  新到一个社区你**无论怎么**小心翼翼**也不过分**。

- You **cannot** be **too** careful in proofreading.

  校对时,**越**仔细**越**好。

- I shall **never** be able to stress **too** much for your kindness.

  无论用什么言辞,**也表达不尽**我对你的感激之情。

- The importance of this conference **cannot be overestimated**.

  这次会议的重要性**无论怎么**强调**也不过分**。

- According to the late Duchess of Windsor, **no** woman **can be too** rich or

too thin.

按已故温莎公爵夫人的说法，女人钱**再**多**也不**多，身材**再**瘦**也不**瘦。

以上各例中第 1 句和第 4 句用"无论怎么……也不过分"结构翻译出了原文的准确意思。其余各例在把握原文意思的基础上灵活处理，适当调整了语气措辞。

第 2 句要是直译为"校对时，你怎么仔细也不过分"，听起来很拗口，用汉语"越……越……"这样一种习惯表达法，省略意译为"校对时，越仔细越好"，语句就通顺了。

第 3 句也是如此，直译为"我怎么感谢你，也将不过分"就不如意译为"无论用什么言辞，都表达不尽我对你的感激之情"更顺口，更符合此处的口气。

第 5 句要是照字面译作"女人不能钱太多或太瘦"，就掉进了否定的"陷阱"，与原文的精神完全背道而驰。用汉语"再……也不……"这一习惯表达法则恰到好处地反映出了原文的意思和精神风貌。

C. all/every/both...not（并非……都）

这一结构不可照字面理解为"都不"（no, nothing, none, nobody），而是"并非……都"、"两者不能同时都"之意，这一点往往很容易被大家所忽视，照字面理解为"（二者）都不"，因而造成翻译的失误。请看下面各例。

- **All** that glitters is **not** gold.

  发光的**不一定都**是金子。

- **All** cities did **not** look alike as they do today.

  在过去，城市**并不都像**今天这样个个千篇一律。

- No, **everything** is **not** straightened out.

  不，**并非每一个**问题都弄清楚了。

- But you see, we **both cannot** go.

  但是我告诉你，我们俩**不能同时都**走。

- **Both** of his children are not college students.

  他的两个孩子**不都是**大学生。

一般来说，英语中的 all...not = not all，翻译成汉语应为"并非……都"，而不是"都不"。我们知道，汉语的"都不"是一种完全否定，其对应的英语字眼应当是 no, nothing, none, nobody, neither 等带否定词根 no 的词语。不过，随着计算机越来越普遍地得到使用，英语与世界其他语言的接轨，all...not 逐渐具有了"都不"的含义，尤其是在科技翻译中。譬如下面两例：

- **All** these various losses, great as they are, **do not** in any way contradict the law of conservation of energy.

  所有这些损失，尽管很大，却都和能量守恒定律**无矛盾**。

- **All** other sources of heat besides the sun **would not** raise the temperature of the earth 1/4 degree F.

  除了太阳的热源以外，**所有**其他热源**都不能**把地球的温度升高华氏 0.25 度。

那么，all...not 在什么情况下译作"并非……都"，什么情况下译作"都不"呢？一般来说，传统的、文学性的语句多译作"并非……都"；新近的、科技的语句多译作"都不"。不过，这只是一般的情况，不是绝对标准，翻译时应当具体问题具体分析，通过上下文语境判断究竟是部分否定还是完全否定。

二、汉译英的正反调换

汉语否定结构中出现频率最高的否定词是"不"和"没（有）"，此外，还有用于名词否定的"无"、"非"，用于命令句的"莫"、"别"、"甭"等字眼。

1. 汉译英正反调换的一般情况

汉语否定结构的翻译一般可套用英语的模式，如：

- 我**不会**做这道题。

  I **can't** work out this problem./I am **unable to** solve the problem.

- **别**告诉他答案。

  Don't tell him the answer.

- 请了他，但他有事**没**来。

  He was invited, but he **didn't** come because he had something else to do.

- 巧妇难为**无**米之炊。

Even a clever housewife can't cook a meal **without** rice.

需要注意的是，在汉语的一些习惯表达法里，"没"是一个赘词，去不去掉否定词"没"意思都不变，如：

- 她**差点儿（没）**从楼梯上摔下来。

  She almost tumbled downstairs.

- 他**好（不）容易**才找到了一个加油站。

  It took him great trouble to find a gas station.

和英语一样，汉语中的双重否定一般也译作肯定，或套用英语的习惯表达结构，如：

- 知识**不**是**不**可以学会的。

  Knowledge **can be** learned **after all**.（将双重否定译作肯定）

- 听到这一消息，全班同学**无不**欢欣鼓舞。

  The whole class is **invariably** elated at this news.（双重否定灵活处理）

- 我想说的**无非**是那么几句话。

  What I want to say is **no more than** (or **nothing but**) a few words.（双重否定套用英语结构）

- 在中国，**没有人不**知道白求恩是一位伟大的国际主义战士。

  There is **no one** in China **but** knows that Norman Bethune is a great internationalist fighter.（双重否定套用英语结构）

另外，从语气、搭配考虑，有时需要进行否定转移才能翻译出原文的准确含义，如：

- 他来的真**不是**时候。

  He **didn't come** at right time.（采用否定转移）

- 他说这话是**无意**的。

  He **didn't say** it intentionally.（采用否定转移）

2. 汉语肯定，英语译作否定

这一类情况比较笼统，主要涉及对原文的准确理解和英语的习惯表达法，翻译时应视具体情况的不同而采用肯定或否定。在有些情况下，汉语的肯定结构要是照字面直译显得比较生硬，便可根据英语的习惯表达将其转换为否定结构。

- 室内**禁止**吸烟！

  No smoking inside the room!

- 警察**立刻**赶到犯罪现场。

  The policemen arrived at the scene of the crime in **no time**.

- 计算机已在全世界**空前**普及。

  Computer has been popularized as **never before** all over the world.

- 我们要到星期四**才能**去。

  We **can't go** until Thursday.

- 活到老，学到老。

  One is **never too** old **to** learn.

- 我们的辛劳全都**白费**了。

  We had all our trouble **for nothing**.

- **再困难**的任务我们都能完成。

  No task is so difficult but (that) we can accomplish it.

- 低脂肪饮食能帮助身体避免多种疾病。

  A diet **without a lot of fat** can help the body avoid many diseases.

- 迄今为止，他**辜负**了党和人民的希望。

  So far, he **has not** lived up to the expectation of the Party and the people.

- 党的十八大充分表明我们党**兴旺发达，后继有人**。

  The 18th Party Congress fully demonstrates that our Party is flourishing and has **no lack of successors**.

3. 汉语否定，英语译作肯定

这种情况与前面的情况正好相反，但目的是一样的，也是为了保证英语译文通顺、地道，符合英语的习惯表达法。

- **别**再找借口了！

  Stop making excuses!

- 很少有人是**无忧无虑**的。

  Few people are **free from care**.

- 我喜欢茶而**不喜欢**咖啡。

  I **prefer** tea **to** coffee.

- 这水果太酸了，**不能**吃。

  The fruit was **too** sour **to** eat.

- 我们在那个问题上跟他们的意见**不同**。

  We **differ** from/with them on/about that question.

- 她**不好意思**提出这么简单的问题。

  She **was ashamed** to ask such a simple question.

- 系主任告诫他**不要**迟到。

  The dean cautioned him **against** being late.

- 俗话说，"男儿有泪**不**轻弹，皆因**未到**伤心处"嘛。

  As the saying goes, "Men **only** weep **when** deeply hurt."

- 居里夫人**不同意**把这些新的发现看作是属于自己的东西。

  Madame Curie **refused** to treat these new discoveries as though they belonged to her.

4. 汉语四字成语的反说正译

汉语成语往往喜欢用四字结构，英语没有这样的语言习惯，翻译时可考虑用意译的方法，套用英语的句型结构、固定搭配或词组短语，将否定转换为肯定。

- 我茫然**不知所措**。

  I am **at a** complete **loss** what to do.

- 她身上有一种**不屈不挠**的精神。

  She has an **indomitable** spirit.

- 诸如此类的事例**不胜枚举**。

  Such instances are **too numerous to mention**.

- 他认为自己的成就**微不足道**。

  He **made light of** his own achievements.

- 欠款必须**不折不扣**地偿还。

  The debt must be paid **in full**.
- **不出所料**，销售部经理今天提出了辞职要求。

  As expected, the sales manager gave in his notice at work today.
- 两个老朋友在飞机上**不期而遇**。

  The two old friends **met by chance** on a plane.
- 过去的**不毛之地**变成了富饶的粮仓。

  That remote **barren land** has blossomed into rich granaries.
- 工作人员将**源源不断**的一系列表格输入打印机。

  The clerk fed a **continuous** form into a printer.
- 他们**不择手段**，最终达到了目的。

  Finally, they attained their goal **by hook or crook**.

思考与练习

一、简要回答以下问题

1. 翻译中为什么要使用正反调换的手段？试举例说明。
2. 常见的英译汉正反调换的手段主要有哪几种？
3. 何谓"否定的陷阱"？在翻译中我们应当怎样避开这些陷阱？
4. 常见的汉译英的正反调换主要有哪些方法？

二、英汉互译翻译练习

1. 英译汉。翻译下列各句，注意使用必要的正反调换。

    1) Better late than never.

    2) I can't thank you enough.

    3) Oil preserves metal from rust.

    4) You can learn in no time at all.

    5) He had an absent-minded manner.

6) One careless move loses the whole game.

7) The machine tool does not function properly.

8) The insecticide should be put out of the child's reach.

9) The author's arguments are ill grounded in facts.

10) Mr. Zhang is bad at getting along with his fellows.

11) I know you didn't do this just to win an election, and I know you didn't do it for me.

12) Blind people never know their hidden strength until they are treated like normal human beings.

2. 汉译英。翻译下列各句，注意使用必要的正反调换。

1）今年冬天不冷。

2）他对这个城镇很陌生。

3）账单数额太大，付不起。

4）直到昨天我才知道他住院了。

5）快点，要不然就来不及了。

6）这孩子辜负了父亲对他的期望。

7）让我们面对现实，不要逃避。

8）令人惊奇的是，他竟然不及格。

9）环境迫使他不得不接受此方案。

10）他每次出去总是会丢失雨伞。

11）他如果不努力学习，就永远不能考及格。

12）白茫茫的大地，除了呼呼的北风外，没有一点声响。

第十单元
翻译的标准与直译、意译问题

前面 9 个单元对常用翻译技巧方法做了详尽的介绍。但翻译技巧本身并不能保证翻译的准确无误，关键是将它们灵活地用于翻译实践。一个句子、一篇文章翻译得好不好，应当以什么为标准来评判呢？本单元将着重就翻译的标准与直译、意译问题展开讲解分析。

一、"信、达、雅"翻译标准

早在 19 世纪末，翻译家严复（1853—1921）就提出了"信、达、雅"的翻译标准："译事三难：信，达，雅。求其信已大难矣，顾信矣不达，虽译犹不译也，则达尚焉……《易》曰：'修辞立诚。'子曰：'辞达而已。'又曰：'言之无文，行之不远。'三者乃文章正轨，亦即为译事楷模。故信、达而外，求其尔雅。……"

严复的"信、达、雅"三字，用现行的说法也就是忠实/准确、达意/流畅、雅致/优美，长期以来一直被视为翻译的标准，备受译界推崇。但也有不少学者指出，事实上，严复本人从来就没有遵循过自己所提出的"信、达、雅"标准。他所译的《天演论》就是一个很好的说明。且以前言第一段为例。

第十单元
翻译的标准与直译、意译问题

Evolution and Ethics

It may be safely assumed that, two thousand years ago, before Caesar set foot in southern Britain, the whole countryside visible from the windows of the room in which I write, was in what is called "the state of Nature." Except, it may be, by raising a few sepulchral mounds, such as those which still here and there, break the flowing contours of the downs, man's hands had made no mark upon it; and the thin veil of vegetation which overspread the broad-backed heights and the shelving sides of the coombs was unaffected by his industry.

严复译《天演论》

赫胥黎独处一室之中，在英伦之南，背山而面野。槛外诸境，历历如在几下。乃悬想二千年前，当罗马大将凯彻未到时，此间有何景物。计惟有天造草昧，人功未施，其借征人境者，不过几处荒坟，散见坡陀起伏间。而灌木丛林，蒙茸山麓，未经刬治如今日者，则无疑也。

现代白话译文《进化与伦理》

可以有把握地想象，2 000年前，当凯撒到达不列颠南部之前，从我正在写作的这间屋子的窗口可以看到整个原野处在一种"自然状态"中。也许除了若干突起的坟墓已在几处破坏了连绵的丘陵的轮廓以外，此地未经人工修葺整治。薄薄的植被笼罩着广阔的高地和峡谷的斜坡，还没有受到人类劳动的影响。

比较对照原文和两个译文之后我们不难发现：为了追求古雅的文风，严复以牺牲"信"为代价，无论是人称、时态还是语气景物描述等方面都对原文做了大量的增删和改造。由此可见，严复对自己提出的"信"并不遵守，却不惜余力地追求译文的"达"和"雅"。

王佐良先生曾经对严复的"雅"做过一番很好的评注：严复的"雅"追求的是古雅的文风，是一层包裹着治疗社会弊病的苦药的糖衣，便于当时的官僚士大夫接受。他显然达到了目的。

翻译究竟需不需要"雅"？这应视情况而定。原文是什么风格，译文就应当保持什么风格，不必刻意去追求"雅"。原文不雅，译文自然就没有雅的道理。

二、忠实与通顺的翻译标准

尽管我国翻译界在翻译标准的认识上没有一个统一的尺度，但有两条标准却是大家所公认的：忠实、通顺（或叫作准确、流畅）。

所谓"忠实"，首先是指译文必须准确如实地传达原文的内容，对原文的意思既不能随便歪曲，也不能任意增减。内容除了指原文中所叙述的事实，说明的道理，描写的景物以外，也包括作者在叙述、说明和描写过程中所反映的思想、观点、立场和感情。"忠实"还指对原文风格的如实传达。译者不得随意改动原作的风格风貌，原作是口语体，就不能译作书面体；原作是粗俗的文体，就不能译成高雅的格调，译者不能用自己的风格去代替原文的风格。

所谓"通顺"，指的是译文的语言必须顺畅易懂，符合汉语表达规范。译文应当按汉语的语法和习惯来用词造句，不应当出现文理不通、结构混乱、逻辑不清的现象。理想的译文应当通顺流畅，避免生搬硬套，在深刻领会原文意思的基础上，尽量摆脱原文形式的束缚，选用符合汉语习惯的表达方法，把原文的意思清楚明白地表达出来。

高校英语专业翻译的教学大纲也认同"忠实、通顺"的标准。《高等学校英语专业高年级英语教学大纲》规定，英译汉、汉译英的评估项目分"忠实"、"通顺"两项。"忠实"具体阐述为"原文的信息全部传达，语气和文体风格与原文相一致"；"通顺"具体阐述为"英译汉断句恰当，句式正确，选词妥帖，段落之间，句子之间呼应自然"，"汉译英句式处理恰当，选词妥帖，英语表达地道"。

三、翻译实例分析讲解

"忠实"与"通顺"这两条标准，看似简略，但要在实际翻译中掌握好、运用好却并没那么容易。我们且以"忠实"为尺度来衡量下面 3 个翻译实例，它们均出自学生练习作业。

例 1：The importance of superconductor in the uses of electricity cannot be overestimated.
译文：超导体在电器应用上的重要性不能被估计过高。

例 2：Titanic struck an iceberg and sank on its maiden voyage in 1912, carrying more than 1,500 passengers to their death.
译文：泰坦尼克号在 1912 年的处女航中撞上冰山沉没，造成全船 1 500 多名乘客死亡。

例 3：If a designer were to design a bracket to support 100 lb. when it should have been figured for 1,000 lb., failure would be forthcoming.
译文：如果设计者所设计的托架能支撑 100 磅，当它被设计为 1 000 磅时，事故一定会出现。

分析：

从"忠实"的角度来看，上述 3 例译文均存在严重问题。

例 1 错在不熟悉英语的特殊句型，将 cannot be overestimated（怎么估计也不会过高）误解为"不能被估计过高"；

例 2 忽视了语境因素，句中的 more than 1,500 passengers 不是"全船 1 500 多名乘客"，而是"船上的 1 500 多名乘客"——根据史料我们知道，全船乘客共计 2 000 多名，其中的妇女儿童大都获救；

例 3 对英语的虚拟语气及连词把握不当，将 were to design（打算设计）和 should have been figured（应当被设计为）误解为"所设计的"和"当它被设计为"。所译上述译文均未能忠实地传达出原文的意思。下面是修改后的正确译文。

例 1：对超导体在电器应用上的重要性怎么估计也不会过高。
例 2：泰坦尼克号在 1912 年的处女航中因撞上冰山而沉没，致使船上 1 500 多名乘客罹难。
例 3：如果一个托架按计算应支撑 1 000 磅，而设计者却将它设计为 100 磅，那么肯定会出事故。

我们再以"通顺"为尺度来衡量下面两个译例。

例 1：The pilot lamp stopped to represent the termination of the operation.
指示灯停止显示操作终止。

例 2：My husband and I didn't leave our hometown until our first son Carl was born.
直到我们的第一个儿子卡尔出生,我的丈夫和我都没离开我们的家乡。

分析：

以上两例译文几乎每个字都对应了英语原文,但读起来却磕磕绊绊,语句不通顺。

例 1 原文中的不定式短语 to represent the termination of the operation 为结果状语,一目了然,而译文的"停止显示操作终止"却含糊不清:停止的是"显示"、"操作",还是"操作终止"?我们不得而知。

例 2 译文拖泥带水,不符合汉语的习惯表达法。英语的人称表达顺序为二、三、一人称,而汉语则是二、一、三(如你、我、他),所以 My husband and I 应将"我"放在前,"丈夫"放在后,代词 my, our 应当省略(参见第五单元"代词的省略");从习惯表达看,our first son 应为"大儿子"而不是"第一个儿子";not...until... 应为"直到……才……"。这两句话的通顺译文应为:

例 1：指示灯熄灭,表示操作终止。
例 2：我和丈夫直到大儿子卡尔出生之后才离开家乡。

忠实和通顺是辩证的统一关系,两者互为依存,不可分割。译文不通顺,读者看不懂,就谈不上忠实。通顺而不忠实,歪曲原意或随意增减,便成了乱译甚至杜撰。因此,要使译文忠实,就必须通顺;反之,译文的通顺,也必须以忠实于原文为前提。我们不能把两者割裂开来,认为忠实只管对原文的准确理解,通顺只负责译文的流畅表达。在整个翻译过程中自始至终都要把握好准确与通顺的关系:既要防止对忠实的片面理解,一味追求形式上的相似,造成逐字死译,产生翻译上的形式主义,又要防止片面追求译文的通顺,随心所欲地增减原文中没有的内容,形成翻译上的自由主义。

四、直译与意译

翻译的过程大体上包括理解和表达两个阶段。准确地理解原文是翻译的前提，没有理解，翻译也就无从谈起。但理解正确并不意味着就能表达无误。有时候，一些我们完全领会了的东西却不能用恰当的汉语表达出来，这就需要借助一些必要的翻译手段、方法来解决具体的翻译问题了。直译与意译便是两种常见的方法手段。

"直译"的英语说法叫作 literal translation，也即是"字面翻译"。但这并不能简单地理解为字对字、词对词的翻译，否则就难免会闹出以下笑话：

How are you?　　＊怎么是你？
How old are you?　　＊怎么老是你？

类似的情况，如将 white wine（白葡萄酒）译作"白酒"，将 restroom（公用厕所，洗手间）译作"休息室"等，也都不是直译而是误译，就像将 eggplant（茄子）译作"蛋植物"那样荒唐可笑。

所谓直译，就是在译文语言条件许可的情况下，使译文尽量保持原文的形式结构、比喻形象和民族文化色彩等。例如，英语中的 be armed to teeth, crocodile tears, chain reaction, win-win 等词组短语翻译成汉语的"武装到牙齿"、"鳄鱼的眼泪"、"连锁反应"、"双赢"，既对应了原文的字面意义，又保留了原文的生动形象。

再如，关于"死"的概念，英汉均有各种生动形象的表达法用于不同的描述对象：breathe one's last（断气），to one's eternal rest（安息），the long sleep（长眠），pass away（去世），see God（见上帝），see one's ancestors（见祖先），see Marx（见马克思），go west（归西），go to heaven（进天国），kick the bucket（蹬腿儿了）……。所有这些，都十分生动形象，用一个简单的"死"或"death"则很难表现出原文的寓意和情趣。

"意译"的英语说法是 free translation，主要用于原文与译文思维或表达方式不同的翻译情况。有时候，译文不便或无法套用原文的句型结构，需要译者用自己的措辞将原文的意思恰如其分地表达出来，就需要采用"意译"。在这种情况下，需要译者在整体上把握原文的思想内容的基础上，摆脱原文的形象特征和句式结构，对原文进行必要的、创造性的加工。例如：

- Don't cross the bridge till you get to it. 不必担心过早。（不必自寻烦恼。）
- Love me, love my dog. 爱屋及乌。
- Her grandson is the apple of her eye. 孙子是她的掌上明珠。
- Do you see any green in my eye? 你以为我是好欺骗的吗？

由于英汉思维或表达方式不同，以上各例均不宜按原文字面意义直接译出，否则会令人感到莫名其妙，不知所云。

除"直译"、"意译"之外，翻译中偶尔还可以借助另一种翻译手段——"音译"（transliteration）。"音译"这种翻译手段我们并不陌生，大家耳熟能详的《国际歌》中的 Internationale（英特纳雄耐尔）就是最典型的一例。

"音译"往往用以翻译两种语言中没有对应的词语的情况，如中国传统文化中的"阴、阳、衙门、叩头"等，英语没有对应的词语，只好音译为 yin, yang, yamen, kowtow；同理，英语中的一些词语，如 humor, logic, club 等，汉语原本缺乏相应的词汇，所以音译为"幽默"、"逻辑"、"俱乐部"。另一方面，"音译"可能会随时代的变化而变化，譬如几十年前，democracy, science, cement 等曾一度音译为"德先生、赛先生、水门汀"，随着时间的推移，逐渐有了"民主、科学、水泥"等固定的译法。同样，一些富有中国文化色彩的词语如"馒头、豆腐、功夫片"等，曾一度意译为 steamed bread, bean curd, martial arts films，显得不伦不类，现在随着中国国际地位的提高，对外交流的加强，音译为 mantou, toufu, gongfu movies，得到了国际社会的普遍认可、接受。请看下面一例。

- He is an old Fox.

译文 A：他是一只老狐狸。（直译）

译文 B：他是一个老奸巨猾的家伙。（意译）

译文 C：他是一位姓福克斯的老先生。（音译）

同一句话中的 Fox，用不同的翻译手法产生了效果截然不同的 3 种译文。直译保持了原文的语言特色，生动地再现原文的修辞比喻形象；意译对 Fox 一词做了适当的解读，准确传达出了原文的内在含义；而音译则反映了英语姓氏中的某一特点，揭示了姓氏翻译的一般规律。需要注意的是，无论英译汉还是汉译英，人名姓氏的翻译通常采用音译，哪怕是两种语言字面意思碰巧相同也不例外。如英语姓氏 King 和 White 我们不译作"王"和"白"，而是分别音译为"金"和"怀特"。同理，汉语中的"老王"、"白先生"，通常音译作 Lao Wang 和 Mr. Bai。

无论采取直译还是意译，都必须结合上下文、根据具体的语境需要来进行翻译。譬如这样一例：Wet paint。按直译法，可将其译作"湿油漆"，可是读者很难理解其意。按意译法，可译作"油漆未干"，亦可根据不同的语境、语气，译作"当心油漆"、"不要触摸"。

再如英语成语 Kill two birds with one stone. 按直译法，可译作"一石二鸟"。原文中的 birds 及 stone 均直接体现在译文中了。按意译法，可译作汉语的成语"一箭双雕"，原文中的 birds 和 stone 已转换了概念，分别被中文的"箭"和"雕"所取代。除此之外，我们还可以撇开"石"与"鸟"、"箭"与"雕"的概念，将此句译作"一举两得"。同一个句子，3 种不同译法，哪一种更可取呢？这自然得结合上下文来考虑了。我们不能说哪一种译法更好，只能说第一种保持了原文的字面形式和比喻形象，更忠实于原文，后两种译法的自由度较大，表现力更强，适用性更广。

此外，直译、意译是一个相对的概念，没有截然明了的划分。譬如，go to bed，大家都知道不能按字面理解为"去上床"，而是"去睡觉"之意，这种译法算是直译还是意译？还有 How are you? How do you do? 之类的日常用语，译作"你好"，算是直译还是意译？一些我们现在认为是天经地义的"直译"的东西，在被人们广泛接受之前，很可能算是"意译"。譬如我们平日最熟悉不过的 Good-bye 一词译作"再见"，究竟是直译还是意译？它和"再见"有什么关系？要弄清它的原本意思，还得追溯到古英语的用法：Be God with yee，直译成现代汉语，也就是"愿上帝与你同在"之类的话。我们不能因此而得出结论，说将 good-bye 译作"再见"是意译而不是直译。

简而言之，无论是直译、意译还是音译，均须以理解原文为前提，准确传达出原文的意思。在处理手法上，直译要近情理，便于读者理解、接受，否则就会变成硬译、死译；意译应当注重事实依据，不能无中生有、随意杜撰，否则就会变成胡译、乱译；音译必须约定俗成，符合规范，否则会自行其是，令读者不知所云。译者应当善于把这几种翻译方法手段有机地结合起来，在不失原文本意的前提下，灵活机动地选用或交替使用这些手段去解决翻译中的具体问题。

思考与练习

一、简要回答以下问题

1. 翻译的标准是什么？你对严复的"信、达、雅"标准持什么看法？
2. 你怎样理解"忠实"与"通顺"之间的关系？试举例说明。
3. 什么是直译、意译与音译？试举例说明。
4. 使用直译、意译需注意哪几点？你自己常用哪种译法？试举例说明。

二、翻译练习

1. 以"忠实"、"通顺"为标准指出下列各句翻译中的失误，并加以改正。

    1) I know he meant business. 我知道他的用意在生意。

    2) Your company must make good any loss. 贵公司必须转祸为福。

    3) It is a wise man that never makes mistakes. 从不犯错误的人是聪明的人。

    4) We can not estimate the value of modern science too much. 我们不能过高地估计现代科学的价值。

    5) Presidents come and go, but for more than half a century, the queen has always been the queen. 总统们来来去去，但半个多世纪以来，女王一直总是女王。

    6) Less than a decade ago, the city of Beijing was an industrial wasteland. 不到 10 年前，北京城还是一座工业废墟。

    7) Practically every Olympic construction project is running ahead of schedule. 事实上，许多奥林匹克的建设工程都走在了时间表的前面。

    8) People felled trees to make room for steel plants in the

administrative capital. 在这一行政首都人们砍倒树木为钢铁厂修房子。

9) Seven years and $40 billion later, the Chinese have had remarkable success on many fronts. 7年和400亿美元后，中国人在许多方面都取得了卓越的成功。

10) China has only 16 months before 550,000 overseas visitors pile into a city of more than 15 million. 在55万海外游人涌入这个拥有1 500万余人口的城市之前中国只有16个月了。

11) It's not hard to see why these two larger–than–life figures—one the world's most powerful man, one the richest—didn't become fast friends: the two Bills are as different as the two ends of the baby–boom generation they represent. 不难看出为什么这两位高于生活的人物———一个是世界上最有权的人，另一个是全球最有钱的人——没有很快成为朋友。因为两个比尔大不一样，他们代表了战后生育高峰这一代人的两个极端。

12) Yet the basic problems are the same everywhere. Mr. Black recalls an acquaintance from China teaching him a Chinese saying, "rice paddy to rice paddy in three generations". 然而，基本问题每个地方都一样。布莱克先生想起一位中国朋友教给他的一句中国谚语："三代家业田挨田"。

2. 英译汉。用直译或意译翻译以下各句。

1) No dish suits all tastes.
2) Every second counts.
3) A fox cannot hide its tail.
4) A bargain's a bargain.
5) Hunger is the best sauce.
6) He's got more money than taste.
7) The early bird gets/catches the worm.
8) He is a ruined man.

9) She read his thoughts.
10) He's married to his work.
11) We decided to return blow for blow.
12) The beauty of the plan consists in its simplicity.

第十一单元
专有名词的翻译问题

翻译是一门涉及范围广、知识覆盖面宽的学科，不但需要译者对语言、语法、词汇了解得非常透彻，还要对中国和英语国家的背景知识有所把握，对各行各业、各个领域的知识有所了解，需要具有广博的百科综合知识。

譬如专有名词的翻译问题。翻译中我们不时会碰到一些诸如人名、地名、机构组织名称、专业术语等专有名词。在翻译这类专有名词时须倍加小心，否则一不留神就会闹笑话。曾有这样一例有关美国的网络大学（webcentric university）的情况介绍：

"King University" is an institution of higher education in Nashville, Tennessee, born of a merger of three historically black colleges and universities. （"路德·金大学"是一所位于田纳西州首府纳什维尔的高等学府，由以前只招收黑人学生的3所院校合并而成。）

相当多的同学由于缺乏相关知识，不知道此处的 King 是指著名的黑人领袖 Martin Luther King（马丁·路德·金），将其误解为"国王"，结果将 King University 译成了"国王大学/大型大学"。由此可见，要做好翻译，除了需要具备较高的英语水平外，广博的百科综合知识也是一个不可忽视的重要因素。

下面向大家介绍一些有关英语专有名词、汉语地名、住址的一般翻译方法和注意事项，以及汉语拼音与韦氏拼法的差异。

一、英语专有名词的翻译方法

英语专有名词的翻译方法主要采用音译、意译和混合式翻译。

1. 音译法

这种方法主要用于人名、地名的翻译，如：Karl Marx 卡尔·马克思、Bill Clinton 比尔·克林顿、Mr. Black 布莱克先生、Mr. White 怀特先生、New York 纽约、Washington 华盛顿等。需要注意的是，在翻译某些历史人物的时候，需要采用约定俗成的译法，如著名的国际主义战士 Bethune 译作"白求恩"而不是目前流行的"贝休恩"；喜剧演员 Chaplin 译作"卓别林"而不是"查普林"。这样做是为了尊重历史，避免造成不必要的混乱。

2. 直／意译法

主要用于机构组织名称及其缩写、地名、术语、书名、影片名等翻译，视不同情况可采用直译或意译，如：

UN United Nations 联合国（直译）
WHO World Health Organization 世界卫生组织（直译）
Oxford University 牛津大学（Ox 牛＋ford 渡口，津）（直译）
RAM Random Access Memory 随机存取存储器（意译）
Red Star Over China《西行漫记》（意译）

有时候，根据不同的情况，同一作品可能有不止一个译名，如：

Gone with the Wind《飘》（小说名，意译）／《乱世佳人》（电影名，意译）
Oliver Twist《奥列弗·退斯特》（小说名，音译）／《雾都孤儿》（电影名,意译）

3. 混合式

这种模式是将直译、意译和音译结合起来，组合成汉语词组，如：

Cambridge University 剑桥大学（音译 Cam＋直译 bridge）
AIDS Acquired Immune Deficiency Syndrome 艾滋病（音译 AIDS＋意

译"病")

Wall Street 华尔街（音译 Wall+ 直译 Street）

二、汉语地名的翻译方法

汉语地名翻译通常采用汉语拼音加直译的方法。

1. 一般专名加通名构成汉语地名的翻译方法

这类情况通常将专名译作汉语拼音，然后再意译通名，例如：

- 石家庄市 Shijiazhuang City
- 天安门广场 Tian'anmen Square
- 王府井商业街 Wangfujing Shopping Mall
- 青藏高原 the Qinghai-Tibet Plateau
- 云贵高原 the Yunnan-Guizhou Plateau
- 准噶尔盆地 the Junggar Basin
- 洞庭湖 the Dongting Lake
- 壶口瀑布 Hukou Waterfalls
- 雅鲁藏布江 the Yarlung Zangbo River
- 四川盆地 the Sichuan Basin
- 京杭运河 the Beijing-Hangzhou Canal
- 神农架自然保护区 Shennongjia Nature Reserve

2. 由单字专名加通名构成汉语地名

这类情况通常将通名视为整个地名的组成部分，先音译并与专名连写，再重复意译通名，例如：

- 恒山 the Hengshan Mountain（河北、山西）
- 淮河 the Huaihe River（河南、安徽、江苏）
- 巢湖 the Chaohu Lake（安徽）

- 渤海 the Bohai Sea（辽宁、山东）
- 韩江 the Hanjiang River（广东）
- 礼县 Lixian County（甘肃）
- 沙市 Shashi City（湖北）

3. 通名专名化的英译法

通名专名化主要指单音节的通名，如山、河、江、湖、海、港、峡、关、岛等，这类情况按专名处理，与专名连写构成专名整体，例如：

- 都江堰市 Dujiangyan City（比较：都江堰 the Dujiang Weir）（四川）
- 绥芬河市 Suifenhe City（比较：绥芬河 the Suifen River）（黑龙江）
- 白水江自然保护区 Baishuijiang Nature Reserve（比较：白水江 the Baishui River）（甘肃）
- 青铜峡水利枢纽 Qingtongxia Water Control Project（比较：青铜峡 the Qingtong Gorge）（宁夏）
- 武夷山自然保护区 Wuyishan Nature Reserve（比较：武夷山 Wuyi Mountain）（福建）

4. 通名为同一个汉字的多种不同译法

通名是单音节的同一个汉字，根据意义有多种不同英译法，在大多数情况下，这些英译词不能互相代换。譬如，一见到"山"字，我们就马上想到英语的对应词 mountain。其实，除 mountain 之外，"山"可视情况译作 mount、hill、peak、rock 等，有时候还可以省略"山"字，如：喜马拉雅山译作 the Himalayas。

- mountain（连绵的山脉、大山）
  长白山 the Changbai Mountains，唐古拉山 the Tanggula Mountains，秦岭 the Qinling Mountains
- mount（高山，一般放在前面）
  泰山 Mount Taishan，黄山 Mount Huangshan，华山 Mount Huashan，峨眉山 Mount Emei
- hill（小山、丘陵）

香山 Xiangshan Hill，象鼻山 the Elephant Hill，阳明山 the Yangming Hill
- peak（山峰）

  莲花峰 the Lotus Peak，独秀峰 the Singular Beauty Peak，玉屏峰 the Jade Screen Peak
- rock（山岩、公园假山）

  狮子山 Lion Rock，冠云峰 Cloud-Capped Rock，天心岩 Heaven's Heart Rock

5. 通名为不同汉字的同一种译法

与前面相反，根据通名意义，不同的汉字在很多情况下可英译为同一个单词。譬如"江、河、川、水、溪"都统一英译为 river，如：
- 长江 the Yangtze River
- 黄河 the Yellow River
- 嘉陵江 the Jialing River
- 汉水 the Hanshui River
- 螳螂川 the Tanglang River
- 古田溪 the Gutian River

一些小河、溪流可译作 creek，brook，如美国纽约大学石溪分校就叫做 State University of New York at Stony Brook。

"湖、泊、海（非海洋类）、池、潭"在很多情况下都统一英译为 lake，如：
- 洞庭湖 the Dongting Lake
- 梁山泊 the Liangshan Lake
- 洱海 the Erhai Lake
- 滇池 the Dianchi Lake
- 日月潭 the Sun-Moon Lake

需要注意的是，诸如泻湖、环礁湖之类的咸水湖一般叫做 lagoon，如 Venetian Lagoon 威尼斯泻湖；而较小的湖泊、池塘可译作 pond，如美国作家梭罗的《瓦尔登湖》，其原名就叫做 Walden Pond。

三、中文地址的翻译方法

在前面第五单元谈到，英汉两种语言有着不同的行文造句特点和表达习惯，英语的句式结构习惯于由点及面，由小到大，由近及远，而汉语恰恰相反。如：中国北京清华大学 28 号楼 502 室应翻译为 Room 502, Dormitory Building 28, Tsinghua University, Beijing, China。以家庭住址为例，中文地址的排列顺序是由大到小，如：× 国 × 省 × 市 × 区 × 路 × 号；英文地址则刚好相反，由小到大，先是门牌号码，然后街道、城市、州、国家，如：

● 中国上海虹口区西康路 125 弄 34 号 201 室

Room 201, No. 34, Lane 125, Xikang Road, Hongkou District, Shanghai, P. R. China

中文家庭地址翻译成英文的顺序是：× 室、× 号、× 路／街、× 区／× 县、× 市、× 省，最后是中国。其汉英对照如下：

× 室 Room ×

× 号 No. ×

× 单元 Unit ×

× 号楼 Building No. ×

× 路／街 × Road/Street

× 区／县 × District/County

× 市 × City

× 省 × Province

中国 P. R. China

中文的人名、路名、街道名等翻译一般用拼音，邮政编码放到所在城市后面。

中文地址翻译示例：

● 473004 河南省南阳市中州路 42 号

Room 42, Zhongzhou Road, Nanyang City, 473004, Henan Province, P. R. China

● 528400 广东中山市东区亨达花园 7 栋 702

Room 702, Building No.7, Hengda Garden, East District, Zhongshan City, 528400, Guangdong Province, P. R. China
- 266042 山东省青岛市开平路 53 号国棉四厂二宿舍 1 号楼 2 单元 204 室 Room 204, Unit 2, Building No. 1, the 2nd Dormitory of the No. 4 State-run Textile Mill, 53 Kaiping Road, Qingdao, 266042, Shandong Province, P. R. China

四、汉语拼音与韦氏拼法

汉语拼音通常用来翻译专有名词（人名、地名），使用起来非常方便。而 20 世纪 50 年代之前，中国人名地名采用的是威妥玛拼音（Wade-Giles），又称威玛式拼音或韦式拼法，是由英国人威妥玛在 1870 年代发明的，如：北京 Peking、香港 Hong Kong、赵元任 Chao Yuen Ren、杨振宁 Chen Ning Yang、李政道 Tsung-Dao Lee、李嘉诚 Lee Ka-shing、董建华 Tung Chien-hua 等。

随着汉语拼音方案在中国大陆地区的广泛推广，威妥玛拼法停止了使用，但在中国大陆以外的台湾地区、港、澳特别行政区及海外一直沿用至今。因为尽管汉语拼音非常简便，但有些拼音规则与英美读音不兼容，给外国读者造成很大困难，有些姓氏如：任 Ren、邱 Qiu、徐／许 Xu 等，英语中没有近似的发音，按韦式拼法，分别写作 Jen/Yum、Ch'iu、Hsü，这样便化解了汉语的读音困难。在翻译专有名词时需注意这一现象，以免阴差阳错、张冠李戴。

另外，汉语拼音书写需要注意两个特殊符号。一是隔音符号'，这种符号用在 a，o，e 开头的音节连接在其他音节后面的时候，以免发生音节界线的混淆，如 pi'ao（皮袄）。地名中的隔音符号如果省略就会造成读音甚至语义错误，例如：
- 西安市 Xi'an City（如果省略隔音符号，就成为 Xian，可以读成仙、贤、险、县等）
- 兴安县 Xing'an County（如果省略隔音符号，就成为 Xingan County 新干县）

二是汉语拼音 ü 的韵母跟声母 n，l 拼的时候，ü 上面的两点不能省略。如果省略，就会造成误解。例如：

- （山西）闾河 the Lühe River（如果省略 ü 上面的两点，就变成 the Luhe River 芦河，在江西）
- （台湾）绿岛 Lüdao Island（如果省略 ü 上面的两点，就变成 Ludao Island 鹭岛，在黑龙江海林）

为了便于计算机键盘操作，汉语拼音 ü 往往用英语字母 v 取而代之，这样也就省了不少麻烦，如：

- 旅顺港 Lvshun Port
- 吕梁地区 Lvliang Prefecture

思考与练习

一、简要回答以下问题

1. 英语专有名词有哪几种翻译方法？
2. 汉语地名的翻译需要注意哪些方面？
3. 中文地址的翻译与英语有什么不同？
4. 什么是韦氏拼法？它与汉语拼音有何差异？

二、翻译练习

1. 翻译下列各句，注意专有名词的译法。

    1) Adam's apple
    2) Achilles' heel
    3) *The Sun also Rises*
    4) *Waterloo Bridge*
    5) *Wuthering Heights*
    6) *Uncle Tom's Cabin*
    7) *Steel Meets Fire*
    8) United Nations Security Council

9) World Health Organization

10) International Monetary Fund

11) Massachusetts Institute of Technology

12) National Aeronautics and Space Administration

2. 汉译英，指出下面译文的错误。

1) 时间非常宝贵。 *Time is very valuable.

2) 他眼睛近视。 *His eyes are short-sighted.

3) 她正在照镜子。 *She is looking at the mirror.

4) 我与律师联系上了。 *I have contacted with my lawyer.

5) 我们坚决反对战争。 *We strongly oppose to the war.

6) 他的英语水平比我高。 *His English level is higher than I.

7) 为我们的成功干杯。 *Let's drink for our success.

8) 寒冷的气候影响了庄稼。 *Cold weather influenced the crops.

9) 这是一个不幸的悲剧。 *That was a unfortunate tragedy.

10) 这孩子学习成绩不太好。 *The boy's study result is not so good.

11) 我们在学校学了很多知识。 *We have learned many knowledges at school.

12) 过度饮酒会损害你的身体。 *Over-drinking may injure your body.

第十二单元
谨防"假朋友"的陷阱

翻译的实践性很强,因此翻译能力的形成不能单靠学习理论知识、方法技巧,而更重要的是需要扎扎实实的双语功底及大量的翻译实践。我们知道,作为译者,在翻译过程中自始至终要受到两方面的因素的干扰。一方面,他必须熟悉源语的语言文化,凭语感直觉把握原文的精神;另一方面又必须排除源语的语言模式的干扰,谨防英语中的"假朋友"避开翻译中的"陷阱",用地道的目的语进行翻译创作,敏锐地发现并处理好各类相似语句中的些微差别。

一、切忌"望文生义"

所谓"望文生义"是指在没弄清词句的真正含义的情况下,仅从字面牵强附会也作出片面理解,因而造成译文的失误。据统计,翻译中的失误相当大一部分与"望文生义"有关,其中大都是我们非常熟悉的字眼。有些表达法在英汉语中看上去似乎很吻合,但实际上意义全然不同。这就形成了英语中的"假朋友"(false friends)。假朋友貌合神离,给翻译布下一道道陷阱。轻者译文不通,词不达意,重者完全牛头不对马嘴,扭曲了原文的本意。请看下面各例:

1. Peter had a stopwatch.　　* 彼得有一只不走的表。
2. She always sleeps very late.　　* 她总是睡得很晚。

第十二单元
谨防"假朋友"的陷阱

3. The bike is as good as new.　＊这部自行车和新的一样好。

4. His father has gone to his rest.　＊他父亲已经去休息了。

5. Your words are over my head.　＊你的话在我头上嗡嗡作响。

6. There are friends and friends.　＊到处都是朋友／我们的朋友遍天下。

7. Mr. Johnson got a woman with child.　＊约翰逊先生得到一个带孩子的女人。

8. He went behind the wall and made water against a tree.　＊他走到墙后，造水毁掉一棵树。

评析：

1. 正译：彼得有一只跑表。

英语的 stopwatch 指的是体育比赛时用的跑表，而不是"停止不走的表"。英语中这种跟汉语貌合神离的词汇不少，如：white wine 白葡萄酒（不是"白酒"），rest room 公用厕所,洗手间（不是"休息室"），goldbrick 偷懒的人（不是"金砖"），brown sugar 红糖（不是"棕色糖"），等等。

2. 正译：她总是起床很迟。

这句话完全扭曲了原文的意思，sleep very late 意为"睡到很晚"或"睡懒觉"。"睡得晚"的英语说法是 go to bed late/stay up late。

3. 正译：这部自行车几乎是新的。

短语 as good as 的意思是"和……一样；差不多"，如：The house was as good as sold. 房子差不多卖掉了。

4. 正译：他父亲已经去世了。

名词 rest 一般作"休息，歇息，静止"之意，如：to take a rest 休息，go to rest 去休息［睡］；但加上 his, her 之类的修饰语,往往就有了"长眠、去世"的含义。如：He was called to his eternal rest. 他已长眠地下。

5. 正译：我听不懂你的话。

此处的 over sb.'s head 意思是"太深而超过某人的理解"，如：They talked over our heads. 他们讲得我们莫名其妙。

6. 正译：朋友有各种各样，有真朋友，也有假朋友。

此处的 and 用以表示"同一类事物，但优劣不同"；如：There are books and books. 书有种种，有好书，也有坏书。

7. 正译：约翰逊先生使一女子怀孕了／结交了一个孕妇。

with child 意为"怀孕的"，它跟 with a child 或 with the child 意思完全不同。而 get 既可指"弄到，得到"，又可指"使……"。请看以下表达方法，特别注意单数可数名词前有无冠词：

- with child 怀孕／with a child 带着一个孩子
- in the class 在那个班上／in class 在课堂上
- in a word 简言之／in word 口头上
- at the school 在那个学校／at school 上学
- out of question 毫无疑问／out of the question 不可能

8. 正译：他走到墙后，冲着一棵树小便。

此处的 make water 意为"小便"，不可照字面译作"造水"；against prep. 逆着，与某个方向或过程相反；如：advance against difficulties 迎着困难上；row against the current 逆水行舟。

附：英语中的常见"假朋友"

a baker's dozen 十三；an afternoon farmer 拖拉的人；an apple of love 西红柿；apple-pie order 整整齐齐；as good as gold 很乖，很规矩；a bad sailor 晕船的人；bring down the house 博得全场喝彩；cat-and-dog life 吵架的生活；Chinese rose 月季花；dog days 三伏天；dog-eared（书）卷角的；eat one's hat 不信，才怪；every Tom, Dick and Harry 普通百姓；feet of clay 致命弱点；fishwife 泼妇；fly a kite 试探反应；four hundred 社会名流；forty winks：打盹，小睡；go against the grain 不合常理；go to the wall 碰壁，失败；hand in glove 相互勾结，密切合作；hard cheese 不走运，倒霉；hat in hand 恭恭敬敬地；have a ball 狂欢，玩得开心；have a bone in one's throat 难于启齿；have two left feet 笨手笨脚；help a lame dog over a stile 助人渡过难关；hold the baby 把责任推卸给别人；in Dutch 处境困难，碰到麻烦；in one's birthday clothes 裸体；in repair 状况良好；in the green 年富力强的；in the wind 即将；into the bargain 除……以外；labour of love 心甘情愿的工作；now or never 勿失良机，机不可失；odd jobs 杂活；paint the lily 画蛇添足；pigtail 辫子；powder room 女厕所，化妆室；priceless 价值连城的；rat race 激烈的竞

争；red type 繁文缛节；ride the high horse 盛气凌人；rose-colored 乐观的；rule of thumb 凭经验；salt of the earth 社会的中坚力量；say uncle 讨饶；sea cucumber 海参；shoestring 小本，微薄；sit on the fence 不表态；skeleton in the cupboard 家丑；smell fishy 可疑，觉得不太对头；sporting house 妓院，赌场；swan song 绝唱，最后的作品；take French leave 不辞而别；take one's medicine 忍受不愉快的事情；take sb. for a ride 上当受骗；take the cake 名列第一，列榜首；ten to one 很可能；throw the book at sb. 给某人定重罪；toilet water 花露水；under the weather 感到不舒服，身体不适；wet behind the ears 无经验的，不成熟的；white feather 胆怯；wild goose chase 白费力气；wipe sb.'s eye 先发制人；yellow boy 金币；zero hour 关键时刻

二、学会比较对照

翻译中我们常常会发现这样一种情况，有些句型结构从字面上看极为相似，有时候，句与句之间仅仅差一个冠词、介词，甚至一个字母、一个标点符号，其意思就完全不同了。这就需要学会比较对照，辨清造成差别的原因，在理解的基础上再动手，将翻译失误降低到最小程度。请看以下各组近似的句子。

1) A. She bought **a red and yellow** dress. 她买了一条红黄两色的裙子。

   B. She bought **a red and a yellow** dress. 她买了一条红裙子，一条黄裙子。

   （a red and a yellow dress 各一件；a red and yellow dress 就一件）

2) A. He is **not a** child. 他已不是孩子了。

   B. He is **no** child. 他绝不是个孩子。

   （not a child 表明事实"不是孩子";no child 表示强烈语气"绝不是孩子"）

3) A. This tool is **no** more useful than that one. 这工具和那个工具都不管用。

   B. This tool is **not** more useful than that one. 这工具不比那个工具管用。

   （no more than 同……一样不；not more useful than 不比……更）

4) A. Quite **properly**, he was punished. 他受到了处罚，这完全恰当。

B. He was punished quite **properly**. 他受到了恰如其分的惩罚。

（Quite properly 完全恰当地；be punished quite properly 受到恰如其分的惩罚）

5) A. **Although** he is busy, Henry is in high spirits. 虽然亨利很忙，但心境极佳。

B. He is busy, **but** Henry is in high spirits. 他很忙碌，但亨利心境极佳。

（A 中的 he 和 Henry 为同一人；B 中的 he 和 Henry 为不同两人）

6) A. They say David is mad, and so **he is**. 他们说大卫疯了，他果然疯了。

B. He says Jane is mad, and so **is he**. 他说简疯了，而他自己也疯了。

（and so he is 他果然疯了；and so is he 他自己也疯了）

7) A. This cup of tea is **fairly** hot. 这杯茶很热乎。

B. This cup of tea is **rather** hot. 这杯茶太烫。

（fairly hot 热乎，正好喝；rather hot 太烫，不能喝）

8) A. He is **anything** but a teacher. 他绝不是一位老师。

B. He is **nothing** but a teacher. 他只不过是一位老师罢了。

（anything but 绝不是；nothing but 只不过是……罢了）

9) A. You **may** as well say so. 你完全可以这样说。

B. You **might** as well say so. 你不妨这样说。

（may as well say so 完全可以这样说；might as well say so 不妨这样说）

10) A. You have offended the girl as deeply as **I**. 你像我一样深深地冒犯了这女孩。

B. You have offended the girl as deeply as **me**. 你像冒犯我一样深深地冒犯了这女孩。

（as deeply as I 像我一样深深地冒犯；as deeply as me 像冒犯我一样深深地）

11) A. His success is **out of question**. 他必然会成功。

B. His success is **out of the question**. 他不可能成功。

（out of question 不成问题；out of the question 成问题）

12) A. It has been raining **continually** for two hours. 雨断断续续地下了两小时。

第十二单元
谨防"假朋友"的陷阱

B. It has been raining **continuously** for two hours. 雨连续不断地下了两小时。

（continually 不住地，断断续续地；continuously 连续不断地）

13) A. I regret **to say** he was wrong. 我遗憾地说，他错了。

    B. I regret **saying** he was wrong. 我后悔自己说他错了。

    （regret to say 遗憾地说；regret saying 因说了……而感到遗憾）

14) A. She spoke to the boy **as** a mother. 她作为母亲和男孩谈话。

    B. She spoke to the boy **like** a mother. 她像母亲一样和男孩谈话。

    （as a mother 作为母亲；like a mother 像母亲一样）

15) A. He stood there **to watch** the train come in. 他站在那里等着看火车开进站。

    B. He stood there **watching** the train come in. 他站在那里看见火车开进站。

    （to watch the train come in 等着看火车开进站；watching the train come in 看见火车开进站）

16) A. I, as well as you, shall not do this test. 我和你一样，都不会做这个测试。

    B. I shall not do this test as well as you. 我不会像你那样做这个测试。

    （I, as well as you, shall not 我和你都不会；I shall not...as well as you 我不会像你那样）

17) A. The children who wanted to play soccer ran to an open field. 这群孩子中想踢球的人朝野外跑去。

    B. The children, who wanted to play soccer, ran to an open field. 这些孩子想踢球，他们朝野外跑去。

    （The children who wanted to play soccer 孩子中想踢球的人；The children, who wanted to play soccer 这些孩子都想踢球）

三、当心"异常"结构

翻译中我们常常会发现这样一种情况：有些词语、句式结构与常规语法或搭配习惯似有出入。对于这类看似超越"常规"的"异常"结构，翻译时应特别小心，否则也会掉入"陷阱"。请看以下各例带＊号的误译。

1. 冠词

1）He always talks shop.　＊他经常谈商店的事。

2）They often talk horse.　＊他们常常谈论马。

3）That girl student is in the green.　＊那个女学生身着绿装。

4）The boss gave her the sack.　＊老板给了她一个麻袋。

冠词是引导名词的标志，除了抽象名词、固定搭配之外，一般名词前都应带有冠词。talk shop, talk horse 为习语固定搭配，因此不能理解为"谈商店"、"论马"，而是"说行话，三句话不离本行"、"吹牛，说大话"之意；而 in the green, the sack 中的定冠词，与一般意义上的 in green, a sack 也大不一样，而是"青春，活力"、"解雇"之意。各句的正确的译文是：

1）他三句话不离本行。

2）他们常常吹牛。

3）那女学生正值豆蔻年华。

4）老板解雇了她。

2. 介词

1）That woman walks the streets.　＊那个妇女常在那些街上走。（in the streets）

2）The machine is in repair.　＊那台机器正在修理之中。（under repair）

3）Don't make a fuss of them!　＊别对那些事大惊小怪！（make a fuss about）

4）We'll stand up to the project.　＊我们都赞成这个工程。（stand up for）

5）I'll report that official.　＊我要向那位官员报告。（report to）

6）She is in the dock.　＊她在码头上。（at the docks）

介词搭配是外语学习中最令人头痛的一项。以上各句之所以造成误译，均是因为将特定的介词结构误解为常规的用法（如括号中所示）。如：walk the streets 走遍大街，其引申含义为"当妓女"；in (good) repair 维修状况良好；make a fuss of/over sb. 娇养某人，过分关怀某人；stand up to 勇敢地面对，抵抗；report *vt.* 告发，揭发（He reported me to the head. 他向领导告发我。）；in the dock 在被告席受审。以上各句正确的译文分别是：

1）那个妇女是妓女。

2）那台机器状况良好。

3）别讨好他们！

4）我们将抵制这个计划。

5）我要检举那位官员。

6）她在被告席受审。

3. 名词的单复数

1）I bought some salts yesterday.　＊我昨天买了一些食盐。

2）The man is in the dumps.　＊那个人在垃圾堆里。

3）Don't call him names!　＊别叫他的名字！

名词的单复数问题看似简单，翻译中往往也是一个棘手的难点。关键应把握两点：一是不可数名词加了复数，那么必是另有所指。如 water（水）/ waters（海域），sand（沙）/ sands（沙滩），wood（木材）/ woods（树林），等等；二是一些只能用复数形式的名词，如：remains（残骸），means（手段），species（种，类），等等。上述1）属于第一类，而2）、3）则属于第二类。salts 泻盐；in the dumps 心情沮丧；call names 骂人，咒骂。以上各句的正确的译文分别是：

1）我昨天买了一些泻盐。

2）那个人神情沮丧。

3）别骂他！

4. 名词的大小写

1）He is the Speaker. *他是讲演者。

2）Where is the Book? *那本书在哪？

3）Why thank me? Thank Him above. *为什么谢我？应该感谢上面的他。

4）Do you know anything about japan? *你了解日本吗？

大小写的问题相对比较容易解决，遇到不合常规的情况，注意格外留心就行了。在必要的时候，不妨查查词典，疑虑一般就能化解。the Speaker 议长，主席；the Book 圣经；Him 他（指上帝）；japan 日本漆，天然漆。以上各句的正确的译文分别是：

1）他是议长。

2）圣经在哪儿？

3）为什么谢我？应该感谢上帝。

4）你了解日本漆吗？

5. 其他搭配

1）The woman in labor is his wife. *那个劳动的妇女是他的妻子。

2）We charged him to do it. *我们指控他干了那个事。

3）They surprised him doing it. *他们惊吓得他做那个事。

4）I have seen him through. *我看透了他。

其他类搭配包括介词短语、不定式与动名词或分词的区别、介词与副词的区别等。in labor 在分娩；charge sb. to do sth. 责令某人干某事；surprise sb. doing sth. 撞上某人干某事；see sb. through 帮助某人克服困难等。以上 4 句的参考译文分别是：

1）分娩的妇女是他的妻子。

2）我们责令他干那事。

3）他们撞上他做那个事。

4）我帮助他过难关。

四、语音歧义、词汇歧义和语法歧义

歧义是指结构或句子的语义模棱两可，一句话、一个词语可以作两种或多种解释。这些歧义往往会给翻译造成很大障碍。英语中的歧义大致可分为三类：语音歧义、词汇歧义和语法歧义。

1. 语音歧义

英语中有许多同音异义词，其发音相同而拼写和意义不同，如：

1) Seven days' hard work makes one week/weak.

   译文 A：7 天辛勤工作刚好一周。

   译文 B：辛勤地工作 7 天使人虚弱无力。

2) (In a restaurant) Waitress: "Anything wrong with the fish?"
   Customer: "Long time no see/sea."

   （在一家餐馆）女服务员："鱼有什么不对劲吗？"

   顾客："好久没有见 / 出海了。"（一语双关，借 Long time no see 的句型，谐 sea 的音，暗示久未出海，餐桌上的鱼不新鲜）。

2. 词汇歧义

词汇歧义在英语歧义现象中较为常见。在英语中，一个词经常有两种甚至多种词性和含义，这就使话语产生了歧义，在语境不明的情况下很难判断这类句子的真正含义。

1) Mr. Wang is a bachelor.

   译文 A：王先生是一个学士。

   译文 B：王先生是一个单身汉。

2) She can't bear children.

   译文 A：她没有生育能力。

   译文 B：她无法容忍孩子。

3. 语法歧义

语法歧义亦称结构歧义，因句子成分不同的排列顺序和组合层次，以及它们在句中不同句法功能而引起。

1) They called me a cook.

译文 A：他们为我找来一个厨师。

译文 B：他们称我为厨师。

2) The wolf is too small to kill.

译文 A：这只狼太小了，不要捕杀。

译文 B：这只狼太小了，还不会捕杀猎物。

排除歧义往往需要通过上下文分析来解决，如：

1) He hit the man with a stick.

是"他用棍子打那人"，还是"他打了拿棍子的那个人"？根据上下文，一看情况就清楚了。有时候，作者玩文字游戏，故意造成歧义，则可用灵活的翻译技巧方法作适当的变通处理，保留原文的情趣，如：

2) Why is an empty purse always the same? Because there is never any change in it.

为什么空钱包老是一成不变？因为里面从来就没有一个子儿。

此句中的 change 既可理解为"改变"，也可以理解为"零钱"，用"一成不变"和"没有一个子儿"，两层意思也就大致翻译出来了。

思考与练习

一、简要回答以下问题

1. 什么是翻译中的"望文生义"？
2. 我们应当怎样利用比较对照来减少翻译失误？
3. 什么是翻译的"陷阱"？我们怎样才能避开它们？
4. 什么是语音歧义、词汇歧义和语法歧义？为什么它们对翻译造成很大障碍？

第十二单元
谨防"假朋友"的陷阱

二、翻译练习

1. 翻译下列各句，注意避免已给出错误译文中的"望文生义"。

   1) His refusal is final. *他的拒绝是最后的。

   2) Don't tell him home truth. *不要告诉他家里的真实情况。

   3) He is the last person for the job. *他是最后一个做这份工作的人。

   4) This couple led a cat-and-dog life. *这对夫妇过着猫狗不如的日子。

   5) I hope you'll soon be in the pink again. *我希望你早日再度穿上粉红衣服。

   6) She told me that she was in deep water. *她告诉我说，她曾落入深水差点送命。

   7) Finally, Mr. White had to eat his own words. *怀特先生最终不得不自食其言。

   8) I feel she has a couple of skeletons in her cupboard. *我觉得她的食橱里有几个骷髅。

   9) He faced the music even in times of great adversity. *即使在危难时刻，他也欣赏音乐。

   10) The boy refused to say uncle no matter how they threatened him. *无论他们怎样恐吓，孩子都不肯叫一声叔叔。

   11) Price is soaring. If it goes on like this, we shall not be able to keep the pot boiling. *价格高升，如果继续这样下去，我们将不能烧不开锅里的水了。

   12) Thomas isn't just some nature nut in his birthday suit—he's one of a growing number of hikers. *托马斯不仅身穿生日套装喜欢自然坚果，他也是越来越多的徒步旅行者之一。

2. 翻译下列各句，注意句子的歧义。

   1) It is a long tale/tail.

   2) Put down your arms.

   3) He cut the meat on the table.

   4) I know him better than you.

5) He was seated by the chairman.
6) Flying planes can be dangerous.
7) She didn't dance to please her mother.
8) The criminal lawyer committed suicide.
9) Time flies like an arrow and fruit flies like a banana.
10) They pray for you today and pray on you tomorrow.
11) We must all hang together, or we shall all hang separately.
12) Mary liked the vase in the cupboard which she had bought the day before.

第十三单元
翻译能力的培养与提高

外语学习中的翻译是一个日积月累的过程，需要经过长期不懈地努力才能获得预期的成效。不少同学可能会说，从中小学到大学，我们的外语学习少则七八年，多则十几年，为什么成效不大，尤其是翻译，总是难以取得显著的进步？

原因是多方面的。有的同学学得多，但真正掌握得少；有的学得死，灵活性不够；还有的人学外语只是为了应付考试，一旦侥幸过关，刚学到手的一点皮毛知识就抛到了九霄云外。

外语学习的关键不在于学会了多少生词，做了多少练习，背了多少课文，而在于是否真正具备了对这门语言的实际运用能力——这就涉及学习态度和方法问题。英语学习中听、说、读、写、译五大技能的培养不能单靠啃词典、抠语法、找窍门、背范文，最重要的是将学到的知识融会贯通、灵活运用，在语言的实际运用中不断改进、提高，最终形成自己的独立运用能力（包括应试能力）。尤其是翻译能力的形成，不能单靠学习理论知识、强化技巧训练，而是需要扎扎实实的双语功底及大量的翻译实践。因此，从某种意义上讲，一个人的翻译能力不是课堂上讲出来的，也不是翻译技巧所能造就的，而是要靠自己脚踏实地地翻译出来。

下面我们就翻译能力的培养与提高提出以下几点供大家参考借鉴。

一、扎实的词汇语法功底

扎实的词汇语法功底是做好翻译的前提。英语的词汇犹如砖瓦材料，语法则是黏合剂，将零乱的材料组合一起，形成有序的语言文字。砖瓦材料越多修建的大厦越高，语法越扎实黏合得越牢。因此，没有一个扎实的语法词汇功底，外语学习无异于空中楼阁、纸上谈兵，更不用说翻译了。从某种意义上说，词汇语法的把握能力是衡量一个人英语水平的一把重要标尺。当然，我们所说的词汇把握能力，不仅是指能够认识或记住多少词汇，懂得多少语法规则，而更重要的是对所学词汇的灵活把握和应用，能够听得懂，说得出，写得对，译得准。

1. 把握词语的搭配意义

很多同学花不少精力去死记硬背英语生词难词，而忽略了一些简单的词语的丰富的含义。而英语中最难以掌握的不是复杂的字眼，而是一些最常用的单词。譬如 take 一词，《新英汉词典》所收入的词义为：及物动词 23 义，不及物动词 9 义，名词 8 义，总共 50 义；而《英汉大词典》所收入的词义为：及物动词 36 义，不及物动词 15 义，名词 12 义，总共 63 义；如果再加上数十个固定词组短语的数百项各种不同用法，其含义就更广了。《大学英语课程教学要求》列出的要求掌握的 take 词组短语就有整整一页，从 take a chance, take a delight in,... 到 take turns, take up, take...with a grain/pinch of salt，共 56 条，每条都非常重要。因此，我们在平常的学习过程中，对英语词汇的理解不要停留在表面的字词对应关系，而是要抓住其实质特征，熟悉各种搭配意义，就连平日最常见、最熟悉的词语也不例外。只有这样，才能从根本上把握词义，准确地译出原文的意思。

以我们平日最熟悉不过的两个词 and 和 when 为例，在以下各例中 and 都不宜照常规译作"和"、"与"、"并且"，when 都不宜译作"当"、"当……时候"，否则就算不上真正掌握。

And

1) Two and two makes four.

2) Let's go and play basketball.

3) He is so rich and lives like a beggar.

4) The sun came out and the grass dried.

5) She read for an hour and went to bed.

6) I went to his house, and he came to mine.

7) One step more, and you are a dead man.

8) He did the work, and he did it very well.

9) These parts are made of woods or plastics and not metals.

10) Rust is abrasive and can cause damage to the injection components.

译文：

1）二加二得四。（将 and 译作动词"加"）

2）我们去打篮球吧。（省译 and）

3）他那么有钱，却生活得像个乞丐。（表示转折，"却"）

4）太阳一出，草就干了。（表示时间连贯，"一……就"）

5）她看了一个钟头的书，然后就睡觉了。（表时间先后顺序，"然后"）

6）我上他家去，而他却到我家来。（表对照，"而"）

7）再挪一步，（那么）就要你的命。（表结果，"那么"）

8）他干了这件工作，并且干得挺好。（表递进，"并且"）

9）这些零件是用木材或塑料制成的，而不是金属制成的。（表对比关系，"而不是"）

10）锈具有腐蚀性，所以能损坏喷射元件。（表结果，"所以"）

When

1) I stayed till noon, when I went home.

2) I can't tell you when you won't listen.

3) He usually walks when he might ride.

4) When you cross the river you are safe.

5) When the wind blows, all the doors rattle.

6) Why are you here when you should be in school?

7) When one is older, one is also more experienced.
8) They had only three transistors when they needed five.
9) He stopped trying, when he might have succeeded next time.
10) We'll go to there in June, when the summer harvest will start.
11) Turn off the switch when anything goes wrong with the machine.
12) When the teacher had left the classroom, the pupils started talking.

译文：
1）我一直待到中午，然后就回家了。（表时间先后顺序，"然后"）
2）既然你不想听，我就不告诉你了。（表原因，"既然"）
3）虽然有车可乘，他通常总是步行。（表转折，"虽然"）
4）一旦过了河，你便安全了。（表假设，"一旦"）
5）只要风一吹，这门就吱嘎作响。（表条件关系，"只要"）
6）你本该在学校里的，却为何在这里？（表责怪，"本该"）
7）一个人的经验随年龄的增长而增长。（表示伴随关系，"随……而"）
8）他们需要5只晶体管，可是只有3只。（表示转折，"可是"）
9）他不再试了，其实他可能下一次就成功。（表示推测，"其实"）
10）我们6月要去那里，那时夏收就要开始了。（表将来，"那时"）
11）万一机器发生什么故障，就把电源关上。（表推测，"万一"）
12）老师一离开教室，学生们就喧哗起来。（表示时间连贯，"一……就"）

2. 利用构词法扩大词汇量

通过构词分析可以加深我们对词汇的理解、把握，收到事半功倍的效益。构词法的核心是词根和词缀（包括前缀和后缀），有效地利用词根、词缀，不仅有助于确定词的词性、词义，更重要的是可以帮助我们滚雪球似地扩大词汇量。譬如，利用词根 act 及其各种前后缀，便可轻松地掌握以下几十个词：

action *n.* 活动，行为，作用（-ion 为名词后缀）
activate *vt.* 使活动起来，使开始起作用（-ivate 为动词后缀）
active *a.* 有活力的，积极的，主动的（-ive 为形容词后缀）

activist *n.* 活动分子，积极分子（-ist 为"行为者"后缀）

activity *n.* 活动；所做的事，活动性，活跃（-ivity 为名词后缀）

actor *n.* ①男演员②行动者（-or 为"动作者"后缀）

actress *n.* 女演员（-ess 为阴性后缀）

actual *a.* 事实上的，实际的（-ual 为形容词后缀）

interact *vi.* 互相作用，互相影响（前缀 inter- 为"互相"之义）

interaction *n.* 互相作用，互相影响（前缀 inter-，后缀 -ion）

react *vi.* ①反应②起作用，有影响（前缀 re- 表示"再、又、重新"之义）

reaction *n.* ①反应②化学反应，反作用（力）③反动（前缀 re-，后缀 -ion）

reactionary *a.* 反动的（前缀 re-，后缀 -ion, -ary）

reactivity *n.* 反应，反应性

coact *vi.* 协作，共同行动

coactor *n.* 共同合作者

coaction *n.* 合作，强迫

coactive *adj.* 强制的，限制性的

deactivate *vt.* 解除动员，使无效

enact *vt.* 制定法律，颁布，扮演

enactive *adj.* 有制定权的；制定法律的

enactment *n.* 制定（法律），颁布

enactable *adj.* 能实行的，能演出的

enactory *adj.* 制定法律的

inaction *n.* 无行动，不活动，无为

inactivate *vt.* 使不活动；使不活泼

inactivator *n.* 抑制剂；钝化剂

inactive *adj.* 不活跃的；不活动的

inactivity *n.* 静止；不活泼；休止状态

inactiveness *n.* 钝性；不活泼

……

依此类推，掌握了名词后缀 -ion，便可举一反三：记住了动词 decide（决

定），就可知名词 decision；记住了动词 divide（分开），就可知其名词 division；知道动词 corrode（腐蚀），就可知其名词 corrosion。再如，某些以 c 为结尾的名词，添加词尾 -ian，就变成相应的名词：logic 逻辑 -logician 逻辑学家，magic 魔术 -magician 魔术家，music 音乐 -musician 音乐家，physic 药品 -physician 内科医生；某些以 y 为结尾的名词去 y 后加上 -ze，就变成相应意义的动词，如：apology 道歉 -apologize 道歉，energy 能量 -energize 给予能量，sympathy 同情 -sympathize 同情；等等。某些名词加后缀 -less，便成为意思相反的形容词，再加上后缀 -ness，便成为该词的抽象名词，如：

daunt 畏惧 dauntless 无畏的 dauntlessness 无畏
hope 希望 hopeless 绝望的 hopelessness 绝望状态
match 比较 matchless 无与伦比的 matchlessness 无与伦比
self 私心 selfless 无私的 selflessness 无私
weight 重量 weightless 失重的 weightlessness 失重状态

通过使用这种方法，甚至连最复杂、最冗长的词语也可化难为简，便于把握。譬如 pneumonoultramicroscopicsilicovolcanokoniosis 一词，长达 45 个字母，既费解，又难记。要是利用构词法将其分解为 8 部分，就很容易把握了：pneumono（肺的）+ultra（超）+ micro（微）+scopic（观察的）+silico（硅的）+volcano（火山的）+ coni（尘埃）+ osis（病症）；即：硅酸盐沉着病，矽肺病。

二、敏锐的分析判断能力

敏锐的分析判断能力包括语法分析、上下文语境分析、句式结构分析、逻辑分析等。语法分析是翻译中不可或缺法宝。不少同学不善于使用语法分析，因而犯下了一些本来可以避免的翻译失误。语法分析通常可从以下几处着手。

1. 词类鉴别分析

英语中不同的词类具有不同作用，充当不同的句子成分。因此，通过词类辨

析有助于把握原意,消除误解。譬如下面几例:

- He **saw** a man **sawing** trees with a **saw**.

第一个 saw 为动词 see 的过去式,中间的动名词 sawing 为 man 的宾语补足语,表示"锯"这一动作;后一个 saw 为名词"锯子"。

译文:他看见一个人正在用锯子锯树。

- Eat what you **can** and **can** what you **cannot**.

前后两个 can 为情态动词"能够",中间的 can 是实义动词"装罐",为名词 can(罐头)的词类转换形式。

译文:你能吃多少吃多少,吃不了的做成罐头。

2. 时态语态分析

时态语态分析亦是翻译中的一个重要手段。我们知道,英语有时态、语态的不同形式,而汉语的时态、语态多隐在句子和上下文中,用"着"、"了"、"过"、"被"之类的助词表达不同的时间关系;英语句式紧密,有大量的连词、介词在句与句之间衔接,汉语句式松散,句与句之间缺少连接成分;英语的各类语句的关系靠严密的句法来衔接,浑然一体,汉语的句式不靠句法上的衔接,讲究"不言而喻"。譬如这样一例:

- "Why didn't you reply my phone call?" "I was sleeping."

译文:"你刚才为什么不回我的电话?""我(那会儿)在睡觉。"

英语用了一般过去时 didn't,过去进行时 was asleep,汉语没有时态的说法,因此翻译时我们得添加助词"刚才"和"在",否则,会令人不可思议:在睡觉怎么还能答话呢?

再看下面一例翻译试题:

- But for many, the fact that poor people are able to support themselves almost as well without government aid as they did with it is in itself a huge victory.

同一个句子中两种不同时态,are able to support themselves 和 as they did with it,反映出两种不同的时间状态,因此在翻译时必须加上"现在"和"过去"两个时间状语。才能准确传达出原文的含义。

译文：但对许多人来说，穷人能够不靠政府帮助自己养活自己，而且日子过得几乎和过去靠政府帮助时一样好，这件事本身就是一种了不起的胜利。

语态问题也是语法分析中的一个要点。请看下例：

- If computer could be made as complex as a human brain, it could be the equivalent of a human brain and do whatever a human brain can do.

有同学将此句译作：如果电脑能够被制造得像人脑那样复杂，它完全能够像人脑那样，人脑能干什么，它就能干什么。

此句中的两处 could 均为虚拟语气，不应译作"能够"，而是"倘若"、"可能会"。

译文：倘若电脑被制造得像人脑那样复杂，就可能会与人脑旗鼓相当，完成人脑所能做的一切工作。

3. 上下文语境分析

语境分析是翻译中不可或缺的环节。语境反映在书面材料中叫做上下文，在口语中就是前言后语。语境分析是翻译的重要手段，没有一定的上下文，翻译就无从着手。我们在平常的词汇学习过程中，对英语词汇的理解不要停留在表面的字词对应关系，而是要抓住其实质特征，通过上下文来把握词意。譬如英语动词 develop，很多同学往往喜欢将其与汉语的"发展"画等号。而实际上在不同的上下文中，develop 的译法差异很大，其英语基本意思是 to grow or change into something bigger, stronger, or more advanced（成长或变得更大、更强，或更高级）。由此可见，除了"发展"之外，还具有"滋长、研制、开发、生发、衍变、患病、显影、推移、推进"等含义。只有通过上下文，才能掌握该词在不同情况下的用法。

1) develop a mine **开矿**
2) develop a photograph **冲洗**照片
3) develop a new symptom **出现**新症状
4) develop an idea **详细地说明**一个概念
5) develop light industry **发展**轻工业
6) develop into a good soldier **成长**为一名好战士
7) develop the spirit of democracy **发扬**民主精神

8) develop a taste for opera 培养对歌剧的鉴赏力
9) Plants develop from seeds. 植物由种子**发育**而成。
10) Exercises develop muscles. 运动**促进**肌肉生长。
11) He developed tuberculosis. 他**患上**了结核病。
12) They develop a new cottage industry. 他们**逐渐形成**新的家庭手工业。
13) The author developed the play into a movie. 作者把戏剧**改编**成了电影。
14) Fresh air and exercise develop healthy bodies. 新鲜空气和运动**能使**身体健康。
15) Some children develop more slowly than others. 有的儿童比其他儿童**发育**得慢。
16) Several new products are developing in this area. 几种新产品正在这个地区**研制**。
17) The instructor develops the capabilities of each student. 教师**激发**每个学生的潜能。
18) She developed her thesis in a series of articles. 她用一系列文章逐渐**阐明**了她的论题。

再以英语副词 well 为例，很多同学喜欢将它与汉语的"好"画等号，其实在很多情况下，well 一词表达的是某种程度。譬如在以下各例中，well 都不宜译作"好"。

1) I knew them well.
2) He is well clothed.
3) It may well be true.
4) I remember it very well.
5) The house is well situated.
6) They all speak well of him.
7) I well understand your intentions.
8) Xiao Li gets along well with people.
9) Shake the bottle well before experiment.
10) The investment is well over the estimate.

11) His arguments are well grounded in facts.

12) Examine the account well before you pay it.

13) The bridge was so well built that it lasted for 100 years.

14) I should be well content to do the job together with you.

15) You must be very well connected; you seem to know all the right people.

参考译文：

1）我跟他们很熟。

2）他衣着周正得体。

3）这很可能是真的。

4）这件事我可记得清清楚楚。

5）这房子的地理位置十分优越。

6）大家对他的评价都很高。

7）我完全理解你们的意图。

8）小李与人们相处和睦。

9）实验之前将瓶内液体摇晃均匀。

10）投资大大地超过预计。

11）他的论据事实根据充足。

12）付款之前须仔细核实账目。

13）桥建得很牢，至少能用100年。

14）我很愿意和你一起干这件工作。

15）你一定交际很广，你似乎认识所有相关的人。

此外，英语词义的褒贬不像汉语那样截然分明，同一个词语有时候可能会产生两种截然相反的意义，需要译者自己去权衡取舍。譬如：ambition（抱负，野心），ambitious（雄心勃勃的，野心勃勃的），envy（羡慕，妒忌），envious（羡慕的，妒忌的），luxury（舒适，奢侈），luxurious（舒适的，奢侈的），pride（自豪，骄傲），proud（自豪的，骄傲的），encourage（鼓励，怂恿），protect（保护，庇护），rebellion（反抗，叛乱），uprising（起义，暴乱），等等。所有这些都需要根据不同的上下文语境做出正确的判断，才能译出原文的准确意思。

4. 逻辑分析

钱歌川先生在《翻译的基本知识》中曾谈道:"逻辑是翻译者的最后一张王牌,是他必须具有的基本要素。俗话说的'岂有此理',正是翻译者随时需要的考验。凡是翻译出来的一字一句,一事一物,都必须要合乎逻辑,合乎情理,否则必然有误。太阳不能从西方出来,父亲不会比儿子年少,小器不能容大物,半数不能表全体,诸如此类,凡是违反人情天地的,都是悖理的,也多半是译错的。"

下面我们从逻辑常识来探讨翻译中的几个误译。

- The engine didn't stop because the fuel was finished.

误译:引擎因为燃料耗尽了所以不停止运转。

这是第九单元"正反调换"中谈到的一例典型的"否定的转移",照通常的句子结构翻译,显然不合逻辑。

改译:引擎并不是因为燃料耗尽而停止运转。

- She told me that her 18-year-old son was her baby.

误译:她告诉我她那18岁的儿子是她的婴儿。

"18岁的婴儿"显然不合乎常理,除"婴儿"外,baby在词典释义中还有"(家庭或集体中)年龄最小的人"含义。

改译:她告诉我她那18岁的儿子是家里最小的孩子。

- These songs were sung in the cottages and huts all over the land for hundreds of years afterward.

误译:这些歌曲从此在全国各地村舍传唱,持续了数百年。

此译不合逻辑,因为谁都知道,歌曲的传唱不能"持续"那么长的时间。

改译:此后,这些歌曲便在全国各地村舍中传唱开了,流传了好几百年。

- He was not the eldest son of his father for nothing.

误译:"他作为他爸爸的长子并不是没有道理的。"

作为父亲的长子,究竟有什么道理可言?凭逻辑常识我们知道,此句大有问题。随手翻开《新英汉词典》,我们就能解决这一并不费解的问题。for nothing ① 免费,不要钱;②徒然,没有结果:These investigations are not done for nothing. 这些调查工作自然不是白做的。All efforts of the enemy went for nothing. 敌人的力气完全白费。很明显，此句中的 for nothing 应为释义②。

改译：他作为他父亲的长子**自然不会没有好处**。

- He was full of enthusiasm, said, "Put 50 in a plane naked. It's only three hours!"

误译：他热情极高地说："光着膀子，一架飞机可以装 50 人。反正空中时间只有 3 个小时。"

此例的译文滑稽得近乎荒诞：为了减轻载重负荷，世界上竟然有让人光着膀子登飞机的事！稍加分析，我们不难发现，此处的 naked 所修饰的并不是人，而是飞机。《韦氏大学词典》对 naked 一词的解释是：scantily supplied or furnished, lacking embellishment，即空舱不带座椅装备。

改译：他充满激情地说："**空舱不带座椅装备**，一架飞机塞 50 人没问题。好歹空中就那么 3 小时。"

三、通顺的语言表达能力

翻译学习的最终检验体现在语言表达上。不少同学书面语言表达欠佳，主要表现为三种情况：一是对原文的理解不够；二是能理解，却不会表达；三是勉强能表达，又往往措辞不当，容易生搬硬套，词不达意。

1. 避免生硬晦涩

措辞生硬晦涩是英汉翻译表达的一个常见问题。有些同学的译文尽管意思上没有错误，但读起来非常拗口，不符合中文表达习惯，这就需要加强自身的汉语基本功了。请看下面各例。

1) The boy started to cry.　　*孩子开始哭。
2) She emptied her glass.　　*她倒空了她的玻璃杯。
3) Tom has youthful good looks.　　*汤姆有年轻漂亮的面容。
4) The truth finally dawned on her.　　*真理最终在她身上露出了黎明。
5) Excitement deprived me of all power of utterance.　　*兴奋使我丧失了

说话的力量。

6) He put his arms around his girlfriend and squeezed her.　＊他用他的双臂搂住他的女友用力挤她。

分析：

1）正译：孩子哭了起来。

此句译文虽然每个字都和原文相对应，但读起来十分别扭，完全不像汉语的语句，是典型的翻译腔。

2）正译：她举杯一饮而尽。

这句话有代词 her，这就表明她不是在洗杯子，而是在和别人喝酒或其他饮料，各人有自己的杯子。既然这样，emptied 就不是把杯子里的东西倒掉，而是喝光。

3）正译：汤姆年轻英俊。

译文应尽量避免使用词字对应的机械式翻译。为了符合汉语的习惯表达法，此句应省略动词"有"，名词"面容"。

4）正译：她最终明白了真相。

此句中的 dawn 为"渐渐明白；开始被察觉或理解"之意，如：Realization of the danger soon dawned on us. 不久我们就意识到危险的存在。

英语常常喜欢用非人称主语，其固定句式为 sth.happen/occur to sb. 而汉语则喜欢用人称主语，其句式结构多为"什么人怎么样了"，4）和 5）两例就充分说明了这一问题。所以在做英译汉时，我们应当尽可能考虑到将物称主语转换为人称主语，而在做汉译英时，正好相反，可考虑将人称主语转换为物称主语。

5）正译：我兴奋得说不出话来。

deprive 拿走，抢夺；从……拿走某物，如：The court ruling deprived us of any share in the inheritance. 法庭裁决剥夺了我们全部的继承权。

6）正译：他双臂搂住女友，搂得紧紧的。

此句译文将原文的每个字都译出来了，连 4 处代词也全都照搬不误，读起来怪怪的，不知所云。省略 3 个代词，调整一下句子结构，语句也就通顺了。

综上所述，在很多情况下，英汉翻译的关键往往不在于对原文字面意义的理解、处理，而是对其整体思想的把握和译文的综合表达，即在透彻领会原文的基础上，用通顺、规范的措辞将其表达出来。关于理解、表达与措辞之间的关系，我们不妨听听老前辈翻译家陆殿扬先生是怎样说的：

"我们的忠告是：首先透彻地阅读有关的句子或段落、理解它的意思，在你心中形成一个概念或意象。然后，合上你的书，用中文思考，把它当作你自己的思想表达出来。这样，你就不会受到外国语言的约束或限制，就能够自由地把原文的思想用中文表达出来。"

2. 克服母语影响

母语对翻译的影响通常出现在汉译英。与英译汉所遇到的问题不同，汉译英的很多问题主要归结为两点：一是词汇量不足，汉英翻译力不从心；二是受母语的干扰影响，翻译时自觉或不自觉地用汉语的思维模式、句型结构去套用英语句子。前一种情况需要通过加强词汇学习，扩大词汇量来解决，而后一种情况则需要平日留心观察，通过比较对照，克服母语的负面影响。下面是一些受汉语思维干扰影响的典型译例。

1）这里很冷。　　*Here is very cold.
2）我不喝酒。　　*I don't drink wine.
3）不准拍照。　　*Don't take picture.
4）他拼命敲门。　　*He knocked the door violently.
5）我没有人帮忙。　　*I have no one to help.
6）他的钱比我多。　　*His money is more than mine.
7）他参加了考试。　　*He joined/attended the exam.
8）我们为祖国服务。　　*We serve for our country.
9）王教授向我挥手。　　*Professor Wang waved his hand to me.
10）他们送我到门口。　　*They sent me to the door.
11）杰克，我要送你一件礼物。　　*Jack, I'll send you a gift.
12）请再把命令重复一遍。　　*Please repeat the order again.
13）她是个极其优秀的歌手。　　*She is an extremely excellent singer.
14）太阳每天早晨从东方升起。　　*The sun rises from the east every morning.
15）经济形势将会变好。　　*The economic situation will change better.
16）这座大楼的质量不好。　　*The quality of this building is poor.

17）小学生天天读书写字。 *The pupils read books and write words every day.

18）孩子们很快要去睡觉了。 *The children will go to sleep very soon.

19）我们需要的是最新信息。 *What we need is the newest information.

20）如果你方便的话，我下周一去你那儿。 *If you are convenient, I'll come next Monday.

评析：

1）正译：It is very cold here.

英语用表达时间、距离、天气等用 it 作各种无人称动词形式的主语，如：It is raining. 正在下雨。It is cold. 天气寒冷。

2）正译：I don't drink.

英语的 drink 作不及物动词就有"喝酒"的意思，如：They only drink socially. 他们只在社交场合喝酒。译作 drink wine 为画蛇添足，而且英语的 wine 多指"葡萄酒"。

3）正译：No photographs.

英语表示"禁止、不准"一般不用 Don't... 之类的劝告句型，而是用 No... 之类语气强烈的结构，如：No smoking! 禁止吸烟！ No admission. 禁止入内。

4）正译：He knocked violently on the door.

英语表示"敲门"需要用介词 knock on 或 at，knock 的意思为"使碰撞"，如：He entered without knocking at the door. 他没敲门就进来了。I knocked my head on a low beam. 我的头撞到了一根低梁上。

5）正译：I have no one to help me.

英语的 help 为及物动词，如：I helped her find the book. 我帮她找到了那本书。所以翻译此句需增添宾语 me。

6）正译：He has more money than I（have）.

注意此处的比较对象，英语习惯于将人而不是物作为比较对象，如：He spends more time in English than his brother. 他在英语上花的时间比他哥哥多。

7）正译：He took the exam.

"参加考试"的英语固定搭配为 take exam，join 和 attend 分别为"加入"和"出席"之意；如：join the army 参军，attend (at) a wedding 出席婚礼。

8）正译：We serve our country.

一看到汉语的"为"字，很多同学自然就想到了英语的 for，而 serve 此处为及物动词，不需要介词来连接，如：serve tea 上茶；serve the guests a wonderful dinner 以盛宴招待客人。

9）正译：Professor Wang waved to me.

英语的 wave 本身就有"挥手示意"之意，如：We waved good-bye. 我们挥手道别。所以应当省略 his hand。

10）正译：They saw me to the door.

11）正译：Jack, I'll present a gift to you.

汉语"送"字的翻译大致有以下两种情况：A. 送 = send：往往发生在行为者不亲自到场的情况，由他人"送"。如：寄送礼物（send sb. a present），送孩子上大学（send the child to college）。B. 送 ≠ send：如果行为者亲自到场，赠送、护送、伴送、陪送、发送、递送等，翻译时可考虑将"送"理解为表示方向的 to，只保留"赠、护、伴、陪、发、递"等字眼。如：送礼 present a gift，送客 see a guest off，送信 deliver a letter，而在更多的情况下，汉语的"送"字需要换成其他表达方法来翻译。如：送命（丧命）lose one's life (get killed)，送某人回家（陪护）escort somebody home，送卫星上天（发射）launch a satellite，送葬（参加葬礼）take part in a funeral procession，送罪犯上法庭（移交）hand the criminal over to the court for trial，等等。

12）正译：Please repeat the order.

英语动词 repeat 本来就指"重复"，汉语的"再"字是一个不必要的赘词，所以应当省略 again。

13）正译：She is an excellent singer.

此句与 12）类似，英语的 excellent 本来就是"卓越的，极好的"之意，所以应当省略副词 extremely，类似的情况还有 perfect（完美的），super（极好的）等。

14）正译：The sun rises in the east every morning.

汉语的"从东方"，翻译成英语为 in the east，这是英语介词的习惯搭配。

15）正译：The economic situation will change for the better.

for the better 为英语固定搭配，意为"向着好的情况（转变）"，如：His health has changed for the better. 他的健康状况已有好转。

16）正译：This building was not well built.

一看到"楼的质量"，很多同学自然而然就会想到 quality 一词。而实际上英语的 quality 一般只用于表示性质、品质、品位、特点、特性等，如某种物质、产品或某人都可用 quality，而楼房本身却不具备 quality，因此应当避开这一字眼，译作 not well built。

17）正译：The pupils read and write every day.

英语的 read 和 write 作为不及物动词，本身就带有"读书写字"的意思，译作 read books and write words 实在是画蛇添足。

18）正译：The children will go to bed very soon.

英语 go to sleep 意为"入睡，睡着"，go to bed 才是"去睡觉"。

19）正译：What we need is the latest information.

英语 the latest 意为"最近的，最新的或新潮的事物"如：the latest in electronic gadgetry 最新的电器发明；new 意为"未用过的，没穿过的"，如：a new car 新车；a new hat 新帽子；"最新信息"应属前者，所以译为 the latest information。

20）正译：If it is convenient for you, I'll come next Monday.

英语形容词一般用于修饰时间，事物，而不直接用于人，如：convenient time 方便的时候；Our house is convenient for the shops. 我们家到商店很方便。

通过以上评析可知，汉译英实际上是一个转换思维的过程，翻译出来是英文，就应该用英文去思考，而不能用汉语的模式，因为用汉语思维，译出来的句子往往容易受母语干扰。多想想英美人会怎么说，翻译出来的句子才到位，才符合英语的表达习惯。

四、不懈的翻译实践

关于最后这一点，请参阅各讲的具体内容及相关练习，这里我们就不赘述了。

从某种意义上讲，一个人的翻译能力不是课堂上讲出来的，也不是翻译技巧所能造就的，而是需要长期不懈地努力，通过扎扎实实的翻译实践来逐步体会、把握，将方方面面的知识融会贯通。

　　翻译学习不能急于求成，而要脚踏实地，一步一个脚印。一个字，一个词，一个句子日积月累，不断实践、不断总结经验、不断提高。潜移默化，水到渠成，以上各方面的能力提高了，翻译中的各种问题自然会迎刃而解，最终达到水到渠成、得心应手的境界。

思考与练习

一、简要回答以下问题

　　1. 你认为成功的翻译学习其关键取决于哪些因素？试举例说明。
　　2. 扎实的语法词汇功底体现在哪几个方面？
　　3. 敏锐的分析判断能力包括哪几个方面？
　　4. 培养通顺的语言表达能力需要注意哪些方面？
　　5. 翻译理论／技巧与翻译实践是一种什么关系？试举例说明。

二、英汉互译翻译练习

　　1. 英译汉。

　　　A. 将以下文字翻译成汉语，注意 light 一词的译法：

　　　　Needing some light to see by, the burglar crossed the room with a light step to light the light with the light green shade.

　　　B. 将以下文字翻译成汉语，注意各种颜色的含义：

　　　　Mr. Brown is a very white man. He was looking rather green the other day. He has been feeling blue lately. When I saw him he was in a brown study. I hope he'll soon be in the pink again.

　　2. 汉译英。指出下列各句的翻译失误，并加以改正。

　　　1）我不怕吃苦。　*I don't fear hardships.

2）这棵树不长果实。　*This tree doesn't grow fruit.

3）那座房子全塌了。　*That house completely collapsed down.

4）她总是睡得很晚。　*She always sleeps very late.

5）老板不同意他离开。　*The boss doesn't agree him to leave.

6）这台破电脑没有用。　*This broken computer has no use.

7）请勿乱扔果皮纸屑。　*Please don't throw peels and scraps of paper.

8）护士量了我的体温。　*The nurse measured my temperature.

9）北京国际饭店欢迎您。　*Beijing International Hotel Welcomes You.

10）他应该为这个事故负责。　*He is to be blamed for the accident.

11）这款车在中国卖得很好。　*This model of car is sold well in China.

12）"太感谢您了。""没什么，这是我的职责／这是我应该做的。"

　　*"Thank you very much." "It is nothing. This is my duty/This is what I should do."

第十四单元
《大学英语教学指南》与四、六级翻译考试

一、《大学英语教学指南》对翻译的要求

按照教育部高等学校大学外语教学指导委员会最新发布的《大学英语教学指南》，大学阶段的英语教学要求分为三个层次，即基础目标、提高目标和发展目标。

"基础目标"对英语翻译能力的要求是：能借助词典对题材熟悉、结构清晰、语言难度较低的文章进行英汉互译，译文基本准确，无重大的理解和语言表达错误。能有限地运用翻译技巧。

"提高目标"对英语翻译能力的要求是：能摘译题材熟悉，以及与所学专业或未来所从事工作岗位相关、语言难度一般的文献资料；能借助词典翻译体裁较为正式、题材熟悉的文章。理解正确，译文基本达意，语言表达清晰。能运用较常用的翻译技巧。

"发展目标"对英语翻译能力的要求是：能翻译较为正式的议论性或不同话题的口头或书面材料，能借助词典翻译有一定深度的介绍中外国情或文化的文字资料，译文内容准确，基本无错译、漏译，文字通顺达意，语言表达错误较少；能借助词典翻译所学专业或所从事职业的文献资料，对原文理解准确，译文语言通顺，结构清晰，基本满足专业研究和业务工作的需要。能恰当运用翻译技巧。

尽管《大学英语教学指南》对翻译提出了上述种种要求，但由于时间和条件所限，无论是 CET-4 还是 CET-6，考试题型都不可能对学生的英译汉、汉译英能

力进行全面的综合检测。因此长期以来，四、六级翻译考试均采用单句翻译的形式，给出若干不完整的英语句子，句子中所缺部分给出汉语，要求考生将其翻译补充完整。翻译部分的分值仅为整个考试卷面的 5%。

自 2013 年 12 月起，全国大学英语四、六级考试委员会对四、六级考试的试卷结构和测试题型作了局部调整。调整后，四级和六级的试卷结构和测试题型相同。其试卷结构、测试内容、测试题型、分值比例和考试时间如下表：

试卷结构	测试内容		测试题型	分值比例	考试时间
写作	写作		短文写作	15%	30 分钟
听力理解	听力对话	短对话	多项选择	8%	30 分钟
		长对话	多项选择	7%	
	听力短文	短文理解	多项选择	10%	
		短文听写	单词及词组听写	10%	
阅读理解	词汇理解		选词填空	5%	40 分钟
	长篇阅读		匹配	10%	
	仔细阅读		多项选择	20%	
翻译	汉译英		段落翻译	15%	30 分钟
总计				100%	130 分钟

如上表所示，翻译部分由原单句汉译英调整为段落汉译英，分值比重由 5% 提高到 15%。四级长度为 140-160 个汉字；六级长度为 180-200 个汉字。翻译内容涉及中国的历史、文化、经济、社会发展等。

二、四、六级翻译考试真题详解

1. 四级翻译考试真题详解

2013 年 12 月英语四级翻译

1

信息技术正在飞速发展，中国公民也越来越重视信息技术，有些学校甚至将信息技术作为必修课程。对这一现象大家持不同观点。一部分人认为这是没有必要的，学生就应该学习传统的课程。另一部分人认为这是应该的，中国就应该与时俱进。不管怎样，信息技术引起广大人民的重视是一件好事。（131 字）

重点词语注释：

信息技术 information technology

飞速发展 the rapid development

越来越重视 attach great importance to/put more emphasis on

必修课 compulsory course

持不同观点 hold different views

传统的课程 traditional curriculum

与时俱进 keep pace with the times /advance with the times

不管怎样 anyway/anyhow

引起重视 draw attention from

广大人民 the majority of people

参考译文

With the rapid development of information technology, Chinese citizens are attaching great importance to this technology, and some schools even set it as a compulsory course. However, people hold different views to this phenomenon. Some think it is not necessary, for in their opinion, students should learn traditional curriculum. Others believe it should, because China should / ought to keep pace with the times. Anyway, it is a great event for information technology to have drawn attention from the majority of Chinese people.

2

"你要茶还是咖啡？"是用餐人常被问到的问题。许多西方人会选咖啡，而中国人则会选茶。相传，中国的一位帝王于五千年前发现了茶，并用来治病。在明清期间，茶馆遍布全国。饮茶在六世纪传到日本，但直到18世纪才传到欧美。如今，茶是世界上最流行的饮料之一。茶是中国的瑰宝，也是中国传统和文化的重要组成部分。（145字）

重点词语注释：

用餐 at dinner

常被问到 be frequently asked

西方人 westerners

选咖啡 choose/prefer coffee

相传 according to legend

中国帝王 Chinese emperor

用来治病 be used to cure illnesses

明清期间 during the Ming and Qing Dynasties

遍布全国 widespread throughout China

传到 spread/be introduced to

最流行的饮料 the most popular beverages

瑰宝 the treasure

重要组成部分 an important component /part of

参考译文

"Would you like tea or coffee?" This question is frequently asked at dinner. Many westerners would choose coffee, while the Chinese usually prefer tea. According to legend, tea was discovered by a Chinese emperor 5,000 years ago and it was used to cure illnesses. During the Ming and Qing Dynasties, tea houses were widespread throughout China. Tea-drinking was spread to Japan in the 6th century but it did not introduced to Europe and

America until the 18th century. Today, tea is one of the most popular beverages in the world. Tea is the treasure of China, and it is also an important component of the Chinese tradition and culture.

3

中国结最初是由手工艺人发明的，经过数百年不断的改进，已经成为一种优雅多彩的艺术和工艺。在古代，人们用它来记录事件，但现在主要是用于装饰的目的。"结"在中文里意味着爱情、婚姻和团聚，中国结常常作为礼物交换或作为饰品祈求好运和辟邪。这种形式的手工艺代代相传，现在已经在中国和世界各地越来越受欢迎。（149字）

重点词语注释：

中国结 the Chinese knot

手工艺人 craftsman

不断的改进 constant improvement

优雅多彩的 elegant and colorful

艺术和工艺 arts and crafts

用来记录事件 be used to record events

用于装饰的目的 for decorative purposes

婚姻和团聚 marriage and reunion

作为礼物交换 be exchanged as gifts

作为饰品 as ornaments pray

祈求好运 pray for good luck

辟邪 exorcise/ward off evil spirits

代代相传 be handed down from generation to generation

越来越受欢迎 become increasingly popular

参考译文

The Chinese knot is originally invented by some craftsmen. After several hundred years of constant improvement, it has become an kind of elegant and colorful arts and crafts. In ancient times, it was used to record events, but now mainly used for decorative purposes. "Knot" in Chinese means love, marriage and reunion, Chinese knots are often exchanged as gifts or as ornaments to pray for good luck and ward off evil spirits. Handed down from generation to generation, this form of handicrafts has now become increasingly popular in China and all over the world.

2014 年 6 月英语四级翻译

1

为了促进教育公平，中国已经投入 360 亿元，用于改善农村地区教育设施和加强中西部地区农村义务教育。这些资金用于改善教学设施、购买书籍，使 16 万多所中小学受益。资金还用于购置音乐和绘画器材。现在农村和山区的儿童可以与沿海城市的儿童一样上音乐和绘画课。一些为接受更好教育而转往城市上学的学生如今又回到了本地农村学校就读。（154 字）

重点词语注释：

教育公平 fairness in education/educational equity

投入 invest/put in

教育设施 educational facilities

农村义务教育 rural compulsory education

中西部地区 central and western regions

使……受益 benefit

音乐和绘画器材 musical instruments and painting materials

沿海城市 coastal cities

音乐和绘画课 music and painting classes

接受更好教育 receive a better education

转往城市上学的学生 students transferred to city schools

本地农村学校 local rural schools

参考译文

In order to promote fairness in education, China has invested 36 billion yuan for the improvement of the educational facilities in rural areas and the enhancement of the rural compulsory education in the central and western regions. This fund is mainly spent in improving educational facilities and book purchases and thus benefits more than 160 thousand primary schools and middle schools. Meanwhile, it is also used to supplement musical instruments and painting materials. Nowadays, like the children in coastal cities, those living in rural and mountain areas may also enjoy music and painting classes. As a result, some students who previously transferred to other cities for better education have now come back to their local rural schools.

2

中国应该进一步发展核能，因为核电目前只占其总发电数的 2%。该比例在所有核电国家中居第 30 位，几乎是最低的。

2011 年 3 月日本人核电站事故后，中国的核能开发停了下来，中止审批新的核电站，并开展全国性的核电安全检查。到 2012 年 10 月，审批才又谨慎地恢复。随着技术和安全措施的改进，发生核事故的可能性完全可以降到最低程度。换句话说，核能是可以安全开发和利用的。（169 字）

重点词语注释：

进一步发展 further develop

核能 nuclear energy

核电 nuclear power

占 account for

总发电数 total generating capacity

居第 30 位 rank the thirtieth

停下来 be suspended

中止审批 stop the approval of

安全检查 safety check

谨慎地恢复 prudently resume

技术和安全措施 technology and safety measures

降到最低程度 reduce to the minimum level

换句话说 in other words

开发和利用 tap/exploit and utilize

参考译文

China should further develop its nuclear energy because its current nuclear power accounts for only 2% of the total generating capacity, ranking the thirtieth (almost the lowest) of all nuclear countries.

After Japan's nuclear power accident in March 2011, nuclear power development in China was suspended, so was the approval of new nuclear power plants. At the same time, a national wide safety inspection for the nuclear power was carried out. It wasn't until October 2012 that the approval work was prudently resumed.

With the improvement of technology and safety measures, the possibility for nuclear accident may absolutely be reduced to the minimum level. In other words, it will be safe to tap and utilize nuclear power.

3

中国教育工作者早就认识到读书对于国家的意义。有些教育工作者2003年就建议设立全民读书日。他们强调，人们应当读好书，尤其是经典著作。通过阅读，人们能更好地学会感恩、有责任心和与人合作，而教育的目的正是要培养这些基本素质。阅读对于中小学生尤为重要，假如他们没有在这个关键时期培养阅读的兴趣，以后要培养成阅读的习惯就更难了。（156字）

重点词语注释：

教育工作者 professional educators/teaching staff

早就 longs ago/years ago

认识到 realize/be aware of

读书对于国家的意义 the significance of reading for a nation

全民读书日 national reading day

经典著作 Chinese classics

学会感恩 learn to be grateful

有责任心和与人合作 be responsible and cooperative

基本（个人）素质 basic personal quality

中小学生 primary and secondary school students

关键时期 crucial period

培养成阅读的习惯 form a habit of reading

参考译文

Professional educators in China were aware of the significance of reading for a nation years ago. Early in 2003, some of them suggested that we should have a national reading day. They emphasized that people ought to read good books, especially Chinese classics. Through reading, we may learn better how to be grateful, responsible and cooperative, while the goal of education is to cultivate these basic personal qualities. Reading is especially important for primary and secondary school students. Therefore, if they fail to develop the interest of reading at this crucial period, it will be harder for them to form a habit of reading in the future.

2. 六级翻译考试真题详解

2013 年 12 月英语六级翻译

1

中国人自古以来就在中秋时节庆祝丰收，这与北美地区庆祝感恩节的习俗十分相似，过中秋节的习俗于唐代早期在中国各地开始流行。中秋节在农历八月十五，是人们拜月的节日。这天夜晚皓月当空，人们合家团聚，共赏明月。2006 年，中秋节被列为中国的文化遗产，2008 年又被定为公共假日，月饼被视为中秋节不可或缺的美食，人们将月饼作为礼物馈赠亲友或在家庭聚会上享用。传统的月饼上带有"寿"、"福"或"和"等字样。（193 字）

重点词语注释：

自古以来 since ancient times/down the ages

中秋时节庆祝丰收 celebrate the mid-autumn harvest season

与……十分相似 similar to that of

感恩节 Thanksgiving

过中秋节的习俗 the custom of observing Mid-Autumn Festival

唐代早期 the early Tang Dynasty

开始流行 come into vogue

农历八月十五 the fifteenth day of the eighth lunar month/August 15 of the Chinese lunar calendar

拜月的节日 a festival for the people to worship the moon

皓月当空 a bright moon hangs high in the sky

合家团聚 people get together

共赏明月 enjoy the moment of family reunion

被列为中国的文化遗产 be listed as China's cultural heritage

被定为公共假日 be designated as a public holiday

月饼 the mid-autumn moon cake

被视为不可或缺的美食 be regarded as an indispensable delicacy

作为礼物馈赠亲友 be presented as a gift among friends

在家庭聚会上享用 shared at family gatherings

带有……等字样 decorated with such Chinese characters as…

"寿"、"福"或"和" Shou (longevity), Fu (blessing) or He (harmony)

参考译文

Since ancient times (Down the ages), it has been a custom for the Chinese people to celebrate the mid-autumn harvest season, similar to that of celebrating Thanksgiving in North America. The custom of observing Mid-Autumn Festival came into vogue around the early Tang Dynasty all over China. It is on the fifteenth day of the eighth lunar month (It is on August 15 of the Chinese lunar calendar)—a festival for the people to worship the moon. On the very night when a bright moon hangs high in the sky, people would get together, enjoying the moment of family reunion. In 2006, the Mid-Autumn Festival was listed as China's cultural heritage. In 2008 it was designated as a public holiday. The mid-autumn moon cake is regarded in China as an indispensable delicacy that is commonly presented as a gift among friends, or shared at family gatherings. Traditional moon cakes are usually decorated with such Chinese characters as *Shou* (longevity), *Fu* (blessing), *He* (harmony), etc.

2

闻名于世的丝绸之路是一系列连接东西方的路线。丝绸之路延伸 6 000 多公里，得名于古代中国的丝绸贸易。丝绸之路上的贸易在中国、南亚、欧洲和中东文明发展中发挥了重要作用。正是通过丝绸之路，中国的造纸术、火药、指南针、印刷术等四大发明才被引介到世界各地。同样，中国的丝绸、茶叶和瓷器也传遍全球。物质文化的交流是双向的。欧洲也通过丝绸之路出口各种商品和植物，满足中国市场的需要。（178 字）

重点词语注释：

闻名于世的丝绸之路 the world-renowned Silk Road

一系列连接东西方的路线 a series of routes connecting the East and the West

延伸 extend

得名于 named after

古代中国的丝绸贸易 ancient China's silk trade

南亚、欧洲和中东 South Asia, Europe and the Middle East

文明发展 the development of civilization

发挥重要作用 play an important role

造纸术、火药、指南针、印刷术 papermaking, gunpowder, compass and printing

中国的四大发明 the four great inventions of ancient China

引介到 be introduced to

同样 similarly

瓷器 porcelain

物质文化 material culture

双向交流 two-way exchange

出口各种商品和植物 export various goods and plants

满足中国市场的需要 meet the needs of the Chinese market

参考译文

The world-renowned Silk Road is a series of routes connecting the East and the West. Named after ancient China's silk trade, it extended more than 6,000 kilometers and played an important role in developing civilizations in

China, South Asia, Europe and the Middle East. It was through the Silk Road that the four great inventions of ancient China, i.e. papermaking, gunpowder, compass and printing were introduced to other countries in the world. Similarly, Chinese silk, tea and porcelain spread all over the world via the Silk Road. As the result of a two-way exchange of material culture, Europe also exported various goods and plants through the Silk Road to meet the needs of the Chinese market.

3

中国园林是经过三千多年演变而成的独具一格的园林景观。它既包括为皇室成员享乐而建造的大型花园，也包括学者、商人和卸任的政府官员为摆脱嘈杂的外部世界而建造的私家花园。这些花园构成了一种意在表达人与自然之间应有的和谐关系的微缩景观。典型的中国园林四周有围墙，园内有池塘、假山、树木、花草以及各种各样由蜿蜒的小路和走廊连接的建筑。漫步在花园中，人们可以看到一系列精心设计的景观犹如山水画卷一般展现在面前。（198字）

重点词语注释：

中国园林 Chinese gardens

演变 evolvement

独具一格的景观 unique landscape

为皇室成员享乐而建造的 built as entertainment venues for royal family

卸任的政府官员 retired government officials

摆脱嘈杂的外部世界 get rid of the noisy outside world/secluded retreats

私家花园 private gardens

微缩景观 miniature landscape

人与自然之间应有的和谐关系 a proper harmony between man and nature

四周有围墙 surrounded by enclosing walls

有池塘、假山、树木、花草 with ponds, rockeries, trees, and flowers

蜿蜒的小路和走廊 winding trails and corridors

一系列精心设计的景观 a series of elaborately designed landscape

山水画卷 landscape picture scroll

展现在面前 unfold before one's eyes

参考译文

After 3,000 years of evolvement, Chinese gardens have become a unique landscape. They include both large gardens built as entertainment venues for royal family, and private gardens as secluded retreats for scholars, merchants and retired government officials. These gardens have constituted a miniature landscape that is designed to display a proper harmony between man and nature. A typical Chinese garden is surrounded by enclosing walls, with ponds, rockeries, trees, and flowers inside it, and a various structures linked by winding trails and corridors. Strolling in such a well-designed garden, one could see a series of elaborately designed landscape, as if a landscape picture scroll being unfolded before one's eyes.

2014年6月英语六级翻译

1

　　中文热词通常反映社会变化和文化，有些在外国媒体上愈来愈流行。例如，土豪和大妈都是老词，但已获取了新的意义。

　　土豪以前指欺压佃户和仆人的乡村地主，现在用于指花钱如流水或喜欢炫耀财富的人，也就是说，土豪有钱，但是没有品位。大妈是对中年妇女的称呼，但是现在特指不久前金价大跌时大量购买黄金的中国妇女。

　　土豪和大妈可能会被收入新版的牛津英语词典，至今约有120个中文词加进了牛津英语词典，成了英语语言的一部分。（196字）

重点词语注释：

热词 hot words/buzzword

反映社会变化和文化 reflect social changes and culture

外国媒体 foreign media

愈来愈流行 be increasingly popular

老词 old word

获取新的意义 get different meanings

欺压佃户和仆人 oppress the tenants and servants

花钱如流水 spend money like water

炫耀财富 show off one's wealth

没有品位 have no taste

特指 refer in particular to

大跌 plunge/tumble

新版牛津英语词典 the latest Oxford English Dictionary

加进词典 add to the entries

参考译文

The Chinese hot words usually reflect social changes and culture, some of which are getting increasingly popular in foreign media. For example, *tuhao* and *dama* are both old Chinese words, but they get different meanings now.

The word *tuhao* used to mean rural landlords who oppress their tenants and servants, while now it refers to people spending money without limits or those who like to show off their wealth. In other words, a *tuhao* is very rich but has no taste. The word *dama* is used to call middle-aged women, but now it refers in particular to the Chinese women who rushed for gold when gold plunged not long ago.

Both *tuhao* and *dama* may be included in the latest Oxford English Dictionary. Up to now, about 120 Chinese words have been added to its entries, becoming a part of English language.

2

最近中国科学院出版了关于其最新科学发现与未来一年展望的年度系列报告。系列报告包括三部分:科学发展报告,高技术发展报告,中国可持续战略报告。第一份报告包含中国科学家的最新发现,诸如新粒子研究与H7N9病毒研究的突破。该报告还突出强调了未来几年需要关注的问题。第二份报告公布了一些应用科学研究的热门领域,如3D打印和人造器官研究。第三份报告呼吁加强顶层设计,以消除工业升级中的结构性障碍,并促进节能减排。(196字)

重点词语注释：

中国科学院 Chinese Academy of Sciences

最新科学发现 the latest scientific discoveries

年度系列报告 a series of annual reports

中国可持续战略报告 China's sustainable strategy

新粒子研究 new particle research

H7N9 病毒研究 the probe into H7N9 virus

突破 the breakthroughs in

突出强调 highlight

需要关注的问题 the matters that call for our attention

应用科学研究 the research of applied science

热门领域 hot fields

3D 打印 3D printing

人造器官研究 research on artificial organs

呼吁 calls for

加强顶层设计 strengthen the top-level design

工业升级 industrial upgrading

结构性障碍 the structural obstacles

节能减排 energy conservation and emissions reduction

参考译文

Chinese Academy of Sciences recently published a series of annual reports on its latest scientific discoveries and the prospect of the next year. The series consists of three parts, i.e. report on science development, report on high-tech development, and report on China's sustainable strategy. The first report includes the latest discoveries by Chinese scientists, such as the breakthroughs in new particle research and the probe into H7N9 virus. Furthermore, it highlights the matters that call for our attention in next few years. The second one announces some hot fields in the research of applied science, such as 3D printing and research on artificial organs. The third one calls for strengthening the top-level design, so as to get rid of the structural obstacles in industrial upgrading and promote energy conservation and emissions reduction.

3

北京计划未来三年投资 7 600 亿元治理污染，从减少 pm2.5 排放入手。这一新公布的计划旨在减少四种主要污染源，包括 500 万辆机动车的尾气排放、周边地区燃煤、来自北方的沙尘暴和本地的建筑灰尘，另外 850 亿元用于新建或升级城市垃圾处理和污水处理设施，加上 300 亿元投资未来三年的植树造林。

市政府还计划建造一批水循环利用工厂，并制止违章建筑，以改善环境。另外，北京还将更严厉地处罚违反减排规定的行为。（182 字）

重点词语注释：

投资 invest

治理污染 curb environmental pollution

从……入手 start with

旨在减少四种主要污染源 aim at reducing four main pollutants

机动车的尾气排放 exhaust from motor vehicles

周边地区燃煤 coal burning in surrounding areas

沙尘暴 sandstorm

建筑灰尘 construction dust

垃圾处理和污水处理设施 facilities used to process garbage and sewage

植树造林 afforestation

水循环利用工厂 plants for water recycling

违章建筑 illegal constructions

更严厉地处罚 tougher punishment

违反减排规定 violate the emission reduction regulations

参考译文

In the next three years, Beijing plans to invest 760 billion yuan to curb environmental pollution, starting with cutting down the emission of pm 2.5. This newly announced project aims at reducing four main pollutants, including exhaust from 5 million motor vehicles, coal burning in surrounding areas, sandstorms from the north, and local construction dust. In addition, another 85 billion yuan will be used to establish or upgrade the facilities used to process garbage and sewage of the city. Moreover, 30 billion yuan will be invested in the afforestation program in the next three years.

To improve the environment, the municipal government also plans to construct some plants for water recycling, and ban illegal constructions. Besides, Beijing will propose tougher punishments for those who violate the emission reduction regulations.

三、四、六级翻译考试题备考思考题与训练

2013年6月之前的四、六级翻译考试为单句补充，即给出若干不完整的英语句子，句子中所缺部分给出汉语，要求考生将其翻译补充完整。这实际上是对考生句子整体理解、组合与表达能力的综合考查。这样的试题英译汉、汉译英兼顾，在注重英语的句型结构、习惯表达法的同时，也需要一定的翻译方法技巧。从2013年12月开始，翻译部分由原单句汉译英调整为段落汉译英，分值比重由5%提高到15%。四级长度为140~160个汉字；六级长度为180~200个汉字。翻译内容涉及中国的历史、文化、经济、社会发展等。这样一来，对考生的翻译要求就大大提高了：考生除了需要掌握一般的遣词用字、句式结构等翻译方法技巧，还必须抓住全文的主旨要点、篇章结构；通过上下文，把握好句与句之间的前后衔接、段落过渡等，形成准确通畅的英译文。

做好单句翻译是篇章翻译的基础。在此我们给出以下单句翻译练习120例，其中的大部分为历年四、六级翻译考试的真题，旨在帮助大家把握好英汉翻译的基本句型，作为考前训练，为参加考试打下一定的基础。第二部分的段落翻译练习30篇，内容涉及中国的历史、文化、经济、社会发展等，可作为翻译考试新题型模拟训练，为大家提供了有针对性的考前实战翻译素材。

第十四单元
《大学英语教学指南》与四、六级翻译考试

1. 思考题
（1）大学阶段的英语教学要求分为哪三个层次？分别有哪些具体要求？
（2）《大学英语课程教学要求》对翻译提出了什么要求？考试采用什么样的形式？
（3）你认为四、六级翻译考试难在何处？为什么？

2. 翻译备考训练

单句翻译练习 120 句

翻译下列各句，注意根据不同的句型使用相关翻译技巧方法。

练习 1
1. 有朝一日家庭将由安装在地下室的小型反应堆供热。
2. 他在讲话中特别强调提高产品质量。
3. 我们正准备去度假，汽车就出了毛病。
4. 我的汽车尽管用了一年多了，可几乎还是新的。
5. 他把整个情况给老师讲了，原原本本，一字不差。
6. 一切生物，不管是动物还是植物，都是由细胞组成的。
7. 能不能提前完成计划呢？
8. 我不得不推迟原定的计划，这使我深感失望。
9. 万一有紧急情况，请按红色按钮以切断电源。
10. 据估计到 2025 年之前，世界人口中的三分之二可能住在面临严重缺水的国家。

练习 2
1. 我理所当然地认为，你会来跟他谈这件事的。
2. 从他告诉我的话我知道，他比我懂的英语多。
3. 无论他如何努力尝试，最后也失败了。
4. 他开车时心不在焉，差一点造成交通事故。
5. 讲话者提高声音，以便让听众听到。
6. 很抱歉，因为雨太大，参观博物馆得推迟到明天。
7. 要是你昨天来了，你就会在这里看到他的。

8. 他此行所见所闻都给他留下了深刻的印象。

9. 借助一架显微镜，就可以看到集成电路被分离和被测试的情况。

10. 全世界的石油将会用尽，人们将使用从原子分裂获得的这种更为方便的动力。

练习 3

1. 如果某物具有适应环境的能力，我们就说它具有智力。

2. 要不是我亲眼看见，我本来是不会相信的。

3. 他希望写一篇能够引起公众对此事注意的文章。

4. 艾滋病是全球第四大死因，它使很多家庭丧失了父母和孩子。

5. 他们决心坚决执行计划，不论他们将会面临什么样的障碍。

6. 如果食物中缺少了某些重要成分，即使其中不含有任何有害物质，也会引起严重疾病。

7. 在经过30年的改革开放之后，中国现在已经进入现代化的一个关键阶段。

8. 火箭必须获得每秒大约五英里的速度，以便能够把卫星送入轨道。

9. 地球上的任何物体都会落下来，除非它受到一个大小与其重量相等的力的支撑。

10. 即使是最精确的实验，也没有希望获得无任何误差的实验结果。

练习 4

1. 真奇怪，她竟然没有看出自己的缺点。

2. 在他还没来得及阻拦我之前，我已经跑出教室。

3. 年轻的作家将自己的成功归功于老师的鼓励。

4. 如果你仔细比较，你就会发现它们之间的不同之处。

5. 不论用什么方法做实验，他所得到的结果都相同。

6. 我已经提前完成了交给我的工作，他也提前完成了交给他的工作。

7. 问题越是难，我越不可能回答得出来。

8. 全世界的科学家都在寻找净化空气、防止空气污染的有效方法。

9. 不过，问题还是圆满地解决了，这说明计算很准确。

10. 由于历史、政治和经济上的原因，全世界讲英语、用英语的人为数最多。

练习 5

1. 不管是否加热，这种物质都不溶于水。
2. 他不仅向我收费过高，而且修得也不好。
3. 与我的相比，你今年生意上的损失根本算不了什么。
4. 工人们认为遵守安全规则很重要。
5. 相反，美国母亲更可能把孩子的成功归因于自然天赋。
6. 最要紧的是我们在月底前签订合同。
7. 令我们高兴的是，她进大学一个月就适应了大学生活。
8. 新政府被指责未兑现其降低失业率的承诺。
9. 据说，游客在利兹旅游时，平均每天的花费只及在伦敦旅游所花费的一半的钱。
10. 消费者抱怨说，他刚试着使用这台机器，它就不运转了。

练习 6

1. 从事跨文化研究的专家认为，适应不同文化中的生活很不容易。
2. 自从童年时代我就发现没有什么比读书对我更有吸引力。
3. 要是受害者被及时送到医院，他本来有机会活下来。
4. 一些心理学家声称，人们出门在外时可能会感到孤独。
5. 这个国家的人口继续以每年 1 200 万人的速度增长。
6. 这项研究的结果未能将人们的睡眠质量考虑在内。
7. 预防和治疗艾滋病是我们可以合作的领域。
8. 由于腿受伤，该运动员决定退出比赛。
9. 如要捐赠，或想了解更多的信息，请按以下地址和我们联系。
10. 60 多岁的时候，我注意到的一个变化是我比以前更容易累了。

练习 7

1. 你最好带上毛线衫，以防天气变冷。
2. 通过这一工程，很多人受到训练，并决定自己创业。
3. 抗病毒剂直到一名医生偶然发现了它之前一直不为人知。
4. 要是你听从了我的忠告，你就不会陷入麻烦。
5. 夫人满面泪水地看着她受伤的儿子被送进手术室。

6. 恐怖袭击之后，旅游者被劝告暂时不要去该国旅游。

7. 我喜欢通过写电子邮件而不是打电话与顾客交流。

8. 直到截止日他才寄出申请表。

9. 只有在小城镇他才感到安全和放松。

10. 这些汽车生产厂家发现它们正在同外国公司竞争市场的份额。

练习 8

1. 这绝对不公平，这些孩子被剥夺了受教育的权利。

2. 我们多年的艰苦工作都白费了，更别提我们所花费的大量金钱了。

3. 黑人和妇女问题最近几十年受到公众相当大的关注。

4. 要不是有了移动电话，我们的通信就不可能如此迅速和方便。

5. 在对付尴尬局面时，没有什么比幽默感更有帮助的了。

6. 外交部长说他要辞职，但他拒绝进一步解释这样做的原因。

7. 人类行为主要是知识的产物，动物的行为主要依靠本能。

8. 目击者被告知，在任何情况下他都不应该对法庭说谎。

9. 玛丽准是还没有收到我的信，否则她上周就该回信了。

10. 对于毕生致力于诗歌的人，我们有很多的话可说。他们热情洋溢、性格冲动、举止独特。

练习 9

1. 估计南茜至少已在两星期前做完化学实验。

2. 自从 40 年前结婚以来，老两口就从未相互争吵过一次。

3. 一个国家未来的繁荣在很大程度上有赖于教育的质量。

4. 他设计了第一座吊桥，把美与功能完美地结合起来。

5. 天很黑，但是玛丽似乎本能地知道该走哪条路。

6. 我认为家长剥夺孩子们课余时间的自由是不明智的。

7. 日常活动频率高的老年人精力更充沛，与不那么活跃的人相比死亡率要低。

8. 通过证明为什么你是某个特定职位的最佳人选，你的简历会吸引将来老板的注意。

9. 这些花看起来好长时间没有浇水了。

10. 弗雷德上周买了一辆小车，比我的车便宜 1 000 英镑。

练习 10

1. 这个电视节目太乏味，我们不妨听听音乐。
2. 他慌忙离开办公室，灯亮着，门开着。
3. 据说这部著名的小说已经被译成多种语言。
4. 我认为这顿餐不打折扣完全值 80 美元的价。
5. 面对来自其他公司的激烈竞争，汽车制造商正考虑推出促销活动。
6. 至于业余爱好，珍妮和她妹妹几乎没有什么共同之处。
7. 只是经过多次的失败之后我才认识到仅凭运气是不能成功的。
8. 几乎所有的生物要不是都具有生存的本能，那么更多的物种就可能已经在地球上灭绝了。
9. 一个人的品行不取决于这个人如何享受胜利，而是怎样经受失败。
10. 她觉得受到侮辱，显然任何劝她留下来的企图都是徒劳的。

练习 11

1. 无论我要做出什么样的牺牲我都要追求这一事业。
2. 我喜欢网上购物而不喜欢上百货商店，因为这更加方便和省时。
3. 大多数父母所关心的是尽量为他们的孩子提供最好的教育。
4. 如果研究的结果能应用于新技术的开发，那么我们的努力将不会白费。
5. 我现在打不开我的计算机了。一定是操作系统出了毛病。
6. 一个人离开了自己的工作，无论是什么工作，都是一个艰难的改变，即便对那些盼望退休的人来说也一样。
7. 与我成长的地方相比，这个城镇更繁荣、更令人兴奋。
8. 直到他完成使命才意识到自己得了重病。
9. 医疗研究人员痛苦地意识到，很多医学问题他们至今还没有答案。
10. 很多美国人靠贷款生活，他们的生活质量是用他们能够借到多少来衡量的，而不是他们能够挣多少来衡量。

练习 12

1. 不管中国变得多么强大，它不会对任何国家构成威胁。
2. 如果他知道会发生这种事，也许会以不同方式行事。
3. 从字里行间看，我想说的是，政府更担心他们会承认。

4. 近年来，随着他的生意红红火火，他给慈善事业捐了一大笔钱。

5. 任何驾驶员血液中酒精含量高将被指控为醉驾，并面临严厉的处罚。

6. 很多人已经变得如此沉迷于网上购物，以至于他们情不自禁每天都要访问购物网站。

7. 你是我们组织的执行委员会成员，所以你说的话有分量。

8. 要充分理解作者的动机和意图，你真的必须仔细从字里行间去解读。

9. 人生的成功并不那么多地取决于一个人的学习成绩，而是取决于勤奋和坚持。

10. 没有大气层，我们将被迫寻找躲避太阳的藏身处，因为没有任何其他东西可以保护我们免受其致命光线的伤害。

段落翻译练习 30 篇

1. 中国

我们中国是世界上最大国家之一，它的领土和整个欧洲的面积差不多相等。在这个广大的领土之上，有广大的肥田沃地，给我们以衣食之源；有纵横全国的大小山脉，给我们生长了广大的森林，贮藏了丰富的矿产；有很多的江河湖泽，给我们以舟楫和灌溉之利；有很长的海岸线，给我们以交通海外各民族的方便。从很早的古代起，我们中华民族的祖先就劳动、生息、繁衍在这块广大的土地之上。（186 字）

2. 中国国土

中国的陆地国土面积为 960 万平方千米，仅次于俄罗斯、加拿大，居世界第三位。另外，还拥有 300 万平方千米的海洋国土。

目前，中国有 23 个省、5 个自治区、4 个直辖市和两个特别行政区。首都是北京。

中国国土辽阔、资源丰富、江山多娇。中国是世界四大文明古国之一，中华民族在这块广阔的土地上，创造了光辉灿烂的东方文化。（147 字）

3. 中华民族

中国以其人口密集、疆域辽阔而著称。作为一个多民族国家，中国共有 56 个民族，总人口约 14 亿人。汉族是中华民族的主体民族，约占全国人口的 92%。

主要分布在东部和中部。而其他少数民族居住相对分散，主要分布在中国的西南、西北和东北部地区。每个少数民族都有与众不同的特点、悠久的传统文化和独特的风俗习惯。中国政府长久以来一直提倡和发展平等、团结的民族关系，强调各民族共同发展、共同繁荣。（184字）

4. 中国文化

在17世纪和18世纪，中国的艺术、建筑和哲学在西方很受欣赏。此外，中国的丝绸、茶叶和瓷器在西方也备受欢迎，并在一定程度上改变了许多西方的生活方式。进入20世纪后期，西方人再次转向中国文化。他们除了喜欢中国菜肴外，还学习汉语，尝试中国医药，练习中国武术，观看功夫电影。（134字）

5. 龙的传说

龙是中国人自古以来一直崇拜的神异动物。在中国的民间传说中，龙是多种动物的综合体，具有多种动物的特长。尽管中国龙是一种现实中并不存在的动物，但它在中国人的心里占据着不可替代的位置。在过去，龙长期被古时的中国人当作能够控制自然界的神。在封建社会，龙是权力和帝王的象征。在现代社会，龙已经成为吉祥物，象征腾飞、成功、开拓精神和创造。因此在中国人的日常生活中，到处都能看到龙的形象。（187字）

6. 中国的气候

冬季，中国南北的气温差别较大。中国北方，冬季是千里冰封、万里雪飘的一片银装素裹的洁白世界。当北方的哈尔滨人冒着严寒参观"冰灯游园会"时，南方的广州却是百花盛开，春意盎然。

夏季，全国大部分地区普遍炎热，降水较多，雨热同季，给农业带来了极大好处。全国的降水量，地区分布不均匀，从东南沿海向西北内陆逐渐减少。（150字）

7. 中国的经济

中国自1978年实行改革开放的政策以来，经济获得了持续快速的发展。目前经济总量已位居世界第二。预计到21世纪中叶，中国将基本上实现现代化，达到中等发达国家的水平。

中国经济发展水平的地区差异较大，东部沿海地区比较发达，经济和科学技术发展水平较高，工业、农业、交通运输业和通讯设施基础好，西部地区相对落后。但是，从长远来看，西部地区资源丰富，有发展工农业的广阔空间。（176字）

8. 中国的铁路

铁路是中国最重要的运输方式,到2012年年底,全国铁路营业里程达到9.8万公里,居世界第二位。

中国铁路干线可以分为南北干线和东西干线两大组,在南北干线和东西干线的交叉或衔接处,形成了许多重要的铁路枢纽。

青藏铁路从青海西宁经格尔木到西藏拉萨,全长1 956千米,是世界上海拔最高的铁路。2006年7月1日,青藏铁路全线开通并试运营。青藏铁路的建成使西藏交通运输的落后面貌得到质的改善,为西藏今后经济可持续发展提供了可靠的保证。(198字)

9. 翻译的作用

在人类历史发展的长河中,在世界多元文化的交流、融会与碰撞中,在中华民族伟大复兴的进程中,翻译始终都起着不可或缺的先导作用。所有的国际活动和语言文化交流都离不开翻译。假如这世界有一天没有了翻译,联合国将不复存在,世贸组织将无法运行,一切国际机构都会瘫痪。翻译工作者及其工作就像电线里流动的电流、水管中流动的水流:他们默默无闻地把一个语言文化带到另一个语言文化中,使隔膜变成透明。(187字)

10. 长城

长城是世界七大奇观之一,是世界上修建时间最长、工程量最大的军事性防御工程,是炎黄子孙血汗与智能的结晶,也是中华民族坚毅、勤奋的象征。它以宏大的气势和壮美的英姿享誉世界,吸引天下的游人,现已被联合国列入世界文化遗产名录。

长城是中国古代用作军事防御的一项宏伟建筑。长城最早大约出现于公元前7~前5世纪。其规模和基础是秦朝奠定的。以后,汉、南北朝、隋、唐、辽金、明、清等朝代都曾修筑过长城。(190字)

11. 长江

长江发源于青藏高原,全长6 300多千米,是中国第一大河、世界第三长河。

长江上游落差大,水流急,有许多高山耸立的峡谷地段。中游的平原地区江面变宽,水流减缓,多曲流、多支流、多湖泊。长江下游地区地势低平,江阔水深,是著名的鱼米之乡。长江入海口,江面宽达80~90千米,水天一色,极为壮观。中国大部分的淡水湖分布在长江中下游地区。

长江流域物产丰富，经济发达。上海、南京、武汉、重庆等大城市都分布在这里。（192字）

12. 黄河

黄河发源于青海省，全长5 400多千米，是中国的第二长河。从地图上看，黄河的形状是一个巨大的"几"字。

黄河上游有许多峡谷，这些峡谷地带水力资源丰富，建有多座大型水电站。

黄河中游经过黄土高原，这里水土流失严重，河水中的泥沙含量大，河水浑浊呈黄色而得名黄河。

黄河下游主要流经低缓的华北平原，这里河道宽阔，水流变缓，泥沙大量沉积，形成了河床比两岸高的"地上河"。（174字）

13. 四大发明

中国的四大发明包括指南针、火药、造纸术和印刷术：它们在人类文明史上占有重要地位。第一个指南针产生于战国时期，是利用天然磁石来辨别方向的一种简单仪器。火药发明于隋唐时期，主要应用于军事领域。造纸术于东汉年间由蔡伦改进，使纸成为人们普遍使用的书写材料。印刷术，又称活字印刷术，大大促进了文化的传播：四大发明对世界经济的发展和人类文化的进步做出了巨大的贡献。（176字）

14. 丝绸之路

丝绸之路是中国古代最著名的贸易路线：在这条路上运输的商品中，丝绸占很大部分，因此得名"丝绸之路"。丝绸之路起点始于长安，终点远达印度、罗马等国家。丝绸之路从汉代开始形成，到唐代达到鼎盛，骆驼曾是丝绸之路上的主要交通工具。中国的造纸、印刷等伟大发明通过这条路传播到了西方，而佛教等宗教也被引入中国。丝绸之路不仅仅是古代国际贸易路线，更是连接亚洲、非洲、欧洲的文化桥梁。（183字）

15. 青铜器

中国的青铜器时代从夏开始，经历商、西周到春秋时期，前后持续了1 500多年的时间。大量出土的青铜器物表明，中国创造了灿烂的青铜文明。这些青铜器物不仅有丰富的政治和宗教内涵，而且还具有很高的艺术价值。今藏于中国历

史博物馆的大盂鼎是中国青铜器时代的代表性作品之一。它是西周康王时期的作品，距今大约有3 000多年。（153字）

16. 孔子

孔子是春秋时期的大思想家、大教育家和儒家学派的创始人，是古代中国人心目中的圣人。孔子的言论和生平活动记录在由他的弟子或再传弟子编成的《论语》一书中。《论语》是中国古代文化的经典著作。在孔子之后几千年的中国历史上，没有哪一位思想家、文学家和政治家不受《论语》的影响。不研究《论语》，就不能真正把握中国几千年的传统文化。（158字）

17. 辛亥革命

1911年，中国爆发了历史上的第一次资产阶级革命——辛亥革命，它推翻了中国封建社会的最后一个朝代——清朝，废除了中国延续了2 000多年的封建帝制，建立了中国的第一个民主共和国——中华民国。民国政府成立以后，要求全国人民都剪掉头上的辫子，选择自己喜欢的发型。至此，在中国延续了280多年的辫子法令终于被解除。（139字）

18. 北京

北京是中华人民共和国的首都，是全国的政治、文化和科技教育的中心，也是全国的交通和国际交往中心。

中华人民共和国成立60多年来，首都北京的建设日新月异，发生了巨大的变化。现代化建筑如雨后春笋般相继崛起。

北京科技力量强大，有中国科学院、北京大学、清华大学等世界著名科研机构和高等学府。同时，北京正大力发展高新技术产业，人才密集的中关村被称为中国的"硅谷"。（174字）

19. 上海

上海位于长江入海口，是中国最大的城市，同时也是一座历史文化名城和著名的旅游城市。上海是中国最大的经济中心，是全国最重要的工业基地，也是重要的贸易、金融和文化中心。

今日的上海，交通四通八达，是中国最大港口、华东地区最大的交通枢纽，沪宁、沪杭两条铁路干线的起点，又是中国重要航空中心和国际航空港之一。这里有发达的商业，是中国特大型综合性贸易中心和国际经济、金融、贸易中心之

第十四单元
《大学英语教学指南》与四、六级翻译考试

一。(185字)

20. 台湾岛

台湾是中国的第一大岛,位于中国东南沿海的大陆架上,是中国与太平洋地区各国海上联系的重要交通枢纽。

台湾岛气候冬季温暖,夏季炎热,雨量充沛。这里盛产稻米,主要经济作物是蔗糖和茶,还有"水果王国"美称,同时产名贵木材。台湾岛四周是海,渔业资源丰富。台湾有丰富的水力、森林、渔业资源。

台湾经济发达,交通便利,美丽富饶,名胜古迹众多,如阿里山、日月潭、乌来瀑布等都是著名的旅游胜地。台湾是中国的"宝岛"。(196字)

21. 杭州风光

杭州位于浙江省北部,钱塘江北岸,大运河的南端,是中国古老的风景名城。蜿蜒曲折的钱塘江,穿过浙西的崇山峻岭到这里之后,江面开阔,景色壮丽。特别是每年中秋前后有钱塘江潮,怒涛奔腾,激流汹涌,蔚为天下大观。

迷人的西湖,位于市区的西面,总面积5.6平方公里。纵贯南北的苏堤和横贯东西的白堤,把全湖分成外湖、里湖、岳湖、西里湖和小南湖五个部分。湖面波光闪闪,湖边茂林修竹,景色四季宜人。北宋苏东坡在咏潮的诗篇中,把西湖比作古代美女西施,西湖就更加名扬四海了。(222字)

22. 北京大学

北京大学于1898年成立,原名为京师大学堂。北大的成立标志着中国近代史上高等教育的开始。在中国近代史上,它是进步思想的中心,对中国新文化运动、五四运动及其他重要事件的发生颇有影响。今天,国内不少高校排行榜将北京大学放入国内顶尖大学之列。北京大学重视教学和科学研究。为提高本科生教育和研究生教育质量、保持其领先研究机构的地位,学校已做出很大努力。此外,学校尤以其校园环境及优美的中国传统建筑而闻名。(194字)

23. 清华大学

清华大学是中国著名的高等学府。改革开放以来,先后于1984年和1985年成立了研究生院和继续教育学院。为了适应世界范围内兴起的新技术革命,适应现代科学技术发展和社会进步出现的不同学科间交叉综合的新趋势,学校的系科设置结构不断进行调整,创立了一批高技术及新兴系科专业,增设了理科、经济管理学科和文科，恢复了理学院、法学院，成立了经济管理学院、人文学院和信息科学技术学院，并入了美术学院，新建了医学院。（193字）

24. 中国菜

中国菜是中国各地区、各民族各种菜肴的统称，也指发源于中国的烹饪方式。中国菜历史悠久，流派众多，主要代表菜系有"八大菜系"。每一菜系因气候、地理、历史、烹饪技巧和生活方式的差异而风格各异。中国菜的调料丰富多样，调料的不同是形成地方特色菜的主要原因之一。中国菜强调色、香、味俱佳，味是菜肴的灵魂。中国饮食文化博大精深，作为世界三大菜系之一的中国菜，在海内外享有盛誉。（180字）

25. 北京烤鸭

北京烤鸭是自封建帝王时代就在北京城流行的著名菜肴，如今它被认为是中国的一道国菜。这道菜以它薄而脆的酥皮，以及厨师们在客人面前片鸭子的真实情形而著称。专门用于制作烤鸭的鸭子在养殖65天后就被屠宰了，鸭子在烤制前要先用调料腌制，然后才送进焖炉或者挂炉。鸭肉通常配上葱、黄瓜和甜面酱，用薄饼卷着食用。（146字）

26. 春节

农历正月初一是春节,在西方称之为"中国新年"，是中国最重要的传统佳节，神州大地，举国欢庆。

除夕之夜的年夜饭是必不可少的程序。全家人围坐一张桌子一同分享佳肴，人多的话兴许不止一张桌子。家人还会为没能赶回家的亲人留些座位，仿佛他们也在一起吃似的。年夜饭过后，大家会坐在一起，观看中央电视台的春节特别节目，等待新年的到来。午夜将近时，特别节目也接近尾声，这时家家户户都到户外去放鞭炮。据说这样可以驱妖除魔。(199字）

27. 端午节

公元前278年，也就是屈原62岁那年，他在汨罗江边，听到秦国军队攻破了楚国的国都，便怀着悲痛的心情，抱了一块石头，投汨罗江自杀了。那天正好是农历五月五日。

楚国人民非常热爱屈原。他们担心屈原的遗体被江里的鱼虾吃掉，就划着船，把包好的粽子扔到江里去给鱼虾吃。以后每到农历五月五日这一天，中国人家家

户户都包粽子，吃粽子，表示对伟大诗人屈原的纪念。这就是中国人民的传统节日"端午节"。（186字）

28. 月饼的传说

关于吃月饼这个传统的来历有两个传说。一个是唐朝的神话故事，说的是美丽的嫦娥忍受不了丈夫后羿的暴行，于是偷走了他的长生不老药，飞上了月亮，从此就有了嫦娥奔月的传说。

另一个传说讲的是在元朝，朱元璋领导的起义军决定用起义的方式来摆脱蒙古族的统治。他们用月饼传递情报。掰开月饼就可以读到里面的密信。起义军通过这种方式成功地发动了起义，赶走了元朝的统治者。这场起义发生在8月15日，这就是为什么人们要在这一天吃月饼。（202字）

29. 十八大

中国共产党第十八次全国代表大会，是在我国进入全面建成小康社会决定性阶段召开的一次十分重要的大会。大会的主题是：高举中国特色社会主义伟大旗帜，以邓小平理论、"三个代表"重要思想、科学发展观为指导，解放思想，改革开放，凝聚力量，攻坚克难，坚定不移沿着中国特色社会主义道路前进，为全面建成小康社会而奋斗。(149字）

30. 文化实力和竞争力

文化实力和竞争力是国家富强、民族振兴的重要标志。要坚持把社会效益放在首位、社会效益和经济效益相统一，推动文化事业全面繁荣、文化产业快速发展。发展哲学社会科学、新闻出版、广播影视、文学艺术事业。加强重大公共文化工程和文化项目建设，完善公共文化服务体系，提高服务效能。促进文化和科技融合，发展新型文化业态，提高文化产业规模化、集约化、专业化水平。构建和发展现代传播体系，提高传播能力。增强国有公益性文化单位活力，完善经营性文化单位法人治理结构，繁荣文化市场。（226字）

附 录

各单元翻译练习参考译文及解析

第一单元　翻译知识与翻译技巧

1. 英译汉参考译文

A

Look out! 字面的意思是：向外望；此处为"注意，当心，留神"之意；
Didn't you hear me call "look out"？你刚才没有听见我喊"look out"吗？
Yes, and that's what I did. 听见了，我就是那样做的啊。

解析：

不管这个故事是真是假，它说明学习英语不可死抠字眼。一些十分简单的英语词语，一旦组合成为成语之后，词义就变了。Look out! 字面意思为"向外望"，而此处的实际意思却是"注意，当心，留神"。自己没听懂人家的警告差点出了险，还振振有词，由此产生了这一经典笑话。

B

小明：对不起!

外宾：我也对不起!

小明：我再三对不起!

外宾：你为什么说再三对不起呢?

小明：我说五遍对不起!

外宾：!!??

解析：

产生这一笑话的原因是小明没听懂外宾回答，误将副词 too（也）理解为同音词 two（二），将介词 for（为了）理解为同音词 four（四）；由此产生了一系列的连锁笑话，使得外宾一头雾水，完全摸不着头脑。

2. 汉译英参考译文

1) No Photos!
2) Watch your head!
3) Engine room: No unauthorized access.
4) Please come again.
5) Comments and criticisms are welcome.
6) Please turn the computer off.
7) Don't forget your personal belongings.
8) In case of emergency, please call 110.
9) Slow on bridge in case of rain or snow.
10) Make sure to lock the doors and windows when leaving your car.
11) No Smoking. Penalties for violation.
12) Be civilized and keep the public places clean.

解析：

1）"禁止拍照"之类严禁的口吻一般用 **No**+*n*. 结构；如：**No Smoking**（禁止吸烟）；**No visiting**（谢绝参观）等。

2）"当心碰头"的实际意思也就是"当心别碰着头"，不可译作 **Carefully bump**（仔细地、小心地碰）。根据不同语境，也可以译作 **Mind your head, Look out overhead**。

3）"重地"的意思重要而需加防护的场所，不宜译作 **serious place**（严肃的地方）；翻译时通常可考虑省略"重地"二字；"闲人免进"意译为 **No unauthorized access**（未经授权不得进入）。

4）**Welcome again** 的意思是"再次表示欢迎"；"欢迎再来"应当是 **Please come again**。

5）"欢迎大家批评指正"按英语习惯表达法应当用被动语态，而不用无主句。

6）汉语的"开"和"关"视情况可译作 open/close 或 turn on/turn off；"关闭计算机"属于电源的关闭，所以用 turn off，而不是 close the computer。

7）"随身物品"也即是 personal belongings（个人的东西），用"正说反译"使译文准确通顺。

8）"紧急情况"也即是"万一有紧急情况"，所以应当用增词法译作 In case of emergency（万一发生意外）；in case 假使，如果，万一；如：He took along an umbrella, just in case. 他随身带一把伞，以防万一。

9）"下雨或雪天"为"万一下雨或下雪"的省略，与 8）相似，故译作 in case of rain or snow。

10）"关门"在一般情况下可译作 close the door；此处的"关好车窗门"也即是"锁好车门"，所以应当译作 lock the doors and windows。

11）这句话有两层意思，所以翻译成两个句子。"违者罚款"（penalties for violation）；penalty n. 处罚，罚款；如：the penalty for speeding 驾车超速罚款。后半句也可考虑译作：Any violator will be fined. fine v. 罚款；如：He was fined 200 dollars for violation of traffic regulation. 他因违反交通规则被罚款 200 美元。

12）Visit in civilization, pay attention to hygiene 这句话的字面意义是：在文明中访问，对卫生注意。此处应当用祈使句译出，省略"游览"二字；"环境"指的是"公共场所"（the public places），而不是 environment（自然环境）。

第二单元　遣词用字与词义判定

1. 英译汉参考译文

1）她大为震惊。

2）他本应该当一名医生。

3）这件区区小事不值一顾。

4）老人观点固执，一成不变。

5）孙子是她的掌上明珠。

6）那个水手满肚子都是冒险故事。

7）她告诉我她将永久移居欧洲。

8）曼纳特医生被无端投入监狱。

9）更糟的是，狮子甚至有可能把婴儿叼走。

10）浏览一下这本书，这儿看几眼，那儿看几眼就足够了。

11）不过，这个国家要想恢复到以前那样，得要100多年。

12）生活中最美好的东西是可尽情享用的：阳光、欢笑、与朋友伴着美妙音乐的乡间漫步。

解析：

1）此句不宜照字面直译，而是打破原文的结构，用意译将 the surprise of her life 简化为汉语四字结构"大为震惊"。surprise of one's life 一生中最吃惊的事。

2）此句中的 supposed 为形容词，意为"假定的，推测的"；如：The supposed prince was really a beggar in disguise. 那个被认为是王子的人，原来是个乔装的乞丐。根据此处的过去时态，译为"他本应该"。

3）此句需注意 trifle 和 beneath 两词的翻译。trifle n. 小事，琐事；译为"区区小事"；beneath prep. 不值得；不屑于，如：It was beneath me to beg. 这事不值得我去乞求。所以将 beneath our notice 译为"不值一顾"。

4）rigid adj. 坚硬的；僵直的，固执的；如：rigid ideas 固执的看法；结合此句的系表结构，译为"观点固执，一成不变"。

5）apple of (one's) eye 宠物，珍爱物，此处译为汉语成语"掌上明珠"，不可照字面翻译成"眼中的苹果"。

6）stock n. 贮存，储存，存货；如：We have a large stock of tinned fruit. 我们储存了大量的水果罐头。此处 a rich stock of 也即是"大量的存货"，所以意译为"满肚子都是故事"。

7）for good 永久地，一劳永逸地；如：It seems she'll stay here for good.

她似乎要永远待在这里不走了。

8）**put in prison** 投入监狱；**for no good reason** 没有任何正当理由，简化翻译为"无端"。

9）**carry** *vt.* 携带，运送，拿，提，扛，背……；根据上下文 **the lion** 和 **in its mouth**，将 **carry off** 译作"叼走"。

10）**dip into** 浏览，稍加研究；**read bits here and there** 用重复手段译作"这儿看几眼，那儿看几眼"。

11）这句话的字面翻译：但是，（要让）这个国家再度开始看起来像它过去的模样之前，将会有 100 多年过去了。这样的语句读起来磕磕巴巴，所以对其措辞结构做了调整组合。

12）**free** *adj.* 自由的，免费的，空闲的，丰富的；此处根据上下文译为"可尽情享用"；**walks in the beauty of the country, friends and music** 直译为"在美丽的乡村散步、朋友和音乐"，根据上下文译为"与朋友伴着美妙音乐的乡间漫步"。

2. 汉译英参考译文

1) This book is not available here.
2) This fellow abounds in courage.
3) What are the total losses?
4) This village boasts three shops.
5) My old car has served me well.
6) Smoking is bad for (harmful to) your health.
7) This course carries three credits.
8) The snow is likely to persist in most areas.
9) If I made a mistake, I will try to remedy it.
10) Do you qualify for the vote?
11) The yard is fenced around.
12) Is there any chance of the team winning this week?

附 录
各单元翻译练习参考译文及解析

解析：

一看到"有"、"没有"，不少同学就马上会想到 have 和 there be 句型，实际上关于"有"、"没有"的译法远不止这两个，很多乍看来似乎与"有"字不相关的词语，往往却是最佳选项，我们在翻译时应结合上下文做出必要的取舍。

1）available *adj*. 可得到的；可利用的；如：I'm sorry; those overcoats are not available in your color and size. 对不起，这种外套没有你要的颜色和尺码。These tickets are available on (the) day of issue only. 这种车票仅在发售当天有效。

2）abound *vi*. 有许多；充满；如：Streams abound with fish. 小溪里有很多鱼。Forests abound in that region. 那个地区有很多森林。

3）"有多少"之类的问句，一般用 What..., How many..., How much... 等疑问句型就行了，与 have 和 there be 并无什么相干。

4）boast *v*. 以拥有……而自豪；如：a region that boasts bountiful coal fields 一个拥有丰富煤炭矿藏的地区；该校有着辉煌而悠久的历史。This school boasts a long brilliant history.

5）很有用：serve sb. well；well 很有效；如：The sleeping pills work well. 安眠药很有效。

6）有害于：be bad for.../harmful to...；类似的结构：be beneficial to 有益于；be helpful to 有助于；等。

7）有3个学分：carry three credits，carry *vt*. 包含，含有；如：harsh words that carry a threat of violence 含有暴力威胁的严厉言辞。

8）可能还有：is likely to persist，此处的"有"也即是"存在"，可译作 there be，there exist 等字眼。

9）有错：make a mistake，也即是"犯了错"，不宜照字面译作 have a mistake，因为 have a mistake 可以指别人的错。

10）有……资格：qualify for...；类似的结构：possess great tact 有智谋；be entitled to 有资格；be empowered to 有权；等。

11）围有篱笆：be fenced around，类似的结构：be armed with 装备有；be equipped with 配备有；be installed with 安装有；等。

12）有没有机会：Is there any chance，亦可换作 Is it possible for... 之类的结构。

第三单元　词类转换与句子成分转换

1. 英译汉参考译文

1）这鞋我穿正合适。
2）他与我意见一致。
3）如果房间里没人，灯将熄灭。
4）村民们奋起反抗侵略者。
5）她一见那只死老鼠就感到恶心。
6）我承认他说的是事实。
7）她的病需要很长时间才能痊愈。
8）一些学生随琼斯教授去野外郊游。
9）我们在那个问题上跟他们的意见不同。
10）母亲去世后，这所房子就归他了。
11）法国人在见面问好和相互告别时接吻比英国人更频繁。
12）在过去的60多年，我国的体育运动取得了可喜的成绩。

解析：

1）将动宾结构 adapt me 转换成主谓结构"我穿"。
2）将动词 accord 转换成表语"与……一致"。
3）将副词 off 转换成动词"熄灭"。
4）将介词 against 转换成动词"反抗"。
5）将介词短语 at the sight of 转换成动词"一见"。
6）将名词短语 the truth of his statement 转换成句子"他说的是事实"。
7）将介词及宾语 from the illness 转换主语"她的病"。
8）将介词短语 on a field trip 转换成动词短语"去野外郊游"。
9）将动词 differ 转换成表语"意见不同"。

10）将介词短语 on his mother's death 转换成句子"母亲去世后"。

11）将句子 French people kiss each other hello and goodbye 转换成状语"在……时"。

12）将主语 Gratifying achievements 转换成宾语；状语 in physical culture and sports 转换成主语。

2. 汉译英参考译文

1) The master worker showed me around the factory.
2) His voice trembled with rage.
3) Susan got a divorce from John last year.
4) There seems to be some fault in the computer.
5) The boy behaved very well last night.
6) All our work was in vain.
7) The principal has a very tight schedule.
8) The company advertised for a new secretary.
9) These fish vary in weight from 3 lb to 5 lb.
10) My father values honesty beyond all things.
11) This glass of ice tea will refresh you.
12) China has now reached a new stage in its modernization drive after 35 years' reforming and opening to the outside world.

解析：

1）将连动式结构"带我参观"转换成动、宾、状语结构 showed me around。

2）将动词短语"气得发抖"转换成动词＋介词＋宾语：trembled with rage。

3）将动词"离了婚"转换成名词 a divorce。

4）将主语"这台电脑"转换成状语 in the computer。

5）将名词"表现"转换成动词 behave。

6）将谓语动词"白费了"转换成系表结构 was in vain。

7）将主语"日程"转换成宾语，将表语"满满的"转换成定语 tight。

8）将动词"招聘"转换成介词 for。

9）将表语"从……不等"转换成动词 vary。

10）将"把诚实看得"转换成动宾结构 values honesty；状语"比什么都重要"转换成介词＋宾语 beyond all things。

11）将主谓结构"你会感到清凉"转换成动宾结构 refresh you。

12）将定语"中国的"转换成主语 China；将句子主语"现代化建设"转换成状语 in its modernization drive。

第四单元　增添技巧的运用

1. 英译汉参考译文

1）两个男孩动手打起来了。

2）那就是我们的分歧之所在。

3）音乐会使你的整个生活丰富多彩。

4）城市的街道上满是行人车辆。

5）他个子矮小，戴着一副厚厚的眼镜。

6）他生来本是个自由人，现在却戴上了镣铐。

7）库克是第一位测绘出东海岸地图的人。

8）人们常常认为残疾就是完全残废。

9）这个国家 2/3 的区域属气候干燥区或沙漠地区。

10）她对买不买这衣服下不了决心。

11）他跌入荆棘丛，全身伤痕累累。

12）残疾人不仅能读书、写字、绘画、油漆和烹饪，而且他们还能学习、上大学、参加考试和工作。

解析：

1）增添宾语、语气助词，将 fought 增译为"动手打起来了"，否则不通顺。

2）增添语气助词，将 where 增译为"分歧之所在"，比直译为"地方"更清楚。

3）修辞性增词，将 enrich（使丰富）增译为"使……丰富多彩"。

4）修辞性增词，将 traffic（交通）增译为"行人车辆"，以符合汉语的表达习惯。

5）增添名词"个子"、量词"一副"和动词"戴着"。

6）增添背景说明词语"生来本是"、转折副词"却"、动词"戴上"。

7）增添表语，将 the first 增译为"第一位……的人"；将 map 增译为"测绘出……地图"。

8）重复性增词，将 total 增译为"完全残废"。

9）完善性增词，将 dry or desert 增译为"气候干燥地区或沙漠地区"。

10）增添语气词使译文语气连贯，将 a decision about the dress 增译为"买不买这衣服"。

11）修辞性增词，将 was covered with scratches 增译为"全身伤痕累累"。

12）增添宾语，将 read, write 增译为"读书、写字"；助动词"能"、"还能"。

2. 汉译英参考译文

1) Eliminate the false and retain the true.

2) She performed the worst of all.

3) The apples in the orchard are ripe.

4) In case of trouble, you may dial the police.

5) He was weak in mathematics, but good at English.

6) As the saying goes, the latecomers surpass the early starters.

7) The driver took a sudden turn to the left.

8) Don't blame it on him, but on me.

9) Our manager retired from the business when he was 60.

10) A beggar cheated him out of 100 yuan.

11) The pilot nearly lost his life in the accident.

12) This policy concerns the national welfare and the people's livelihood.

解析：

1）增添两处定冠词 the，连词 and；将"去伪存真"增译为 Eliminate the false and retain the true。

2）增添修饰成分，准确表达出原文的意思，将"最糟"增译为 the worst of all。

3）增添两处定冠词 the，介词 in，动词 are；将"熟了"增译为 are ripe。

4）增添介词短语 in case of trouble（万一遇到麻烦），代词 you；情态动词 may；将"找民警"意译为 dial the police（给警察打电话），而不是 look for policeman（寻找警察）。

5）增添动词 was；介词 in，at；将"数学差，但英语好"增译为 weak in mathematics, but good at English。

6）增添背景说明词语，将"俗话说"增译为 As the saying goes；将"后来居上"增译为 the latecomers surpass the early starters。

7）增添宾语、冠词 a, the，将"突然向左转"增译为 took a sudden turn to the left。

8）增添介词 on，连词 but；将"怪某人"增译为 blame on sb.。

9）增添地点状语 from the business；将"退休"增译为 retire from the business。

10）增添介词 out of，将"骗了他 100 元"增译为 cheat him out of 100 yuan。

11）增添两处定冠词 the，代词 his；将"在事故中"增译为 in the accident；将"丧命"增译为 lost his life。

12）增添定冠词 the，连词 and；将"国计民生的大问题"增译为 the national welfare and the people's livelihood。welfare *n.* 幸福，福利；如：social welfare 社会福利；livelihood *n.* 生活，生计；如：He wrote for a livelihood. 他以写作为生。

第五单元 省略技巧的运用

1. 英译汉参考译文

1）入乡随俗。

2）他不敢投资。

3）老王 16 岁便开始独立谋生。
4）张教授精通法语。
5）这种奇怪的动物会生蛋，同时还用奶哺乳幼仔。
6）小李成天忙于回信。
7）发言人转变了话题。
8）现在旧金山市区和郊区的人口已是 1906 年的 10 倍以上了。
9）新西兰面积比广东省大，而人口却少得多。
10）这些发展中国家，土地辽阔，人口众多，资源丰富。
11）如果一个人每次都是一进入梦境就被叫醒，即使总睡眠量不少，也会烦躁不安。
12）他们进入餐室用餐。美酒佳肴，顿受感染。言谈间不但没有恶言恶语，甚至还充满友好之情。

解析：

1）省略译作汉语成语。如果照字面直译为"当在罗马的时候，按照罗马人那样做"，会显得文句啰唆、不通顺。

2）省略介词 about，宾语 money；将 timid about investing money 省略译为"不敢投资"。

3）省略介词 when，代词 his，he，动词 was；将 to earn his living when he was 16 years old 省略译为"16 岁便独立谋生"。

4）省略冠词 a，the，介词 of，宾语 command；将 has a good command of 省略译为"精通"。

5）省略两处代词 its；将 feeds its young on its milk 省略译为"用奶哺乳幼仔"。

6）省略代词 himself，将 busied himself with 省略译为"忙于"；将 all day long 省略译为"成天"。

7）句子结构省略，将 switched the conversation from one subject to another（将谈话从一个题目转到另一个）省略译为"转变了话题"。

8）省略冠词 the，代词 it，句子结构省略，将 ten times more than it was in 1906 省略译为"1906 年的 10 倍以上"。

9）省略状语 In size，句子结构省略，将 yet has a much smaller population 省略译为"人口却少得多"。

10）省略动词 cover、encompass、abound；连词 and，冠词 a。

11）省略代词 they，their；句子结构省略，将 they are likely to become irritable 省略译为"会烦躁不安"；将 they begin a dream phase of sleep 省略译为"一进入梦境"。

12）省略代词 It，Its，they，them；句子结构省略，将 It was excellent, and the wine was good. 省略译为"美酒佳肴"；将 Its influence presently had its effect on them（酒的影响力很快就在他们身上起了作用）省略译为"顿受感染"。

2. 汉译英参考译文

1) One world, one dream.
2) The gardener is digging in the garden.
3) The lid sprang open.
4) The coat was a real buy.
5) He did what the teacher asked him to do.
6) Food is essential to life.
7) He goes from one extreme to the other.
8) My sister bought her friend a present.
9) She alone was sitting still in the corner of the classroom.
10) The children are singing, dancing and playing in the park.
11) People use science to understand and change nature.
12) Solids expand and contract as liquids and gases do.

解析：

1）省略形容词"同"，量词"个"，将"同一个"省略译为 one，使译文简洁明快。

2）省略宾语"地"，将"挖地"省略译为 digging，以符合英语表达习惯。

3）省略详细的描述；将"啪的一声"省略，"弹开"译为 sprang open。

4）省略动词；将"买得便宜"省略译为 a real buy；buy *n.* 合算的购买，便宜货。

5）省略重复词语，省略句子结构；将"他就干什么"省略译为 He did。

6）省略句子结构成分；将"对于维持生命不可或缺"省略译为 essential to life；essential *adj.* 必要的、必需的。

7）省略重复词语"极端"；将"一个极端走到另一极端"省略译为 one extreme to the other。

8）句子结构省略，将"买了一件礼物给她的朋友"省略译为双宾语 bought her friend a present；也可译为 bought a present for her friend。

9）句子结构省略，将"她一个人"省略译为 She alone，将"动也不动"省略译为一个副词 still（不动地）。

10）省略宾语，将"唱歌、跳舞、做游戏"省略译为 singing, dancing and playing，以符合英语表达习惯。

11）省略重复的宾语，将"了解自然，改造自然"省略译为 understand and change nature。

12）句子结构省略，将"如同液体和气体一样"省略译为 as liquids and gases do；省略情态动词"也能"。

第六单元　句式结构调整

1. 英译汉参考译文

1）他浑身都湿透了。
2）这里的天气几乎每天都变化无常。
3）我说这话真傻。
4）要评价它的功绩为时尚早。
5）2003 年最突出的事件是"非典"。
6）在公共汽车上总共有 8 个人。
7）见他起得这么早我感到惊讶。

8)从来没有人来看过这个老太太。

9)敌人一阵猛攻后占领了这个城镇。

10)这时候传来了他走在楼梯上的脚步声。

11)坐在海滩边,看着轻拍的海浪,令人感到心境安宁。

12)科学家担心有朝一日旧金山周围地区还会发生更大的地震。

解析:

1)前后对调,将状语 to the skin 调整到前面,译作"浑身"。

2)调整状语的位置,将状语 here、almost daily 调整到前面,谓语动词 alters 放到句末,译作"变化无常"。

3)前后对调,将 silly of me 调整到后面,译作"真傻";将 to say such a thing 调整到前面,译作"我说这话"。

4)采用逆序法,将 to evaluate its success 提前,由形式主语 It 引起的句子 It's too early 调整到后面,译作"为时尚早"。

5)采用逆序法,将主语 SARS 放到句末作为强调,宾语 all the events of 2003 调整到前面,译作"2003 年最突出的事件"。

6)调整状语的位置,将地点状语 in the bus 前置,程度副词 Altogether 后置,译作"在公共汽车上总共"。

7)采用逆序法,将原因状语 to see he got up so early 调整到前面,译作"见他起得这么早",被动语态 I was astonished 转为主动,译作"我感到惊讶"。

8)调换主宾结构,如果照字面直译为"这个老太太从来没有来访者",会显得文句生硬,所以按汉语习惯表达,译作"从来没有人来看过这个老太太"。

9)采用时序法,将时间状语 after a violent attack 提前放到主语后面,译作"敌人一阵猛攻后"。

10)调整主谓结构,将 his footsteps sounded(他的脚步声响了)按汉语习惯表达,译作"传来了他的脚步声"。

11)采用逆序法,将由形式主语 It 引起的句子 It's restful 调整到后面,译作"令人感到心境安宁"。

12）调整状语的位置，将地点状语 the area around San Francisco 前置，主语 an even bigger earthquake 后置，按汉语习惯表达，将 an even bigger earthquake will hit the area around San Francisco 译作"旧金山周围地区还会发生更大的地震"。

2. 汉译英参考译文

1) He opened the door with one push.
2) 476 AD saw the ruin of Roman Empire.
3) Slow speed is the chief drawback of sea shipment.
4) Continual practice is necessary to master English.
5) We have determined to get the work done ahead of schedule.
6) The sick child shouted with pain.
7) The scent of the narcissi was in the air.
8) You must be tired after your long journey.
9) Father took the No.5 special express to Beijing.
10) Police searched everyone present at the scene of crime.
11) The scholar is studying the political theory in the West and in the Orient.
12) We have no alternative but to forge ahead.

解析：

1）前后对调，将"门开了"提前，译作 He opened the door；将"他一推"调整到后面，译作伴随状语 with one push。

2）大致保持原文的句式结构，采用无生命的名词充当役使主语（参见第7单元），将"罗马帝国灭亡"译作 saw the ruin of Roman Empire。

3）调整表语的位置，将"速度慢"前置作为句子主语，加以强调，所以译作 Slow speed is...；如果强调的是"最大缺点"，也可以保持原文的语序，译作：The chief drawback of sea shipment is its low speed.

4）结构调整，将"经常不断地练习"译作主语 Continual practice，将"要掌握英语"调整到后面，译作不定式 to master English。

5）调整状语的位置，将"提前"后置，"提前完成工作"译作 get the work done ahead of schedule。

6）调整谓语动词的位置，将"痛得叫了起来"译作 shouted with pain。

7）前后对调，将宾语"水仙花的香味"提前，译作 The scent of the narcissi was in the air. 也可以采用 there be 结构，译作 There was the scent of the narcissi in the air. 但这种译法较为平淡，没有突出主语"香味"。

8）结构调整，理顺因果关系的位置：将"走了这么远的路"译作原因：after your long journey，将"你一定很累"译作结果 You must be tired。

9）结构调整，将系表结构"父亲乘坐的是"译作主谓结构 Father took...，词序调整，将"开往北京的5次特快"译作 the No.5 special express to Beijing。

10）结构调整，将定语结构"在犯罪现场的每一个人"译作 everyone present at the scene of crime。

11）词序调整，将"东西方的政治理论"译作 the political theory in the West and in the Orient。

12）结构调整,将主句"我们没有别的选择余地"提前,将状语"除了继续前进"后置，全句简化译作 We have no alternative but to forge ahead。

第七单元　各类从句的翻译技巧

1. 英译汉参考译文

1）有这种可能，就是每4个吸烟者中有1个要死于抽烟。

2）马铃薯是早期旅行家带回的另外一种植物。

3）电信号的问题是，当它们沿着金属电线传输时，会变得越来越弱。

4）人们相信，早在发明文字之前，中国人就习惯于将若干石块放到一起记事。

5）世界上很多地区曾一度人口众多，生产过大量的农作物，而今已变成了沙漠。

6）行程开始时，被铁链锁在船下面的人约有 1/3 已不见了。

7）在欧盟，81% 的土地用于耕作，食物非常充足。事实上，这些国家的粮食经常供大于求。

8）卫星一进入环绕地球的轨道，电磁帆板就展开以便吸收阳光。

9）如果他们能设法售出大量唱片，那么卖唱片赚的钱就可以用来为非洲购买食品和其他物品。

10）我所做的，是我做得最好、最最好的事情；我想要的，是我所知最安宁、最最安宁的休憩。

11）虽然爱因斯坦结过两次婚，而且有很多挚友，但是在他整个一生中，却乐意孤身一人度过自己大部分时光。

12）事实上，镭不但损害了居里夫妇的健康，而且还使他们的工作实验室设备带放射性。

解析：

1）这是一个带表语从句的复句，可以大致按原文语序翻译。先译出主句 The chance is that（有这种可能），然后再译出表语从句。

2）这是一个带定语从句的复句，可以采用合并法，将定语从句 plant that was taken back by early travelers 并入主句，用"……的"结构译作：马铃薯是早期旅行家带回的另外一种植物。

3）这是一个带表语从句、状语从句的复句，可以先译出主句 The problem with electrical signals is（电信号的问题是），然后再译出状语从句 as they travel along metal wires（当它们沿着金属电线传输时），最后译出表语从句 they get weaker and weaker（它们会变得越来越弱）。

4）这是一个带主语从句的复句，由非人称代词 It 作为形式主语，可按汉语表达的需要先将主句 It is believed that 译作"据信/人们相信"，然后再译出主语从句。before writing was developed 发明文字之前；used to keep records by... 习惯于通过……来记事。

5）这是一个带非限制性定语从句的复句，可以采用替换法，即打破原

213

文的定语结构，将定语从句 which once had large populations and produced plenty of crops 单独译作两句话："一度曾人口众多，生产过大量的农作物"，类似一个插入语结构。

6）这是一个带定语从句的复句，可以采用合并法，将定语从句 the people who had been chained up below 并入主句，用"……的"结构译作：被铁链锁在船下面的人。

7）这是一个带定语从句的复句，可以打破原文的定语结构，将定语从句 In the European Union (EU), where 81% of the land is farmed 单独译作 "在欧盟，81% 的土地用于耕作"，然后再分别译出后面的内容。too much 太多了，此处意译为"供大于求"。

8）这是一个带假设条件状语从句的复句，可以大致按原文语序翻译：一……就。goes into its orbit round the earth 进入环绕地球的轨道，the panels are unfolded 电磁帆板就展开，in order to catch the sunshine 为了吸收阳光。

9）这是一个带条件状语从句的复句，可以大致按原文语序翻译：如果……那么。managed to sell lots of copies 设法售出大量的唱片，the money from the record sales 卖唱片赚的钱，be spent on（被花费在……）转为主动：可以用来购买……。

10）这是一个带定语从句、比较状语从句的复句，可以将定语从句 a better thing that I do 用"……的"结构译作：我做过的最好的一件事。其他照此类推。a far, far better thing that I do 我所做的最最好的一件事情，than I have ever done 比我以前所做的任何事；a far, far better rest that I go to 我想要的最最安宁的休憩，than I have ever known 比我以前所知的。

11）这是一个带让步状语从句的复句，因此可按汉语表达习惯进行结构调整：虽然……，而且……，但是……；却……。All through his life 在他整个一生中，was content to spend most of his time alone 乐意孤身一人度过他的大部分时光，although he married twice 虽然他结过两次婚，and had lots of close friends 而且有很多亲密朋友。

12) 这是一个带定语从句的并列句，可以大致按原文语序翻译：不但……而且……。定语从句 equipment with which they were working 可用"……的"结构译作：他们工作用的实验室设备。the Curies 居里夫妇，made the laboratory equipment radioactive 使实验室设备带放射性，radioactive *adj.* 放射性的；放射引起的；如：radioactive waste 放射性废物。

2. 汉译英参考译文

1) I'm afraid this old radio is beyond repair.
2) If that is true, what should we do?
3) This is the spot where the two trucks collided.
4) He recorded everything that happened on his travel.
5) The moment he spoke we could recognize his voice.
6) It is a project that consumes time and energy.
7) Will you see to it that my room is cleaned while I am out?
8) The committee selected the plan that seemed most feasible.
9) It is well-known that gunpowder is one of the four inventions of the ancient Chinese people.
10) The dog died because there was no way in which it could be brought back to the earth.
11) The fire also destroyed cars which belonged to people who worked in the building.
12) The local evening paper has plenty of advertisements, which help to cut the costs of making the newspaper.

解析：

1）增添主语，将"这台旧收音机没法修了"译作宾语从句 this old radio is beyond repair。 beyond repair 无法修理；beyond *prep.* 超出，为……所不能及；如：This work is beyond my grasp. 这件工作非我力所能及。

2）这是一个带假设条件状语从句的复句，可以大致按原文语序翻译。也可以将条件句后置：What should we do if that is true?

3）用翻译定语从句的方法将"两辆卡车相撞的地点"译作：the spot where the two trucks collided；相撞，碰撞 collide vi. 如：两列火车相撞了。The two trains collided.

4）这也是一个典型的定语从句，可以将"旅途中发生的每件事"译作：everything that happened on his travel，也可以省略译为 everything during his travel。

5）用翻译定语从句的方法将"他一说话"译作：The moment (when) he spoke，也可译作状语：We could recognize his voice whenever he opens his mouth.

6）用翻译定语从句的方法将"一项既耗时又耗精力的计划"译作：a project that consumes time and energy，也可以译为简单句：It is a project requiring a great deal of time and energy.

7）这是一个带时间分句的复句，可以将"我不在家时"反说正译，放到句末：while I am out；"请你把房间收拾干净"根据说话语气可译作 see to it that my room is cleaned，也可译作 Would you please... 句型；see to 注意，留意；如：When you start the engine, you must see to it that the car is in neutral. 开发动机时，一定要使汽车的离合器处于空档位置。

8）用翻译定语从句的方法将"那个似乎最切实可行的方案"译作：the plan that seemed most feasible；切实可行的 feasible adj. 如：一项可行的计划 a feasible plan。

9）将汉语的习惯表达法"众所周知"译作系表结构 It is well-known that，汉语主句实际上译成了英语的主语从句。注意"中国古代四大发明之一"的词语排列顺序：one of the four inventions of the ancient Chinese people。

10）这是汉语中的一个典型因果关系句。翻译成英语习惯上将主句放到前面：The dog died because...；"因为没法把狗带回地球"也可译作 because there was no way to bring it back to the earth. 注意，英语连词的用法一般是"单打一"，如：if..., since..., because...；而汉语连词的用法则是"成双成对",如:因为……,所以……;如果……,那么……,等等。因此,在英译时,应将汉语的连词补充完整。如:if...,如果……,那么……; because...,因为……,所以……; although 虽然……,但是……; unless...,除非……,否则……;而汉译英时则需考虑省略,所以这句话不可译作:Because there was no way to bring the dog back to the earth, so it died.

11) 用翻译定语从句的方法将"大楼工作人员的汽车"增译为 cars which belonged to people who worked in the building;"大楼工作人员"需用增词法译作 people who worked in the building,不能照字面译作 building workers,否则不知所云。

12) 汉语这两句话用逗号隔开,两个主谓结构分别表示两层意思。而按英语的表达习惯,需要用语法手段将这两句话衔接在一起,以表明两句之间的关联意思。非限制定语从句就是这样一种很好的手段。先将"地方晚报刊登大量广告"译成一个完整句:The local evening paper has plenty of advertisements,然后再用 which help to... 这类非限制定语从句加以补充说明。降低成本 cut/reduce the costs。

第八单元 被动语态的翻译技巧

1. 英译汉参考译文

1) 烟雾使他看不见东西。
2) 道路全都被大雪覆盖了。
3) 孩子们被带到一个安全的地方。
4) 钚是用来引爆核弹的。
5) 这个学校的教职员全是大学毕业生。
6) 故事以这种方式从一个人传给另一个人。
7) 应该让学生懂得努力学习的重要性。
8) 第二年春天,种子应该从谷穗中打出来,然后播种。

9）明年的就业前景部分取决于今年签订的合同。

10）数百年以前，就有人用"笔直线"（beeline）这个词来描写蜜蜂在空中飞行的窄细路线。

11）体积不是以平方毫米计量的，而是以立方毫米计量的。

12）1898年通过了一项法律，规定上了某一年限的人，全都按周领取"养老金"。

解析：

1）将被动转为主动，将宾主交换位置，以符合汉语的表达习惯。blind *vt.* 遮住光线，如：Thick shrubs blinded the windows downstairs. 浓密的灌木遮蔽了我们楼下的窗户。

2）保持原文的被动结构，原文的主语处于某种不利的境地，所以按汉语表达习惯将 all covered with snow 译作"全都被大雪覆盖"。

3）保持原文的被动结构，按汉语表达习惯将 were led to a place of safety 译作"被带到一个安全的地方"。

4）将被动语态转换成汉语的系表结构，将 Polonium is used to set off a nuclear bomb 译作"钋是用来引爆核弹的"。

5）将被动语态转换成汉语的系表结构，将 is staffed entirely by 译作"教职员全是……"。

6）将被动转为主动，直接去掉"被"字，将 were passed on 译作"传给"。

7）将被动转为主动，忽略被动结构，用意译来表达出原文的涵义，将 Students should be made to understand 译作"应该让学生懂得"。

8）将被动转为主动，直接去掉"被"字，将 the seeds should be knocked out of the seed-heads and sown 译作"种子应该从谷穗中打出来，然后播种"。

9）将被动转为主动，将 is based in part on 译作"部分地取决于"。

10）将被动转为主动，用增词法表达出原文的涵义，将 the word "beeline" was made to describe 译作"就有人用'笔直线'这个词来描写"。beeline *n.* 直接的、不绕行的路线。

11）将被动语态 is measured in 译作系表结构"是以……计量"。

12）将被动转为主动，以符合汉语的表达习惯。将 In 1898 a law was passed 译作无主句"1898 年通过了一项法律"；将 were paid a weekly "old-age pension" 译作：按周领取"养老金"。

2. 汉译英参考译文

1) The design must be altered.
2) This painting is much admired.
3) The export of gold is forbidden in this country.
4) The enemy was forced to ground arms.
5) The problem is now being studied.
6) Visitors are requested to show their tickets.
7) Motorists should be severely punished for speeding.
8) No register of his death was found.
9) She and her husband have been asked out for the banquet.
10) The soldiers were prohibited from leaving camp after dark.
11) They are prompted by the patriotism of the students.
12) The client was attracted by the novel advertisement.

解析：

1）这是一个不带被动标签的被动结构，翻译成英语时应转换为被动语态，将"必须改动"译作 must be altered/changed。

2）这是一个带有被动标签的被动结构，翻译成英语时可直接译作被动语态，将"备受称颂"译作 is much admired。

3）这是一个主动结构，翻译成英语时应转换为被动语态，将"禁止出口黄金"译作 gold is forbidden，主语"该国"译作状语 in this country。

4）这是一个带有被动标签的被动结构，翻译成英语时直接译作被动语态，将"被迫"译作 was forced，"放下武器"译作 to ground arms。

5）这是一个不带被动标签的被动结构，翻译成英语时应转换为被动语态，将"正在研究"译作 is now being studied。

6）这句话没有被动含义，但出于礼貌考虑，需要将汉语主动结构转为英语被动,将"请来宾出示"译作 Visitors are requested to show...。

7)这是一个带有被动标签的被动结构,翻译成英语时直接译作被动语态,将"应受严惩"译作 should be severely punished。

8)汉语这句无主句没有被动含义,但出于英语表达的方便,需要将汉语主动结构转为英语被动结构,将"他的死亡记录"充当句子主语,将"查到"译作 was found。

9)这句话没有被动含义,但为了便于上下文的衔接,需要将汉语主动结构转为英语被动,将"应邀赴宴去"译作 have been asked out for the banquet。

10)这是一个不带被动标签的被动结构,翻译成英语时应转换为被动语态,将"不准离开"译作 were prohibited from leaving。

11)这是一个带有被动标签的被动结构,翻译成英语时可直接译作被动语态,将"为……所激励"译作 are prompted/stimulated by...。

12)这是一个带有被动标签的被动结构,翻译成英语时可直接译作被动语态,将"被……吸引住"译作 was attracted by...。

第九单元 翻译中的正反调换

1. 英译汉参考译文

1)迟做总比不做好。

2)我对你真是感激不尽。

3)油保护金属不生锈。

4)你马上就能学会。

5)他表现出心不在焉的样子。

6)一着不慎,满盘皆输。

7)这台机床有点毛病。

8)杀虫剂应放在孩子够不到的地方。

9)作者的论点事实根据不足。

10）张先生不善于与同伴相处。

11）你把望远镜调节到适合你的目光之后，你才看得见。

12）盲人只有受到和正常人一样的待遇，才能认识到自己所蕴藏的力量。

解析：

1）保持原文的否定结构，将英语这一谚语用意译表达出其完整的意思。

2）这句话看似否定，实为强烈的肯定语气。将 can't thank you enough 译作"感激不尽"。

3）正说反译，将 preserve metal from rust（保护金属免于生锈）译作"保护金属不生锈"。

4）反说正译，将 learn in no time at all（要不了多少时间）译作"马上就能学会"。

5）正说反译，将 an absent-minded manner（缺乏注意力的样子）译作"心不在焉的样子"。

6）正说反译，将 One careless move（粗心的走棋）译作"一着不慎"。

7）反说正译，将 does not function properly（运转不正常）译作"有点毛病"。

8）正说反译，将 out of the child's reach（孩子范围之外）译作"够不到的地方"。reach *n.* 伸出，伸展的限度，可达到的距离。

9）正说反译，将 ill grounded in facts（糟糕的事实根据）译作"事实根据不足"。ground *vt.* 作为根据；作为基础；如：His arguments are well grounded. 他的说法有充足的根据。

10）正说反译，将 bad at getting along with his fellows（与同伴相处很差）译作"不善于与同伴相处"。get along with 友好相处，和睦相处。

11）否定转换，将 you didn't do this to win an election 和 you didn't do it for me 分别译作"你们这样做并不只是为了赢得大选"和"不是为了我这样做"。

12）反说正译，将 never know...until（直到……之前不知道）译作"只有……，才能认识到"。

2. 汉译英参考译文

1) It's been a mild winter this year.
2) He had never been to the town before.
3) The bill is too big to pay.
4) I did not know that he was hospitalized until yesterday.
5) Make haste, or (else) you'll be late.
6) The child doesn't live up to what his father expects of him.
7) Let's face the facts instead of evading them.
8) To our surprise, he's failed in the exam.
9) The circumstances forced him to accept the plan.
10) He never goes out without losing his umbrella.
11) Unless he studies hard, he will never pass the examination.
12) Except for the howl of the north wind, all was still in the snow-mantled ground.

解析：

1）反说正译，将"冬天不冷"译作 a mild winter，不宜照字面译作 the winter is not cold。

2）正说反译，将"很陌生"译作 had never been，也可译作 He was new to the town，不宜照字面译作 very strange，因为 strange 往往是"奇怪"的意思。

3）反说正译，将"太大，付不起"译作 too big to pay，不宜照字面译作 can not afford。

4）正说反译，将"直到……才知道……"译作 did not know...until...。"住院"也可译作 be in hospital。hospitalize *vt.* 把……送入医院治疗，使入院；如：He hospitalizes patients for minor ailments. 他把生小病的患者也送进医院。

5）反说正译，将"要不然就来不及了"译作 or (else)   you'll be late。

6）正说反译，将"辜负了"译作 doesn't live up to...。live up to 真正做到,

无愧于；如：We will live up to what our parents expect of us. 我们绝不辜负父母对我们的期望。

7）反说正译，将"不要逃避"译作 instead of evading them。evade *vt*. 逃避，躲避；漏（税）；如：evade one's duties 逃避职责；evade income taxes 偷漏所得税。

8）反说正译，将"不及格"译作 failed in the exam。令人惊奇的是 to one's surprise。

9）反说正译，将"迫使他不得不接受"译作 forced him to accept，省略两个"不"字。

10）正说反译，将"每次出去总是会"译作 never goes out without losing，比译作肯定式 always/often lose 更准确。

11）保持原文的否定结构，将"如果不"译作 Unless，"永远不能"译作 Will never。

12）反说正译，将"没有一点声响"译作 all was still。the snow-mantled ground 覆盖着白雪的大地；mantle *vt*. 覆盖；如：Snow mantled the trees. 冰雪覆盖了树木。except for 除了，除……外。

第十单元　翻译的标准与直译、意译问题

1. 以"忠实"、"通顺"为标准指出下列各句翻译中的失误，并加以改正

参考译文：

1）我知道他不是在开玩笑。

2）贵公司必须赔偿任何损失。

3）再聪明的人也难免会犯错误。

4）对现代科学的价值无论如何重视也不过分。

5）总统换了一届又一届，但半个多世纪以来，女王还是同一个女王。

6）八九年前，北京城还是一片饱受工业污染之地。

7）事实上，所有的（奥运）建设项目都正在提前竣工。

8）人们曾在这座都城的辖区里砍伐树木，为兴建钢铁厂腾出地方。

9）在经过7年的努力，投入400亿美元的场馆建设资金之后，中国在许多方面取得了显著的成绩。

10）（奥运期间）将有55万海外游客涌入这座1 500多万人口的城市，而中国的准备时间只剩16个月了。

11）不难看出这两位带有传奇色彩的人物——世界上最有权者和最有钱者——为什么没有成为密友。因为两个比尔禀性大不一样，他们分别代表了战后生育高峰首尾两端出生的这一代人。

12）然而，基本问题在哪里都一样。布莱克先生回想起一位中国老相识教给他的一句中国谚语："富不过三代"。

解析：

1）英语的 business 除了"商业、买卖、交易、生意、营业、商行"等意思之外，还有"严肃的工作或努力"之意，如：get right down to business 开始干正事，言归正传。此处的 mean business 意思是：是当真的，不是随便说说的，故译作"不是在开玩笑"。

2）英语短语 make good 有好几个意思。a. 成功地实施，如：He made good his escape. 他成功地逃脱了。b. 实现：She made good her promise. 她实现了诺言。c. 补偿；弥补：made good the loss 弥补损失。此处的 make good any loss 也就是 c 的含义，故译作"赔偿任何损失"。

3）It be + *adj.* + *noun* + that... 是古英语流传下来的一种特殊句型，不可照字面直译，而应当理解为"再……的……也难免会……"。如：It is a good workman that never blunders. 再好的工匠也难免会出错（智者千虑，必有一失）。It's a good horse that never stumbles. 好马也有失蹄时。故此处译作"再聪明的人也难免会犯错误"。

4）cannot...too 也很容易按字面误译成"不能太……"，而实际上这种表达法是一种"负负为正"的肯定式，其含义是"怎么……也不过分"。（参见第九单元的双重否定）如：The importance of this conference cannot be overestimated. 这次会议的重要性无论怎么强调也不过分。You cannot be too careful in proofreading. 这句话的含义是"校对时，你怎么仔细也不过分",也就是越仔细越好。

5）此处的 come and go 指的是总统不断更迭,不宜照字面译作"来来去去",意译为"总统换了一届又一届"; has always been 一直总是,为了表达通顺,可译作"还是同一个女王"。

6）Less than a decade ago 不到10年前,也即是"八九年前"; an industrial wasteland 一个饱受工业污染之地; wasteland 遭到毁坏之土地,不宜译作"废墟",可译作"饱受工业污染之地"。

7）run ahead of schedule 参见第二单元关于 run 的译例 16）表示工作等"进行、进展"。"走在了时间表的前面"不通顺,故此处译作"所有的建设项目都正在提前竣工"。

8）此处的 room 不是"房间、屋子、寓所"的意思,而是"地盘、空间,被占用或可被占用的地方",如:That easy chair takes up too much room. 那张安乐椅占用太多的空间。make room for steel plants 为建立钢厂腾地方。

9）Seven years and $40 billion later 译作"7年和400亿美元后"固然没错,但不符合汉语的表达习惯,需要用增词法解释清楚,故译作"在经过7年的努力,投入400亿美元的场馆建设资金之后"。

10）这句话太长,为了表达通顺,可以用两句话分别表达出两层意思:(奥运期间)将有55万海外游客涌入,而中国的准备时间只剩16个月了。

11）翻译这句话有三处须加小心: larger-than-life figures 带有传奇色彩的人物; fast friends 忠实的朋友; the two ends of the baby-boom generation 战后生育高峰始末出生的这代人(克林顿生于1946年,盖茨生于1955年)。

12）英语成语 rice paddy to rice paddy in three generations 的意思是:三代时间足够泥腿子来,泥腿子去。此处可意译为汉语谚语"富不过三代";英语类似的成语还有 from rags to riches and back again in three generations; shirtsleeves to shirt sleeves in three generations。

225

2. 英译汉。用直译或意译翻译以下各句

1）众口难调。

2）每秒钟都很重要。

3）狐狸藏不住尾巴。

4）协议总归是协议。／达成的协议决不可撕毁。

5）饥不择食。

6）他有钱却无修养。

7）捷足先登。／疾足者先得。

8）他已不名一文。

9）她看出了他的心思。

10）他一心扑在工作上。

11）我们决定以牙还牙。

12）这个计划妙就妙在简明扼要。

解析：

1）此句采用的是意译。直译：没有任何一道菜能适合所有的口味。文字啰唆，费解，所以意译为汉语成语"众口难调"。

2）此句采用的是直译。count *vi.* 值得考虑；有重要性，如：His opinions don't count. 他的意见不值得考虑。

3）此句采用的是直译。注意省略冠词 A、代词 its。

4）直译：协议总归是协议。意译：达成的协议决不可撕毁。前一种译法保持了原文的简略含蓄口吻；后一种译出了原文的潜在的言外之意。

5）此句采用的是意译。字面直译：饥饿是最好的调料。搭配不当，听起来怪怪的，所以意译为汉语成语"饥不择食"。

6）此句采用的是意译。字面直译：他得到的钱比得到的情趣多。未能反映出原文的真实内涵，因此意译为：他有钱却无修养。

7）此句采用的是意译。early bird 早起者，早到者；字面直译：早飞的鸟能捕到虫子。根据不同语境亦可采用此译。

8）此句采用的是意译。ruin *vt.* 使破产；如：I was ruined by that law case. 我被那场官司搞得倾家荡产。a ruined man 破产的人，也即是"不名一文"。

9) 此句采用的是意译。read *vt.* 看透；确定……的意图或情绪，如：I can read your mind like a book. 我可以像读书一样清楚地看到你的心理活动。

10) 此句采用的是意译。marry *vt.* 紧密地结合，如：His material marries the domestic and the exotic. 他的素材将本土特色和异国情调结合得浑然一体。此句的字面意思是"他紧密地与工作结合"，意译为"他一心扑在工作上"。

11) 此句采用的是意译。return a blow 还击一拳，为了便于表达，此处将 blow for blow "以拳对付拳"转换成汉语成语"以牙还牙"。

12) 此句大致是采用直译。beauty *n.* 美；一种最有效的、令人满意品质或特点，如：The beauty of the venture is that we stand to lose nothing. 这一商业投机妙就妙在我们不会遭受任何损失。

第十一单元 专有名词的翻译问题

1. 翻译下列各句，注意专有名词的译法

参考译文：

1) 喉结

2) 致命伤，致命弱点

3)《太阳照常升起》(小说、电影)

4)《魂断蓝桥》(电影)

5)《呼啸山庄》(小说)

6)《汤姆叔叔的小屋》或《黑人吁天录》(小说)

7)《烈火金刚》(小说)

8) 联合国安全理事会

9) 世界卫生组织

10) 国际货币基金组织

11) 麻省理工学院(美国)

12）国家航空航天局（美国）

解析：

1）Adam's apple 源于宗教故事（《圣经》故事人物亚当偷吃伊甸园的禁果，被上帝发现，将苹果卡在喉以示惩罚）。

2）Achilles 阿喀琉斯，或译阿基里斯，《荷马史诗》中的英雄，传说出生后被其母亲握脚踵倒提着在冥河水中浸过，因此除去未浸泡到水的脚踵外，全身刀枪不入。

3）*The Sun Also Rises*，美国作家海明威（Ernest Hemingway, 1899—1961）小说，1957 年改编为同名电影。此处为采用意译，译作《太阳照样升起》。

4）Waterloo 滑铁卢，比利时城镇，1815 年拿破仑军队战败处；[喻] 惨败。电影 *Waterloo Bridge* 采用意译的手段译作《魂断蓝桥》。

5）*Wuthering Heights*，英国勃朗特三姊妹之一艾米丽（Emily Brontë, 1818—1848）的名著，直译为《呼啸山庄》。

6）*Uncle Tom's Cabin*，美国女作家 Harriet B. Stowe 于1852年发表的小说，直译为《汤姆叔叔的小屋》，意译为《黑人吁天录》。

7）*Steel Meets Fire*，根据作家刘流的小说《烈火金刚》改编的同名影片的英译名。此处为采用意译。

8）United Nations Security Council，通常缩写为 UNSC（安理会）。

9）World Health Organization，通常缩写为 WHO，注意不要与代词 who 相混淆。

10）International Monetary Fund，通常缩写为 IMF。

11）Massachusetts 马萨诸塞：美国东北部的州，简称"麻省"。麻省理工学院通常缩写为 MIT。

12）National Aeronautics and Space Administration，通常缩写为 NASA。administration *n.* 管理，经营，行政部门；（总统、内阁等的）任期；如：Energy Research and Development Administration 能源勘探和发展局；the Bush Administration 布什政府。

附 录
各单元翻译练习参考译文及解析

2. 汉译英参考译文

1) Time is very precious.
2) He is short-sighted.
3) She is looking into the mirror.
4) I have contacted my lawyer.
5) We are strongly opposed to the war.
6) He knows more English than I do.
7) Let's drink to our success.
8) Cold weather affected the crops.
9) That was a tragedy.
10) The boy/girl does not do well in his/her studies.
11) We have acquired a lot of knowledge at school.
12) Over-drinking may injure your health.

解析：

1）valuable 贵重的，重大的，具有可观的用来使用或交换价值的，如：a valuable diamond 贵重的宝石；valuable information 重大的消息；precious 宝贵的，珍贵的，如：precious words 珍贵的话；precious stones 宝石；因此"时间宝贵"用 precious 而不用 valuable。

2）按英语的逻辑思维，"近视"的是人而不是"眼睛"，所以翻译这句话需要用"人"作主语，译作：He is short-sighted. 如果说"他视力不好"，可译作 His eyesight is very poor.

3）"照镜子"的译法是 look into the mirror，look at the mirror 是指"朝镜子看"，介词 at 表示方向。

4）contact 为及物动词，后面应当直接跟名词，如：She contacted me as soon as she arrived. 她一到就和我联系了。注意不要与名词相混淆；contact 作名词时，往往与 with 搭配，如：She comes into contact with many people. 她和许多人有联系。

5）英语可以用来表示"反对"的词语有好几个，如：oppose, against,

229

fight，combat 等，词性及用法各不相同。Fight 和 combat 为及物动词，后面直接跟宾语就行了；against 为介词，需要与动词搭配使用，如：be against, struggle against 等；oppose *vt*. 反对，反抗，对抗；如：Many members of the council opposed the building of the luxury houses in the centre of the city. 许多市议会议员反对在市中心建造豪华型住宅。用于表达观点态度时用 be opposed to sth.，如：My mother is opposed to the new plan. 妈妈反对这个新计划。

6）英语中的 level 的意思是"水平面，级别，层面，层次，程度"等含义，如：the local level of government 地方一级政府；studying at the graduate level 研究生阶段的学习；The garden is arranged on two levels. 花园分两层。因此"英语水平"不宜译作 English level，而是意译为：He knows more English than I do（他英语比我懂得多）。

7）英语"为……干杯"为 drink to... 而不是 drink for...；受汉语影响，往往一看见"为"就联想到 for，其实，英语表达"为了……目的"往往用介词 to，如：a toast to the Queen 为女王而干杯；go out to lunch 出去吃午饭。

8）influence 通常指"通过说服、举例等对行动、思想、性格等产生不易觉察到的、潜移默化的影响"；affect 指"产生的影响之大足以引起反应"，有时含有"对……产生不利影响"的意思。

9）从英语的思维角度，汉语"不幸的悲剧"这一说法表达欠妥：不言而喻，悲剧自然是不幸的，难道还有幸运的悲剧吗？因此应当省略"不幸的"三个字。

10）英语中可用来表达"学习成绩"的词语很多，如：marks, scores, grade, result, achievement 等。此处为泛指，而不是具体的某次考试成绩，所以用 not do well in one's studies。

11）按照英语的思维，"知识"可以"获得"、可以"积累"，但不可"学习"；可以学习的对象应当是具体的学科、专业，如：study math, learn English；所以"学知识"应当译作 acquire/obtain knowledge。

12）此处的"身体"是"身体健康"（health）的省略说法，不可译作 body。

body *n*. 身体，肉体，躯干。这句话的实际意思是：过度饮酒会损害你的健康。所以意译为：Over-drinking may injure your health.

第十二单元　谨防"假朋友"的陷阱

1. 翻译下列各句，注意不要"望文生义"

参考译文：

1）他的拒绝是不可更改的。
2）不要揭他的伤疤。
3）他是最不配干这份工作的人。
4）这对夫妇总是吵吵闹闹。
5）我希望你早日恢复健康。
6）她告诉我说，她有过一段痛苦挣扎的经历。
7）怀特先生最终不得不改口收回前言。
8）我觉得她有几件不可告人的丑事。
9）即使在危难时刻，他也勇于承担后果。
10）无论他们怎样威胁，这孩子都不肯服输。
11）物价直线上升，这样下去，我们都快要揭不开锅了。
12）托马斯不仅是一名裸体自然迷，而且也是日益风行的背包客大军中的一员。

解析：

1）此处的 final 为"不可更改地、决定性地"之意；如：His judgment is final. 他的判决是不可更改的。
2）英语的 home truth 的意思是"使人不愉快的真情实况，逆耳的忠言"；所以不可照字面译作"家里的真实情况"，此处意译为"不要揭他的伤疤"。
3）一见到 last，我们自然而然就将它与"最后的"、"最近的"、"上一次"等意思画上等号，殊不知在某些情况下，last 一词具有"极少可能的"或"最不适合的"之意（特别是与不定式搭配时）。这里面有一个词义的嬗变过程：世界上所有的人或物都轮遍了，最后才轮到某人或某物。而按常理，这种情况是不大可能的，所以也就是"绝不会"。请看下面各例：

● He is the last man to consult. 他根本不值得请教。

● He is the last man to accept a bribe. 他绝不会受贿。

● He should be the last man to blame. 怎么也不应该责备他。

● Bikini was the last thing she'd like to wear. 她最不喜欢穿比基尼泳装。

● He would be the last man to do such foolish things. 他绝不会干这种蠢事。

● This is the last place where I expected to meet you. 怎么也没想到我会在这个地方见到你。

● Money is the last thing he wants, and you won't succeed by offering it. 他绝不想要你的钱，你给他钱也白搭。

4）cat-and-dog 吵吵闹闹的，不和的；不可照字面译作"猫和狗"，而是"不和睦的，吵闹的"。

5）in the pink 即是 in the pink of condition 的省略，即"非常健康"，与"穿上粉红衣服"无关。

6）英语成语 in deep water 的意思是指一个人处于困境，而不是落入深水。

7）英语成语 eat one's own words 的意思是"改口，收回前言"。"自食其言"的相应英语是 break one's promise 或 break one's word。

8）英语成语 skeleton in the cupboard (skeleton in the family closet) 的意思是"家丑，见不得人的事"，故此处译作"不可告人的丑事"。

9）成语 face the music 的意思是"临危不惧，勇于承担后果，尤其是自己行动的结果"，与"欣赏音乐"无关。

10）英语俚语 say uncle 的意思是"认输，服输"，而不是"叫叔叔"。

11）英语成语 keep the pot boiling 的意思是"挣钱糊口，维持生活"，与"锅里的水"无关。

12）此处的 nut 为英语俚语，其意思是"狂热者，迷"，如 a true baseball nut 一个十足的棒球迷；成语 in one's birthday suit 和 in one's birthday clothes 一样，意思是"赤身裸体，一丝不挂"。

2. 翻译下列各句，注意句子的歧义

参考译文：

1）这是一个很长的故事。／这是一条很长的尾巴。

2）放下胳膊。／放下武器。

3）他在桌上切肉。／他切桌上的肉。

4）我了解他甚于了解你。／我比你了解他。

5）主席安排他坐下。／他坐在主席的旁边。

6）开飞机是危险的。／正在飞行的飞机是危险的。

7）为了取悦母亲，她没去跳舞。／她去跳舞并不是为了取悦母亲。

8）那个犯罪的律师自杀了。／那个刑法律师自杀了。

9）时光像箭一样飞逝，水果像香蕉一样飞逝。／果蝇喜欢香蕉。

10）他们今天为你祈祷，明天就会加害于你。

11）我们必须团结在一起，否则我们将被分别绞死。

12）玛丽喜欢前天刚买的那个壁橱里的花瓶。／玛丽喜欢壁橱里的花瓶，那是她前天刚买的。

解析：

1）语音歧义，tale（故事）和 tail（尾巴）读音相同，所以有两种不同的解读。

2）词汇歧义，arms 既可理解为"胳膊"，又可以指"武器"，而 put down（放下）可以与两种意义搭配，由此产生了双关歧义。

3）语法歧义，on the table 既可修饰主语 He（他在桌上），又可修饰宾语 the meat（桌上的肉），由此产生了语法歧义。

4）语法歧义，代词 you 既可作宾语（我了解你），又可作主语 than you (know him)（比你更了解他），由此产生了语法歧义。

5）语法歧义，介词 by 既可理解为接受施动的"被"，又可理解为"靠在……旁"，由此产生了语法歧义。

6）语法歧义，Flying 既可作动名词"开（飞机）"，又可作现在分词"飞行的"，由此产生了语法歧义。

233

7）语法歧义，将 to please her mother 视为目的状语，因此译作"为了取悦母亲"；将这句话理解为"否定转移"（参见第九单元"否定的陷阱"中对否定转移的讲解），亦可译作"她去跳舞并不是为了取悦母亲"，由此产生了语法歧义。

8）词汇歧义，The criminal lawyer 既可理解为"犯罪的律师"，又可理解为"刑法律师"，由此产生了词汇歧义。

9）词汇歧义，前面的 flies like 意为"像……一样飞"，后面的 fruit flies like 既可理解为"水果飞"，也可理解为"果蝇"，like 既可以作介词"像"，也可以作动词"喜欢"，由此产生荒诞的双关歧义。

10）语音歧义，pray（祈祷）和 prey（捕食），发音相同，外形相似，搭配不同的介词，由此产生语音歧义。

11）词汇歧义，前面的 hang together 意为"团结一致"，后面的 hang 意为"绞死"，由此产生了双关歧义。

12）语法歧义，which she had bought 既可以指"壁橱"，又可理解为"花瓶"，由此产生了语法歧义。

第十三单元　翻译能力的培养与提高

1. 英译汉参考译文

A

盗贼需要一点亮光来辨识四周，于是轻步穿过房间，去点亮罩着浅绿色灯罩的灯。

解析：

此句可根据 light 的不同词性来辨别词义。根据不同的语境，light 可以作名词"光，日光，发光体，灯"等，如：You're standing in his light. 你挡住了他的光线。Turn out the lights when you leave. 你离开时把灯灭掉。也可作形容词"轻的，发光的，明亮的，浅的"等，如：light industry 轻工业，as light as a feather 轻如鸿毛；light hair and skin 浅色头发和皮肤；还可作动词"点燃，照亮"等，如：

Fireworks lit the sky. 焰火照亮了夜空。Green wood does not light easily. 新木材不容易点着。A smile lit her face. 微笑使她的脸变得容光焕发。有时候 light 还可以作副词，"轻轻地、轻便地"，如：traveling light 轻装旅行。

这一练习中的 light 的不同含义：Needing some light 需要一点亮光；with a light step 以轻快的步伐；to light the light 点亮这盏灯；with the light green shade 有浅绿色灯罩。

B

布朗先生是个非常正直的人。那天，他脸上颇有病容。近来他一直情绪低落。我见到他时他正在默默沉思。希望他能早日恢复健康。

解析：

此处几个有关颜色的词 white, green, blue, brown, pink 显然都不能根据字面来理解原文。不少同学大致也能猜出原文的意思，但要准确翻译，就必须弄清英汉语言文化在色彩表达上的情感差异。英语中的 white 为"清白、善良、诚实可靠"之意，如：a white spirit 纯洁的心灵；green 意为"脸色难看的，脸色呈病态或不健康的苍白色"；blue 则有"忧郁的、沮丧的"的意思，如：feel blue 感到无精打采，give sb. the blues 使某人情绪低落；而两个短语 in a brown study 和 in the pink 的含义分别是"沉思默想"和"非常健康"之意。如：He is sitting there in brown study. 他坐在那里沉思。Mr. Smith is in the pink of health. 史密斯先生身体极棒。有了这样一些知识，翻译起来便会心中有数了。

2. 汉译英参考译文

1) I can bear hardships.
2) This tree doesn't bear fruit.
3) That house collapsed.
4) She always goes to bed very late/stays up deep into the night.
5) The boss doesn't agree to let him go.
6) This broken computer is useless.
7) Please don't litter.
8) The nurse took my temperature.

9) Welcome to Beijing International Hotel.
10) He is to blame for the accident.
11) This model of car sells well in China.
12) A："Thank you very much." B："It's my pleasure."

解析：

1）此处的"不怕"不是担心害怕之意，而是指承受得住，所以译作 I can bear hardships. 类似的情况如：这种布不怕晒。This cloth can stand the exposure to the sun. 这种手表不怕水。This kind of watch is waterproof.

2）此处的"不长果实"不是"不生长"，而是"不结果实"，所以不用 grow 而用 bear，如：什么样的树结什么样的果。Different trees bear different fruits.

3）英语中的 collapse 意为"倒塌、崩溃"，本身就具有"倒下来、全塌"的意思，所以 completely 和 down 为多余的冗词，应当去掉。如：这座老房子的顶坍了。The roof of the old house collapsed.

4）英语表示"睡得很晚"的词语是 stay up，如：She stayed up till twelve o'clock last night. 她昨晚12点才睡觉。sleep late 的意思是"睡过头，睡懒觉"。

5）英语的 agree 为不及物动词，通常搭配为 agree with sb., agree to sth., agree to do sth.，所以"不同意他离开"应当译作 don't agree to let him go，而不是 don't agree him to leave。

6）英语表示"没有用"的词语是 useless，如：This is a useless knife—the handle has broken. 这是一把没用的小刀,刀把坏了。no use 没益处，没好处，如：There's no use in discussing it. 多说无益。

7）这句话不宜照字面逐词逐字地翻译。英语中的 litter 本身就有"随意弃置果皮纸屑等垃圾"的意思，所以完全可以采用省略法，译作 Please don't litter 就行了。

8）注意使用正确的搭配。英语表示"量体温"的正确说法是 take temperature 而不是 measure temperature，measure 表示"测量,确定大小、尺寸、容量"，如：measure the height of the ceiling 测量了天

花板的高度。

9) 中文中经常会出现"欢迎某人做某事"的句子，按中文语序翻译这样的句子，往往会出现中式英文。Welcome 作动词时有两种形式可用：动词＋宾语，或动词＋宾语＋副词短语。习惯上可以译为 welcome somebody to somewhere，或 welcome to a place。显然上述译法不符合这个英文词的通常表达习惯。所以应译为：Welcome to International Hotel.

10) 汉语的"受责"为被动：受到谴责／责备；而英语则用主动，表示"受责"的词语是 be to blame，如：The children were not to blame. 孩子们不应受到责备。The driver was not to blame for the traffic accident. 那次交通事故不应该责怪司机。

11) 按逻辑思维，"车卖得很好"应当译作被动语态，因为车不能自己卖，只能"被卖"，但英语的 sell 作不及物动词时，其意思为"被出售，销售"，如：an item that sells well 销路很好的商品；Grapes are selling high this season. 在这个季节葡萄卖得很贵。所以此处应译为 This model of car sells well in China.

12) 在受到表扬或感谢时，中国人往往比较谦虚，会说："这没什么。""这是我应该做的。"或者，"哪里，哪里，我还做得很差。"如果直译为 It is nothing. This is my duty. This is what I should do. Well, I have not done very well. There is still much to be improved. 等，外国人听起来会感到非常做作。西方人通常会说：It's my pleasure. 所以翻译这类对待他人的表扬和感谢时，应尽量遵守英语的表达习惯。

第十四单元 《大学英语教学指南》与四、六级翻译考试

单句翻译练习 120 句

练习 1

1. 考点分析

本题的考点是定语从句"有朝一日"（the day will come when）和被动语

态"由……供热"（be heated from...）。

参考译文：The day will come when homes will be heated from a small reactor in the basement.

2. 考点分析

   本题的考点是词类转换，"特别强调"（lay special stress on）和动宾搭配"提高产品质量"（raise the quality of the products）。

   参考译文：In his speech he laid special stress on raising the quality of the products.

3. 本题的考点是时间状语从句，"正准备……就"（just when...）和动宾搭配"度假"（take a holiday）、"出毛病"(broke down)。

   参考译文：The car broke down just when we were starting our holidays/we were about to take a holiday.

4. 考点分析

   本题的考点是让步状语从句"尽管……还是"（even though）和固定搭配"几乎……一样"（as good as）。

   参考译文：My car is as good as new, even though I've had it over a year/even though it has been used over a year.

5. 考点分析

   本题的考点是遣词用字"整个情况"（the whole story），用省略技巧翻译"原原本本，一字不差"（exactly as it had happened）。

   参考译文：He told his teacher the whole story exactly as it had happened.

6. 考点分析

   本题的考点是"不管是……还是……"（whether... or...）以及被动语态"由……组成"（be made up of...）。

   参考译文：All living things, whether they are animals or plants, are made up of cells.

7. 考点分析

   本题的考点是将汉语无主句转换成英语形式主语"能不能"（Is it possible to...），以及固定搭配"提前"（ahead of time）、动宾结构"完成计划"（carry

附 录
各单元翻译练习参考译文及解析

out the plan)。

参考译文：Is it possible to carry out the plan ahead of time?

8. 考点分析

本题的考点是结构调整，将"深感失望"（a keen disappointment）前置，以及短语"推迟原定的计划"（postpone the original plan）。

参考译文：It was a keen disappointment that I had to postpone the original plan.

9. 考点分析

本题的考点是虚拟语气"万一"（Should there be/In case that there is）和动宾结构"切断电源"（switch off the electricity）。

参考译文：Should there be (In case that there is) an urgent situation, press the red button to switch off the electricity.

10. 考点分析

本题的考点是被动语态"据估计"（It is estimated that...）和定语从句"面临严重缺水的国家"（countries that face serious water shortage）。

参考译文：It is estimated that by 2025, two-thirds of the world's population may be living in countries that face serious water shortage.

练习 2

1. 本题的考点是固定搭配"理所当然"（take it for granted），以及宾语从句"你会来跟他谈这件事"（that you will come and talk the matter over with him）。

   参考译文：I take it for granted that you will come and talk the matter over with him.

2. 本题的考点是主语从句"他告诉我的话"（what he told me），以及比较状语的表达"他比我懂的英语多"（he knows more English than I do）。

   参考译文：From what he told me I know that he knows more English than I do.

3. 本题的考点是条件状语"无论如何"（No matter how...）和短语"最后"（at

last)。

参考译文：No matter how hard he tried, he failed at last.

4. 本题的考点是正反转换"心不在焉"（absence of mind），以及动宾结构"造成交通事故"（cause an accident）。

参考译文：His absence of mind during the driving nearly caused an accident.

5. 本题的考点是不定式作目的状语"以便让听众听到"（so as to be heard），以及动宾结构"提高声音"（raise one's voice）。

参考译文：The speaker raised his voice so as to be heard.

6. 本题的考点是被动语态"推迟到明天"（be put off till tomorrow），以及原因状语"因为雨太大"（because of the heavy rain）。

参考译文：I'm very sorry to say, because of the heavy rain, the visit to the museum has to be put off till tomorrow.

7. 本题的考点是虚拟语气"要是你昨天来了，你就会"（Had you come yesterday, you could... ）。

参考译文：Had you come yesterday, you could have seen him here.

8. 本题的考点是主语从句"他此行所见所闻"（Whatever he saw and heard on his trip），以及词语"留下深刻印象"（give /leave a deep impression）。

参考译文：Whatever he saw and heard on his trip gave (left) him a very deep impression.

9. 本题的考点是固定搭配"借助"（With the help of... ）和宾语补足语"看到集成电路被分离和被测试"（watch the integrated circuits being separated and tested ）。

参考译文：With the help of a microscope you can watch the integrated circuits being separated and tested.

10. 本题的考点是被动语态"石油将会用尽"（oil will be exhausted... ）和定语"从原子分裂获得的"（obtained from the splitting of the atom ）。

参考译文：The oil in the world will be exhausted someday, and man will be using the more convenient power obtained from the splitting of the atom.

附 录
各单元翻译练习参考译文及解析

练习 3

1. 考点分析

   本题的考点是条件状语从句"如果某物具有"（If something has），以及词语"适应环境的能力"（the ability to adjust itself to the environment）。

   参考译文：If something has the ability to adjust itself to the environment, we say it has intelligence.

2. 考点分析

   本题的考点是虚拟语气，"要不是……，我本来是不……"（If I had not..., I would not...）以及短语"亲眼看见"（see with one's own eyes）。

   参考译文：If I had not seen it with my own eyes, I would not have believed it.

3. 考点分析

   本题的考点是定语从句，"引起公众对此事注意的文章"（an article that will attract public attention）。

   参考译文：He wishes to write an article that will attract public attention to the matter.

4. 考点分析

   本题的考点是词语"第四大死因"（the fourth leading cause of death），以及固定搭配"使……丧失"（deprive...of...）。

   参考译文：AIDS is the fourth leading cause of death in the whole world; it deprives many families of their parents and children.

5. 考点分析

   本题的考点是词语"决心坚决执行计划"（be determined to carry out their plan），以及条件状语"不论将面临什么样的障碍"（no matter what obstacles they would have to face）。

   参考译文：They were determined to carry out their plan no matter what obstacles they would have to face.

6. 考点分析

   本题的考点是条件状语"如果……，也会"（If..., may also result in...），

以及定语从句"不含有任何有害物质（的食物）"（a diet which contains nothing harmful...）。

参考译文：If certain important elements are missing, a diet which contains nothing harmful may also result in serious disease.

7. 考点分析

   本题的考点是完成时态"中国现在已经进入"（China has now reached），以及词语"改革开放"（reforming and opening to the outside world）、"关键阶段"（a critical stage）。

   参考译文：After 30 years' reforming and opening to the outside world, China has now reached a critical stage in its modernization drive.

8. 考点分析

   本题的考点是目的状语"以便能够"（so that it may...），以及词语"每秒大约五英里的速度"（a speed of about five miles per second）、"送入轨道"（put in orbit）。

   参考译文：A rocket must attain a speed of about five miles per second so that it may put a satellite in orbit.

9. 考点分析

   本题的考点是条件状语从句"除非它受到……支持"（unless it is supported by...），以及词语"地球上的任何物体"（any object above the earth）、"大小与其重量相等的力"（an upward force equal to its weight）。

   参考译文：Any object above the earth will fall unless it is supported by an upward force equal to its weight.

10. 考点分析

    本题的考点是让步状语从句，"即使是……，也没有希望"（Even... offer no hope that...），以及词语"最精确的实验"（the most precisely conducted experiments）、"无任何误差的实验结果"（result without any error）。

    参考译文：Even the most precisely conducted experiments offer no hope that the result can be obtained without any error.

练习 4

1. 考点分析

   本题的考点是 It 作形式主语,"真奇怪"(It is strange that...),以及正反转换"没有看出"(fail to see)。

   参考译文:It is strange that she should have failed to see her own shortcomings.

2. 考点分析

   本题的考点是正反转换"他还没来得及阻拦"(before he could stop me),以及过去完成时"我已经跑出"(I had rushed out of)。

   参考译文:I had rushed out of the classroom before he could stop me.

3. 考点分析

   本题的考点是固定搭配,"将……归功于"(owe... to...),以及词语"老师的鼓励"(teacher's encouragement)。

   参考译文:The young writer owed his success to his teacher's encouragement.

4. 考点分析

   本题的考点是条件状语从句"如果……就……",以及词语"仔细比较"(make a careful comparison)、"不同之处"(the difference)。

   参考译文:If you make a careful comparison you will find the difference between them.

5. 考点分析

   本题的考点是"不论用什么方法"(whichever way),以及词语的顺序调整:"得到的结果都相同"(get the same result)。

   参考译文:He got the same result whichever way he did the experiment.

6. 考点分析

   本题的考点是省略,"他也提前完成了交给他的工作"(and so has he),以及词语"经提前完成"(fulfill ahead of schedule)。

   参考译文:I have fulfilled my assigned work ahead of schedule, and so has he.

7. 考点分析

   本题的考点是比较级"越是难,越不可能……"(the more difficult...the less likely...)。

参考译文：The more difficult the questions are, the less likely I am able to answer them.

8. 考点分析

   本题的考点是正在进行时"都在寻找"（are looking for...），以及不定式作定语"净化空气、防止空气污染的有效方法"（the efficient methods to make the air clean and protect it from pollution）。

   参考译文：Scientists everywhere in the world are looking for the efficient methods to make the air clean and protect it from pollution.

9. 考点分析

   本题的考点是被动语态"圆满地解决"（was solved successfully），以及非限制定语从句"这说明计算很准确"（which showed that the computations were accurate）。

   参考译文：Nevertheless the problem was solved successfully, which showed that the computations were accurate.

10. 考点分析

    本题的考点是结构调整，"全世界讲英语、用英语的人为数最多"（the English language is the most widespread international language in the world），以及词语"由于……原因"（for... reasons）。

    参考译文：The English language is the most widespread international language in the world for historical, political, and economic reasons.

练习 5

1. 考点分析

   本题的考点是被动语态，"不管是否加热"（whether (it is) heated or not），以及词语"不溶于"（does not dissolve）。

   参考译文：The substance does not dissolve in water whether (it is) heated or not.

2. 考点分析

   本题的考点是"不仅……，而且……"（Not only..., but...），以及词语"收费过高"（charge too much/overcharge）、"修得也不好"（didn't do a good repair job）。

参考译文：Not only did he charge me too much/did he overcharge me, but he didn't do a good repair job either.

3. 考点分析

   本题的考点是比较对象，"与我的相比"（compared with mine/in comparison with mine），以及词语"生意上的损失"（losses in trade）。

   参考译文：Your losses in trade this year are nothing compared with mine/in comparison with mine.

4. 考点分析

   本题的考点是 it 作形式主语的结构调整，"很重要"（it is very important to...），以及词语"遵守安全规则"（comply with/follow the safety regulations）。

   参考译文：The workmen think it is very important to comply with/follow the safety regulations.

5. 考点分析

   本题的考点是固定搭配，"把孩子的成功归因于"（to attribute/owe their children's success to），以及词语"相反"（by contrast）、"更可能"（more likely）。

   参考译文：By contrast, American mother were more likely to attribute/owe their children's success to natural talent.

6. 考点分析

   本题的考点是虚拟语气，"最要紧的是"（It was essential that...），以及词语"月底前"（before the end of the month）、"签订合同"（sign the contract）。

   参考译文：It was essential that we (should) sign the contract before the end of the month.

7. 考点分析

   本题的考点是固定搭配，"令我们高兴的是"（to our delight），以及词语"适应"（adapt oneself to）。

参考译文：To our delight, she adapted (herself) to the campus life a month after entering the university.

8. 考点分析

    本题的考点是被动语态，"被指责"（be accused of），以及词语"未兑现承诺"（failure to fulfill its promise）、"降低失业率"（reduce the unemployment）。

    参考译文：The new governor was accused of failure to fulfill its promise to reduce the unemployment.

9. 考点分析

    本题的考点是比较级，"所花费只及……一半的钱"（spend only half as much... as...），以及词语"据说"（it is said）、"平均"（on average）。

    参考译文：On average, it is said, visitors spend only half as much (money) in a day in Leeds as in London.

10. 考点分析

    本题的考点是固定搭配，"刚……就……"（no sooner had... than...），以及词语"抱怨"（complain）、"不运转"（stop working）。

    参考译文：The customer complained that no sooner had he tried to use the machine than it stopped working.

练习 6

1. 考点分析

    本题的考点是 it 作形式主语，"适应不同文化中的生活很不容易"（it is not easy to adapt oneself to life/living in different cultures），以及词语"事跨文化研究"（intercultural studies）。

    参考译文：Specialists in intercultural studies say that it is not easy to adapt oneself to life/living in different cultures.

2. 考点分析

    本题的考点是比较级，"没有什么比读书对我更有吸引力"（nothing is more attractive to me than reading），以及词语"童年时代"（childhood）。

    参考译文：Since my childhood I have found that nothing is more attractive to me than reading.

3. 考点分析

   本题的考点是虚拟语气，"要是……，本来有机会活下来"（would have a chance of survival if he had been taken…），以及词语"及时送到医院"（be taken to hospital in time）。

   参考译文：The victim would have a chance to survive/would have a chance of survival if he had been taken to hospital in time.

4. 考点分析

   本题的考点是宾语从句，"一些心理学家声称"（Some psychologists claim that...），以及词语"在外时"（when they are far from home）、"感到孤独"（feel lonely）。

   参考译文：Some psychologists claim that people might feel lonely when they are far from home/ are not in their hometown/traveling.

5. 考点分析

   本题的考点是固定搭配，"以……的速度"（at a speed/rate of），以及词语"继续增长"（continue to rise）。

   参考译文：The nation's population continues to rise at a speed/rate of 12 million per year/at an annual speed of 12 million.

6. 考点分析

   本题的考点是正反转换，"未能考虑在内"（fail to take into account），以及词语"睡眠质量"（sleep quality）。

   参考译文：The finding of this study failed to take people's sleep quality into account.

7. 考点分析

   本题的考点是定语从句，"我们可以合作的领域"（the field in which we can cooperate），以及词语"预防和治疗"（prevention and treatment）。

   参考译文：Prevention and treatment of AIDS is the field in which we can cooperate/ the field (where) we may cooperate.

8. 考点分析

本题的考点是原因状语,"由于腿受伤"(because of the leg injury),以及词语"退出比赛"(to quit the match)。

参考译文:Because of the leg injury, the athlete decided to quit the match.

9. 考点分析

   本题的考点为不定式目的状语,"如要捐赠,或想了解更多的信息"(to make donations or for more information),以及词语"以下地址"(the following address)。

   参考译文:To make donations or for more information, please contact us at the following address.

10. 考点分析

    本题的考点是表语从句,"我注意到的一个变化是"(one change I notice is that...),以及词语"60多岁"(in one's sixties)、"更容易累"(get tired more easily)。

    参考译文:In my sixties, one change I notice is that I feel/get tired more easily than before.

练习 7

1. 考点分析

   本题的考点是习惯用语"你最好……"(You'd better...),以及词语"以防"(in case)、"天气变冷"(it gets colder)。

   参考译文:You'd better take a sweater with you get colder in case it gets colder.

2. 考点分析

   本题的考点是"受到训练"(have received training),以及词语"自己创业"(start one's own business)。

   参考译文:Through the project, many people have received training and decided to start their own business.

3. 考点分析

   本题的考点是表语从句,"之前一直不"(not... until),以及词语"抗病毒剂"(anti-virus agent)、"偶然发现"(discover accidentally/by chance)。

参考译文：The anti-virus agent was not known until a doctor discovered it accidentally/by chance.

4. 考点分析

    本题的考点是虚拟语气，"要是你听从……，你就不会……"（If you had followed..., you would not have been...），以及词语"陷入麻烦"（put oneself in trouble）。

    参考译文：If you had followed my advice/suggestion, you would not have been/put yourself in trouble.

5. 考点分析

    本题的考点是被动语态用作宾语补足语，"看着她受伤的儿子被送进"（watch her injured son being sent into...），以及词语"满面泪水"（with tears on her face）、"手术室"（the surgery/operating room）。

    参考译文：With tears on her face, the lady watched her injured son being sent into the surgery/operating room.

6. 考点分析

    本题的考点是被动语态，"被劝告暂时不要"（be suggested/advised not to go...），以及词语"恐怖袭击"（the terrorist attack）。

    参考译文：After the terrorist attack, tourists were (have been) suggested/advised not to go to that country/not to choose that country as their destination.

7. 考点分析

    本题的考点是"喜欢……而不是……"（prefer to...instead of...），以及词语"通过"（via/with/through）、"与顾客交流"（communicate with customers）。

    参考译文：I prefer to communicate with my customers via/with/through email instead of telephone.

8. 考点分析

    本题的考点是强调句，"直到……他才感到……"（It was not until...did he...），以及词语"截止日"（the deadline）、"申请表"（application form）。

    参考译文：It was not until the deadline did he send out his application form.

9. 考点分析

本题的考点是倒装句，"只有在……他才……"（Only in... does he feel...），以及词语"安全和放松"（secure and relaxed）。

参考译文：Only in the small town does he feel secure and relaxed.

10. 考点分析

本题的考点是宾语补足语，"发现它们正在竞争"（find themselves competing with...），以及词语"汽车生产厂家"（auto manufacturers）、"市场的份额"（market share）。

参考译文：The auto manufacturers found themselves competing with foreign companies/firms for market share.

练习 8

1. 考点分析

   本题的考点是主语从句，"这绝对不公平"（It is absolutely unfair that...），以及词语"被剥夺"（be denied/deprive of）、"受教育的权利"（the right to receive education）。

   参考译文：It is absolutely unfair that these children are deprived of the right to receive education/ are denied the right to receive education.

2. 考点分析

   本题的考点是固定搭配"更别提"（let alone/not to mention/not to speak of...），以及词语"白费"（in vain）、"花费的大量金钱"（the large sum of money we have spent）。

   参考译文：Our years of hard work are all in vain, let alone/not to mention/ not to speak of the large sum of money we have spent.

3. 考点分析

   本题的考点是"受到相当大的关注"（have received/got great attention from...），以及词语"最近几十年"（in recent decades）。

   参考译文：The problems of blacks and women have received/got great attention from the public in recent decades.

4. 考点分析

本题的考点是虚拟语气，"要不是……，我们的通信就不可能……"（But for...our communication would not have been...），以及词语"移动电话"（mobile phone）、"如此迅速和方便"（so rapid and convenient）。

参考译文：But for mobile phones our communication would not have been so rapid and convenient.

5. 考点分析

   本题的考点是比较级，"没有什么比幽默感更有帮助"（nothing is more helpful than humor），以及词语"对付尴尬局面"（handle an embarrassing situation）。

   参考译文：In handling an embarrassing situation, nothing is more helpful than humor/a sense of humor.

6. 考点分析

   本题的考点是适当省略，"拒绝进一步解释这样做的原因"（refuse to make further explanation），以及词语"外交部长"（the Foreign Minister）、"辞职"（resign）。

   参考译文：The Foreign Minister said he was to resign his post, but (he) refused to make further explanation/to explain further.

7. 考点分析

   本题的考点是并列衔接，"动物的行为"（while animal behavior...），以及词语"知识的产物"（a production of learning）、"依靠本能"（depends /on their instincts）。

   参考译文：Human behavior is mostly a production of learning, while animal behavior depends mainly upon/on their instincts.

8. 考点分析

   本题的考点是被动语态，"被告知"（be told that...），以及词语"目击者"（the witness）、"对法庭说谎"（to lie to the court）。

   参考译文：The witness was told that under no circumstances should he lie to the court/is he allowed to lie to the court.

9. 考点分析

本题的考点是虚拟语气，"准是……，否则……"（couldn't have..., otherwise, ...should have... ），以及词语"收信"（receive a letter）、"回信"（reply to）。

参考译文：Mary couldn't have received my letter, otherwise, she should have replied to me last week.

10. 考点分析

本题的考点是定语从句，"毕生致力于诗歌的人"（those who have devoted their whole lives to poems），以及词语的适当省略："热情洋溢"（passionate）、"性格冲动、举止独特"（impulsive and unique）。

参考译文：We can say a lot of things about those who have devoted their whole lives to poems/who have spent their whole lives on poems. They are passionate, impulsive and unique.

练习9

1. 考点分析

   本题的考点是被动语态，此处的"估计"表达的是"应该，被期望"（be supposed to），以及词语"至少"（at least）、"化学实验"（chemistry experiment）。

   参考译文：Nancy is supposed to have finished her chemistry experiment at least two weeks ago.

2. 考点分析

   本题的考点是结构调整：从未相互争吵过一次（never once has they quarreled），以及词语"结婚"（be/get married）、"老两口"（the old couple）。

   参考译文：Never once has the old couple quarreled with each other since they were married 40 years ago.

3. 考点分析

   本题的考点是固定搭配，"有赖于"（depend on），以及词语"未来的繁荣"（the future prosperity）、"很大程度上"（to a great extent）、"教育的质量"（the quality of education）。

参考译文：To a great extent, the future prosperity of a nation depends on the quality of education of its people.

4. 考点分析

   本题的考点是非限制性定语从句，"吊桥，把……结合起来"（the suspension bridge, which combined...with...），以及词语"完美与功能"（beauty and function）、"完美结合"（perfect combination）。

   参考译文：He designed the first suspension bridge, which combined beauty with function perfectly/made a perfect combination of beauty and function.

5. 考点分析

   本题的考点是不定式作宾语，"知道该走哪条路"（know which way to take），以及词语"本能地"（instinctively/by instinct）。

   参考译文：It was very dark, but Mary seemed to know which way to take instinctively/by instinct.

6. 考点分析

   本题的考点是否定的转移，"我认为……是不明智的"（I don't think it advisable that...），以及词语"剥夺"（deprive of）、"课余时间的自由"（freedom to spend the spare time）。

   参考译文：I don't think it advisable that parents should deprive children of their freedom to spend their spare time as they wish.

7. 考点分析

   本题的考点是比较级，"与不那么活跃的人相比"（compared with less active people），以及词语"日常活动频率高"（have a high level of daily activities）、"精力更充沛"（have more energy）、死亡率（death rate）。

   参考译文：Older adults who have a high level of daily activities have more energy and a lower death rate compared with less active people.

8. 考点分析

   本题的考点是方式状语，"通过证明……，你的简历会……"（Your resume should...by demonstrating...），以及词语"特定职位的最佳人选"（the best one for a certain job）、"将来老板"（a would-be boss）。

参考译文：Your resume should attract a would-be boss's attention by demonstrating why you are the best one for a certain job.

9. 考点分析

    本题的考点是虚拟语气，"看起来没有浇水"（look as if they hadn't been watered），以及状语"好长时间了"（for a long time）。

    参考译文：Those flowers looked as if they hadn't been watered for a long time.

10. 考点分析

    本题的考点是比较级，"比我的便宜 1 000 英镑"（£1,000 cheaper than mine）。

    参考译文：Fred bought a car last week. It is £1,000 cheaper than mine.

练习 10

1. 考点分析

    本题的考点是固定搭配"不妨"（might as well...），以及词语"太乏味"（be quite boring / dull）。

    参考译文：This TV program is quite boring. We might as well listen to the music.

2. 考点分析

    本题的考点是伴随状况，"灯亮着，门开着"（with lights on and doors open），以及词语"慌忙"（in a hurry）。

    参考译文：He left his office in a hurry, with lights on and doors open.

3. 考点分析

    本题的考点是被动语态，"据说"（is said）、"已经被译成……"（to have been translated into...），以及词语"多种语言"（multiple languages）。

    参考译文：The famous novel is said to have been translated into multiple languages.

4. 考点分析

    本题的考点是"完全值……价"（be well worth...），"不打折扣"（without

a discount)。

参考译文：I think that the meal is well worth $80 without a discount.

5. 考点分析

   本题的考点是正在进行时，"正考虑推出促销活动"（is considering launching a promotion campaign），以及词语"面对激烈竞争"（facing fierce competition）。

   参考译文：Facing fierce competition from other companies, the automobile manufacturer is considering launching a promotion campaign.

6. 考点分析

   本题的考点是否定结构"没有什么共同之处"（have nothing in common），以及词语"至于"（as far as... be concerned）。

   参考译文：As far as hobbies are concerned, Jane and her sister have almost nothing in common.

7. 考点分析

   本题的考点是倒转结构，"只是……我才……"（Only after...have I...），以及词语"仅凭运气"（by mere luck）。

   参考译文：Only after many failures have I realized that I cannot succeed by mere luck.

8. 考点分析

   本题的考点是虚拟语气，"要不是……，那么……"（But for..., would have been...），以及词语"生存的本能"（the survival instinct）、"灭绝"（extinct）。

   参考译文：But for the survival instinct which nearly all creatures have, more species would have been extinct from the Earth.

9. 考点分析

   本题的考点是"不取决于……，而是……"（not determined by..., but rather...），以及词语"品行"（character）、"经受失败"（endure defeat）。

   参考译文：A person's character isn't determined by how he or she enjoys victory, but rather how he or she endures defeat.

10. 考点分析

    本题的考点是不定式作定语，"任何企图任何劝她留下来的企图"（any

attempts to persuade her to stay），以及词语"受到侮辱"（be insulted）、"徒劳的"（be of no avail/be in vain）。

参考译文：She felt insulted, and obviously any attempts to persuade her to stay were of no avail.

练习 11

1. 考点分析

   本题的考点是条件状语，"无论……都要……"（no matter what...），以及词语"做出牺牲"（make sacrifice）、"追求事业"（pursue the course）。

   参考译文：I am going to pursue this course, no matter what sacrifice I shall make/whatever sacrifice I will make.

2. 考点分析

   本题的考点是比较状语，"喜欢……而不喜欢……"（would prefer...to...），以及词语"网上购物"（shopping on line）、"省时"（time saving）。

   参考译文：I would prefer shopping on line to shopping in a department store because the former is more convenient and time saving.

3. 考点分析

   本题的考点是主语从句，"大多数父母所关心的是"（What most parents are concerned about is...），以及词语"为……提供"（providing for）、"最好的教育"（the best education possible）。

   参考译文：What most parents are concerned about is providing the best education possible for their children.

4. 考点分析

   本题的考点是条件状语，"如果……，那么……"、被动语态"研究的结果能应用于"（the results of the research can be applied to），以及词语"新技术的开发"（the development of new technology）、"努力将不会白费"（efforts will pay）。

   参考译文：Our efforts will pay if the results of the research can be applied to the development of new technology.

5. 考点分析

   本题的考点是结构调整，"出了毛病"（Something is wrong with...），以及词语"打不开计算机"（can't boot the computer）、"操作系统"（the operating system）。

   参考译文：I can't boot my computer now. Something must have been wrong with its operating system.

6. 考点分析

   本题的考点是条件状语，"无论是……，即便……也"（no matter what..., even for...），以及词语"艰难的改变"（a difficult change）、"盼望退休的人"（those who look forward to retiring）。

   参考译文：Leaving one's job, no matter what job it is/whatever job it is, is a difficult change, even for those who look forward to retiring.

7. 考点分析

   本题的考点是比较级，"与……相比，……更……，更……"（Compared with/In comparison with...is more...），以及词语"我成长的地方"（the place where I grew up）、"繁荣、令人兴奋"（prosperous and exciting）。

   参考译文：Compared with/In comparison with the place where I grew up, this town is more prosperous and exciting.

8. 考点分析

   本题的考点是固定搭配，"直到……才……"（Not until... did...），以及词语"完成使命"（finish the mission）、"得了重病"（be seriously ill）。

   参考译文：Not until he had finished the mission did he realize that he was seriously ill.

9. 考点分析

   本题的考点是宾语从句，"痛苦地意识到……"（be painfully aware that...），以及词语"医疗研究人员"（medical researchers）、"至今"（so far/up to now）。

   参考译文：Medical researchers are painfully aware that there are many problems to which they have no answers so far/up to now.

10. 考点分析

本题的考点是被动语态,"是用……来衡量的"(be measured by...),以及词语"靠贷款生活"(live on credit)、"能够借到多少"(how much they can borrow)。

参考译文:Many Americans live on credit, and their quality of life is measured by how much they can borrow, not how much they can earn.

练习 12

1. 考点分析

本题的考点是让步状语,"不管中国……,它不会……"(No matter China...it will not...),以及词语"构成威胁"(constitute threat)。

参考译文:No matter how strong China becomes it will constitute no threat to any other country.

2. 考点分析

本题的考点是虚拟语气,"如果他知道……,也许会……"(If he had know..., he would have...),以及词语"以不同方式行事"(act differently)。

参考译文:If he had know this would happen, he would have acted differently.

3. 考点分析

本题的考点是宾语从句,"我想说的是……"(I would say that...),以及词语"从字里行间看"(reading between the lines)、"更担心"(be more worried that)。

参考译文:Reading between the lines, I would say that the government is more worried that they will admit.

4. 考点分析

本题的考点是伴随状语,"随着他的生意红红火火,他……"(with his business booming, he...),以及词语"慈善事业"(charity)、"捐了一大笔钱"(donates a large sum of money)。

参考译文:In recent years, with his business booming, he has donated a large sum of money to charity.

5. 考点分析

本题的考点是被动语态,"被指控"(be accused of...),以及词语"血液中酒精含量高"(a high blood alcohol level)、"面临严厉的处罚"(face a severe penalty)。

参考译文:Anyone driving with a high blood alcohol level will be accused of drunk driving and face a severe penalty.

6. 考点分析

本题的考点是结果状语,"如此沉迷于……,以至于……"(so addicted to...that...),以及词语"网上购物"(online shopping)、"情不自禁要访问"(can't help themselves visiting)。

参考译文:Many people have become so addicted to online shopping that they can't help themselves visiting shopping websites every day.

7. 考点分析

本题的考点是主语从句,"你说的话有分量"(what you said weighs a lot),以及词语"执行委员会成员"(an executive council member)。

参考译文:You are an executive council member of our organization, so what you said weighs a lot /what you said matters.

8. 考点分析

本题的考点是不定式作目的状语,"要充分理解作者的动机和意图"(To fully appreciate the author's motive and intention),以及词语"真的必须"(really have to...)。

参考译文:To fully appreciate the author's motive and intention, you really have to understand/read carefully between the lines.

9. 考点分析

本题的考点是"不那么多地取决于……,而是取决于……"(not depend so much on... but on...),以及词语"学习成绩"(one's school records)、"勤奋和坚持"(diligence and persistence)。

参考译文:Success in life does not depend so much on one's school records but on diligence and persistence.

10. 考点分析

本题的考点是虚拟语气,"没有大气层,我们将被迫……"(Without the atmosphere we would be forced to...),以及词语"躲避太阳的藏身处"(a burrow to avoid the sun)、"保护免受伤害"(protect from...)、"致命光线"(deadly rays)。

参考译文:Without the atmosphere we would be forced to look for a burrow to avoid the sun, as there would be nothing else to protect us from its deadly rays.

段落翻译练习 30 篇

1. 中国

重点词语注释:

1. 世界上最大国家之一 one of the largest countries in the world
2. 和整个欧洲的面积差不多相等 about the size of the whole of Europe
3. 广大的领土 the vast country of ours
4. 广大的肥田沃地 large areas of fertile land
5. 给我们以衣食之源 provide us with food and clothing
6. 纵横全国的大小山脉 mountain ranges across its length
7. 广大的森林 extensive forests
8. 丰富的矿产 rich mineral deposits
9. 舟楫和灌溉之利 water transport and irrigation
10. 很长的海岸线 long coastline
11. 交通海外各民族的方便 facilitate communication with nations beyond the seas
12. 从很早的古代起 from ancient times
13. 中华民族的祖先 our forefathers/ancestors
14. 劳动、生息、繁殖 labor, live and multiply

参考译文:

1. China

China is one of the largest countries in the world, her territory being about the size of the whole of Europe. In the vast country of ours there are large areas of fertile land which provide us with food and clothing, mountain ranges across its length and breadth with extensive forests and rich mineral deposits, many rivers and lakes which provide us with water transport and irrigation, and a long coastline which facilitates communication with nations beyond the seas. From ancient times our forefathers have laboured, lived and multiplied on this vast territory.

2. 中国国土

重点词语注释：

1. 国土 land, territory
2. 陆地国土面积 land area
3. 仅次于 second only to/closely behind
4. 居世界第三位 rank the 3rd in the world
5. 海洋国土 sea area
6. 自治区 autonomous region
7. 直辖市 municipalities directly under the central government
8. 特别行政区 special administrative region
9. 国土辽阔 vast territory
10. 资源丰富 abundant resources
11. 江山多娇 numerous scenery beauties
12. 文明古国 countries with ancient civilization
13. 光辉灿烂的东方文化 glorious oriental culture

参考译文：

2. China's Territory

China's land area is 9,600,000km^2, ranking the 3rd in the world closely behind Russia and Canada. It also has a sea area of 3,000,000km^2.

At present, China has 23 provinces, 5 autonomous regions, 4 municipalities directly under the central government and 2 special administrative regions, with

Beijing as its capital.

As one of the four great countries with ancient civilization, China has vast territory, abundant resources and numerous scenery beauties. Chinese people have created glorious oriental culture on this vast land.

3. 中华民族

重点词语注释：

1. 人口密集 dense population
2. 疆域辽阔 vast territory
3. 以……而著称 be noted/famous for
4. 多民族的国家 a multinational country
5. 汉族 the Han Nationality
6. 主体民族 the majority
7. 约占 account for about
8. 分布 distribute
9. 少数民族 ethnic minority/minority ethnic group
10. 相对（居住）分散 dwell extensively
11. 与众不同的特点 distinctive character
12. 独特的风俗习惯 unique convention
13. 长久以来一直 have long been doing
14. 提倡 advocate/promote
15. 平等、团结的民族关系 an equal and united ethnic relationship
16. 强调 highlight/emphasize
17. 共同发展、共同繁荣 mutual development and prosperity

参考译文：

3. Chinese Nation

China is famous for its dense population and vast territory. As a multinational country, China is home to 56 ethnic groups with a total population of about 1.4 billion. The Han Nationality is the majority, accounting for about

92% of the total population which distributes mainly in the east and middle of China; while the ethnic minorities dwell extensively all over China distributing mainly in the southwest, the northwest and the northeast. Each of the minority ethnic groups has a distinctive character, long traditional culture and unique conventions. Chinese government has long been advocating and developing an equal and united ethnic relationship, highlighting the mutual development and prosperity of all ethnic groups.

4. 中国文化
重点词语注释：

1. 很受欣赏 be very much admired
2. 瓷器 porcelain
3. 此外 in addition
4. 备受欢迎 enjoy great popularity
5. 在一定程度上 to some extent/to a certain extent
6. 改变生活方式 transform way of life
7. 20世纪后期 the late 20th century
8. 再次转向中国文化 turn again to Chinese culture
9. 除了……外 apart from
10. 中国菜肴 Chinese cuisine
11. 尝试中国医药 try Chinese medicine
12. 练习中国武术 practice Chinese martial arts
13. 功夫电影 Chinese Kongfu movies

参考译文：

4. Chinese Culture

In the 17 and 18 centuries, Chinese art, architecture and philosophy were very much admired in the West. In addition, Chinese silk, tea and porcelain enjoyed great popularity there, and to a certain extent they transformed many people's way of life in the West. Since the late 20th century, people of the West have turned again to Chinese culture. Apart from their love of Chinese cuisine, they are learning the Chinese language, trying Chinese medicine, practicing Chinese martial arts, and watching Kongfu movies.

5. 龙的传说

重点词语注释：

1. 自古以来 since ancient times
2. 崇拜 worship
3. 神异动物 deified animal
4. 民间传说 folklore
5. 现代社会 contemporary society
6. 多种动物的综合体 a combination of many animals
7. 具有多种动物的特长 possess many animals' special skills
8. 现实中并不存在的动物 a nonexistent animal in reality
9. 不可替代的位置 irreplaceable position
10. 封建社会 feudal society
11. 权利和帝王的象征 the symbol of power and emperor
12. 吉祥物 mascot
13. 腾飞 take off
14. 开拓精神 pioneering spirit
15. 龙的形象 the image of dragon

参考译文：

5. The Legend about Dragon

Dragon has been a deified animal worshipped by Chinese people since ancient times. In the Chinese folklore dragon is a combination of many animals, which possesses those animals' special skills. Chinese dragon is a nonexistent animal in reality, but it has an irreplaceable position in the hearts of Chinese people. In the past, it had long been regarded by the ancient Chinese people as a god who could control the nature. In feudal society, dragon was the symbol of power and emperor. In contemporary society, the dragon has become a mascot, which signifies taking off, success, pioneering spirit and creation. Thus, the image of dragon can be seen everywhere in everyday life of Chinese people.

6. 中国的气候

重点词语注释：

1. 气温差别较大 a big gap between the temperatures
2. 千里冰封、万里雪飘的一片银装素裹的洁白世界 the land is all covered with snow and ice（适当省略）
3. 冒着严寒参观"冰灯游园会" visit ice lantern parks in severe coldness
4. 百花盛开，春意盎然 a blossoming spring（适当省略）
5. 全国大部分地区 the majority of the country
6. 炎热 high temperature
7. 降水较多 heavy precipitation
8. 雨热同季 high temperature and heavy precipitation in the same season（适当增添）
9. 极大好处 benefit a lot
10. 地区分布不均匀 unevenly distributed across the country
11. 东南沿海 the southeast coast
12. 西北内陆 northwest inland
13. 逐渐减少 decrease gradually

参考译文：

6. China's Climate

There is a big gap between the temperatures of north and south China in winter. In north China, the land is all covered with snow and ice in winter. When people in Harbin, a city in north China, visit ice lantern parks in severe coldness, Guangzhou, a southern city, is enjoying a blossoming spring.

In summer, the majority of the country experiences high temperature and heavy precipitation. With high temperature and heavy precipitation in the same season, agriculture benefits a lot. The precipitation is unevenly distributed across the country, decreasing gradually from the southeast coast to northwest inland.

7. 中国的经济

重点词语注释：

1. 实行改革开放的政策 adopt the Reform and Opening-up Policy
2. 持续快速的发展 fast and steady development
3. 经济总量 economic aggregate
4. 位居世界第二 the second largest in the world
5. 预计 it is estimated that
6. 到 21 世纪中叶 by the middle of the 21st century
7. 基本上实现现代化 basically achieve modernization
8. 中等发达国家的水平 the standard of the moderately developed countries
9. 地区差异 regional difference
10. 比较发达 relatively more prosperous
11. 水平较高 higher level of
12. 交通运输业和通信设施 transportation and communication facilities
13. 相对落后 comparatively lag behind
14. 从长远来看 from a long-term point of view
15. 资源丰富 rich resources
16. 有发展广阔空间 have larger space to develop

参考译文：

7. China's Economy

Since China adopted the Reform and Opening-up Policy in 1978, its economy has experienced fast and steady development. At present its economic aggregate is the second largest in the world. It is estimated that by the middle of the 21st century, China will basically achieve modernization, reaching the standard of the moderately developed countries.

Regional difference in China's economic development is considerably large. Coastal area in the east is relatively more prosperous, having a higher level of economy and technological development, and a better foundation of industry, agriculture, transportation and communication facilities. The western area comparatively lags behind. But from a long-term point of view, the western area has larger space to develop its industry and agriculture, thanks to rich resources in this area.

8. 中国的铁路
重点词语注释：

1. 重要的运输方式 a vital transportation mode
2. 铁路营业里程 track in use
3. 居世界第二位 rank the second in the world
4. 铁路干线 trunk railway
5. 可以分为 can be classified into
6. 南北干线 south-north lines
7. 交叉或衔接 crisscross or join each other
8. 重要的铁路枢纽 important hubs
9. 青藏铁路 the Qinghai-Tibet Railway
10. 经格尔木 via Golmud
11. 西藏拉萨 Lhasa in Tibet
12. 海拔最高的铁路 the highest railway
13. 开通运营 put into use
14. 交通运输的落后面貌 backward transportation
15. 质的改善 a fundamental change
16. 可持续发展 sustainable development
17. 提供保证 guarantee

参考译文：

8. Railways in China

Railways provide a vital transportation mode in China. By the end of 2012, there were 98,000 km of track in use. The length ranks the second in the world.

China's trunk railway lines can be classified into two groups, namely south-north lines and east-west ones. There are many important hubs where south-north and east-west lines crisscross or join each other.

The 1,956-km Qinghai-Tibet Railway, from Xining in Qinghai Province to Lhasa in Tibet via Golmud, is the highest railway in the world. On July 1, 2006, this railway was put into use. The successful Qinghai-Tibet Railway marks a fundamental change of Tibet's backward transportation and guarantees a sustainable development of Tibet's economy in the future.

9. 翻译的作用

重点词语注释：

1. 人类历史发展的长河 the long history of human development
2. 多元文化 multiple cultures
3. 交流、融会与碰撞 communication, amalgamation, and collision
4. 中华民族伟大复兴的进程 the course of the national rejuvenation of the Chinese people
5. 起着不可或缺的作用 play an indispensable role
6. 国际活动 international activities
7. 语言文化交流 communications of languages and cultures
8. （交流活动）离不开翻译 be performed without translation
9. 假如这世界有一天没有了翻译 If there were not translation someday（虚拟语气）
10. 将不复存在 would not be able to operate any longer
11. 世贸组织 WTO (World Trade Organization)
12. 会瘫痪 would be at a standstill

13. 电线里流动的电流 the current in the electrical wires
14. 水管中流动的水流 the stream in the pipelines
15. 隔膜 lack of mutual understanding
16. 变成透明 clear up misunderstanding（清除误解）

参考译文：

9. The Function of Translation

Translation has always played an indispensable role in the long history of human development. It serves as the forerunner in communication, amalgamation, and collision of multiple cultures, as well as in the course of the national rejuvenation of the Chinese people. All international activities and communications of languages and cultures could not be performed without translation. If there were not translation someday, the United Nations would not be able to operate any longer, nor could WTO function well, and all the international organizations would be at a standstill. Translators and their efforts are just like that of the current in the electrical wires or the stream in the pipelines: they quietly bring one language and culture into another, clearing up misunderstanding.

10. 长城

重点词语注释：

1. 世界七大奇观 the seven wonders in the world
2. 修建时间最长 take the longest time to be built, repaired and extended（适当增添）
3. 工程量最大的军事性防御工程 the largest piece of military defensive engineering
4. 炎黄子孙 Chinese people（适当省略）
5. 血汗与智能的结晶 the crystallization of the blood, sweat and wisdom
6. 坚毅、勤奋的象征 a sign of their persistence and diligence
7. 宏大的气势和壮美的英姿 its incomparable grandeur（适当省略）
8. 享誉世界 worldwide known for

9. 吸引天下的游人 attract tourists from all over the world
10. 联合国（教科文组织）UNESCO（United Nations Educational, Scientific, and Cultural Organization）
11. 世界文化遗产 the world cultural heritage
12. 军事防御建筑 military defensive architecture
13. 最早大约出现于 date back to
14. 奠定规模和基础 take shape（成形）
15. 汉、南北朝、隋、唐、辽金、明、清等朝代 a number of dynasties such as Han, South and North, Sui, Tang, Liao, Jin, Ming and Qing
16. 都曾修筑过 contribute to the construction of

参考译文：

10. The Great Wall

The Great Wall is one of the seven wonders in the world. It is the largest piece of military defensive engineering in the world which took the longest time to be built, repaired and extended. The Great Wall stands for the crystallization of the blood, sweat and wisdom of Chinese people and also a sign of their persistence and diligence. It is known for its incomparable grandeur, attracting tourists from all over the world. UNESCO lists it as one of the world cultural heritage sites.

The Great Wall is a remarkable military defensive architecture in ancient China. Its genesis dates back to 700 BC to 500 BC. It was in the Qin Dynasty that the Great Wall really began to take shape. Since then, a number of dynasties such as Han, South and North, Sui, Tang, Liao, Jin, Ming and Qing, successively contributed to the construction of the Great Wall.

11. 长江

重点词语注释：

1. 青藏高原 Qinghai-Tibet Plateau
2. 世界第三长河 the third longest river in the world

附　录
各单元翻译练习参考译文及解析

3. 上游 the upper reaches
4. 落差大 big vertical drops
5. 水流急 torrents
6. 高山耸立的峡谷地段 gorges flanked by towering mountains
7. 中游的平原地区 the plain area in the middle reaches
8. 多曲流、多支流、多湖泊 characterized with many crooked streams, branches and lakes
9. 鱼米之乡 land of fish and rice
10. 入海口 estuary/the spot where the Yangtze enters the sea
11. 水天一色 the water and sky blend into a mixture
12. 极为壮观 a grand view of extraordinary splendor
13. 淡水湖 freshwater lake
14. 长江流域 the drainage area of the Yangtze River
15. 物产丰富 rich in products
16. 经济发达 the economy is well developed
17. 分布 distribute

参考译文：

11. The Yangtze River

The Yangtze River originates from the Qinghai-Tibet Plateau. With a length of more than 6,300 km, it is the longest river in China and the third longest river in the world.

The upper reaches of the Yangtze feature big vertical drops, with torrents and many gorges flanked by towering mountains. It gets to the plain area in the middle reaches of the river. Here the river broadens and the flow slows down. This part is characterized with many crooked streams, branches and lakes. Known as the famous land of fish and rice, the lower reaches of the Yangtze River are low and flat, and the water is broad and deep. At the spot where the Yangtze enters the sea, the river is 80 to 90 km wide, and the water and sky blend into a mixture, presenting a grand view of extraordinary splendour. Most freshwater lakes of China are scattered along the middle and lower reaches of the Yangtze.

The drainage area of the Yangtze River is rich in products and the economy is well developed. Many metropolises such as Shanghai, Nanjing, Wuhan and Chongqing are distributed along the river.

12. 黄河

重点词语注释：

1. 第二长河 the second longest river
2. 形状是一个巨大的"几"字 in the shape of huge Chinese character "几"
3. 峡谷 gorge
4. 水力资源丰富 with abundant water resources
5. 大型水电站 large-scale hydroelectric power stations
6. 黄土高原 the Loess Plateau
7. 水土流失严重 a serious problem of soil erosion
8. 泥沙含量大 contain large amount of sand
9. 浑浊 turbid
10. （呈黄色）而得名黄河 hence the name "the Yellow River"
11. 华北平原 the North China Plain
12. 河道宽阔 the river broadens
13. 水流变缓 the flow slows down
14. 泥沙大量沉积 the mud and sand accumulate
15. 河床比两岸高 the riverbed higher than the surrounding land
16. 形成"地上河" form a "suspending river"

参考译文：

12. The Yellow River

Originating from Qinghai Province, the Yellow River, the second longest river in China, is over 5,400 km. Seen from the map, the Yellow River lies in the shape of huge Chinese character "几".

Along the upper reaches of the river there are many gorges with abundant water resources, and large-scale hydroelectric power stations have been built there.

The middle reaches flow through the Loess Plateau, where there is a serious problem of soil erosion. This part of the river contains large amount of sand. The water there is turbid and shows the yellow colour, hence the name "the Yellow River".

The Yellow River flows through the North China Plain in its lower reaches, where the river broadens, the flow slows down, and the mud and sand accumulate to form a "suspending river", with the riverbed higher than the surrounding land.

13. 四大发明

重点词语注释：

1. 四大发明 four great inventions
2. 指南针 the compass
3. 火药 gun powder
4. 造纸术 paper-making technique
5. 印刷术 printing technique
6. 人类文明史 the history of human civilization
7. 占有重要地位 play an important role
8. 战国时期 the Warring States Period
9. 天然磁石 natural magnet
10. 辨别方向 identify/recognize directions
11. 简单仪器 simple device
12. 隋唐时期 Sui and Tang Dynasties
13. 主要应用于军事领域 mainly used in military sphere
14. 东汉年间 the Eastern Han Dynasty
15. 普遍使用的书写材料 a commonly used writing material

16. 活字印刷术 movable type printing

17. 文化的传播 the spread of culture

18. 做出巨大贡献 make tremendous contribution to

参考译文：

13. Four Great Inventions

Four great inventions of China include the compass, gun powder, the paper-making technique and the printing technique. They play an important role in the history of human civilization. The first compass was invented during the Warring States Period. It was a simple device employing natural magnets to identify directions. Gunpowder was invented in Sui and Tang Dynasties and was mainly used in military sphere. The paper-making technique was developed by Cai Lun in the Eastern Han Dynasty, making paper a commonly used writing material. The printing technique, also called movable type printing, promoted the spread of culture significantly. The four great inventions of China made tremendous contribution to the development of the world's economy and the progress of the culture of mankind.

14. 丝绸之路

重点词语注释：

1. 丝绸之路 the Silk Road

2. 贸易路线 trade route

3. 运输的商品 commodities transported

4. 占很大部分 comprise a large proportion of

5. 因……得名 get its name because...

6. 起点始于长安 start at Chang'an

7. 终点远达印度、罗马等国家 extend as far as countries like India and Rome

8. 从汉代开始形成 open up during the Han Dynasty

9. 唐代达到鼎盛 reach its peak in the Tang Dynasty

10. 主要交通工具 the major means of transportation

11. 传播到了西方 spread to the Western world
12. 佛教等宗教 religions like Buddhism
13. 引入 introduce
14. 连接 link/connect
15. 文化桥梁 a cultural bridge

参考译文：

14. The Silk Road

The Silk Road is the most well-known trade route in ancient China. It got its name because silk comprised a large proportion of commodities transported along this road. The Silk Road started at Chang'an and extended as far as countries like India and Rome. The Silk Road was opened up during the Han Dynasty and reached its peak in the Tang Dynasty, with camels being the major means of transportation. Great inventions in China, such as paper-making and printing were spread to the Western world along this road and religions like Buddhism were also introduced to China via the road. The Silk Road was not only an ancient international trade route, but also a cultural bridge linking Asia with Africa and Europe.

15. 青铜器

重点词语注释：

1. 青铜器时代 Bronze Age
2. 夏、商、西周 the Xia, the Shang and Western Zhou Dynasties
3. 春秋时期 the Spring and Autumn Period
4. 前后持续 last（适当省略）
5. 大量出土的青铜器物 large numbers of unearthed artifacts
6. 灿烂的青铜文明 a high level of ancient bronze civilization
7. 丰富的政治和宗教内涵 rich political and religious themes
8. 具有很高的艺术价值 of high artistic value
9. 中国历史博物馆 the Museum of Chinese History

10. 大盂鼎 the Great Ding for Yu

11. 代表性作品 representative example

12. 西周 Western Zhou Dynasty

13. 康王时期 the reign of King Kang

参考译文：

15. The Bronze Age

The Bronze Age in China lasted more than 1,500 years, from the Xia through the Shang and Western Zhou Dynasties, to the Spring and Autumn Period. Large numbers of unearthed artifacts indicate a high level of ancient bronze civilization in the country. They feature rich political and religious themes, and are of high artistic value. A representative example is the Great Ding for Yu, which is now preserved in the Museum of Chinese History. It was cast about 3,000 years ago during the reign of King Kang of Western Zhou Dynasty.

16. 孔子

重点词语注释：

1. 孔子 Confucius

2. 春秋时期 the Spring and Autumn Period

3. 儒家学派 Confucianism

4. 创始人 founder

5. 古代中国人心目中的圣人 sage to the ancient Chinese people

6. 言论和生平活动记录 words and life story（适当省略）

7. 弟子或再传弟子 disciples and their students

8. 编成 be recorded

9. 《论语》 The Analects

10. 中国古代文化 ancient Chinese culture

11. 经典著作 an enduring classic

12. 没有不受影响 influence all of...（反说正译）

13. 思想家、文学家和政治家 thinkers, writers and politicians

14. 不……就不能…… No one could...without...

15. 真正把握 truly understand

参考译文：

16. Confucius

As a great thinker, educator and founder of Confucianism during the Spring and Autumn Period, Confucius is a sage to the ancient Chinese people. His words and life story were recorded by his disciples and their students in *The Analects*. As an enduring classic of ancient Chinese culture, *The Analects* has influenced all thinkers, writers and politicians in the thousand years' Chinese history after Confucius. No scholar could truly understand this long-standing culture of the ancient Chinese without this book.

17. 辛亥革命

重点词语注释：

1. 爆发 break out

2. 资产阶级革命 bourgeois revolution

3. 辛亥革命 the Revolution of 1911

4. 推翻 overthrow

5. 中国封建社会 the Chinese feudal society

6. 清朝 the Qing Dynasty

7. 废除 abolish/do away with

8. 封建帝制 the monarch system

9. 民主共和国 democratic republic

10. 中华民国 the Republic of China

11. 剪掉 cut off

12. 辫子 pigtail/queue

13. 自己喜欢的发型 the haircut one likes

14. 辫子法令 the wearing-queue order

15. 被解除 be abolished

参考译文：

17. The Revolution of 1911

In 1911, the first bourgeois revolution in Chinese history—the Revolution of 1911 broke out. The last dynasty of the Chinese feudal society, the Qing Dynasty, was overthrown and the monarch system that had a history of more than 2,000 years was abolished. The Republic of China, the first democratic republic in China, was founded in 1912. After its foundation, the government of Republic of China required the citizens to cut off their queues and make the haircut they liked. Since then, the wearing-queue order that had lasted for more than 280 years in China has been abolished.

18. 北京

重点词语注释：

1. 政治、文化和科技教育的中心 the political, cultural, scientific and educational center
2. 交通和国际交往中心 the center of transportation and international exchange
3. 中华人民共和国成立 the founding of the People's Republic of China
4. 60 多年 60-odd years
5. 日新月异 change with each passing day
6. 发生巨大变化 great changes have taken place
7. 如雨后春笋般 like mushrooms/like bamboo shoots after a spring rain
8. 相继崛起 spring up（适当省略）
9. 科技力量强大 a strong potential in science and technology
10. 中国科学院 the Chinese Academy of Sciences
11. 世界著名科研机构 world famous scientific research organizations
12. 高等学府 institutions of higher learning
13. 同时 at the same time
14. 大力发展 make efforts to develop

15. 高新技术产业 hi-tech industries

16. 人才密集 a galaxy of talents

17. 中关村 Zhongguancun district

18. 被称为 known/reputed as

19. 硅谷 Silicon Valley

参考译文：

18. Beijing

Beijing, the capital of the People's Republic of China, is the political, cultural, scientific and educational center of the country, and also the center of transportation and international exchange.

In the 60-odd years after the founding of the People's Republic of China, great changes have taken place and the capital has developed quickly. Modern buildings spring up in Beijing like mushrooms.

Beijing has a strong potential in science and technology. It boasts a number of world famous scientific research organizations and institutions of higher learning such as the Chinese Academy of Sciences, Peking University and Tsinghua University, etc. At the same time, Beijing is making efforts to develop hi-tech industries. Its Zhongguancun district, known as China's Silicon Valley, has gathered a galaxy of talent.

19. 上海

重点词语注释：

1. 位于 located/situated
2. 长江入海口 the estuary of the Yangtze River
3. 历史文化名城 a famous city of history and culture
4. 旅游城市 tourist city/city of tourism
5. 经济中心 economic center
6. 最重要的工业基地 the most important industrial base
7. 贸易、金融和文化中心 a hub of trade, finance and culture

8. 交通四通八达 transport lines extending in all directions

9. 交通枢纽 the largest transportation hub

10. 沪宁铁路 Huning (Shanghai-Nanjing) railway

11. 沪杭铁路 Huhang (Shanghai-Hangzhou) railway

12. 起点 the starting point

13. 国际航空港 international aviation port

14. 发达的商业 advanced commerce

15. 特大型综合性贸易中心 super large comprehensive trading center

16. 国际经济、金融、贸易中心 international economic, financial and trading centers

参考译文：

19. Shanghai

Located on the estuary of the Yangtze River, Shanghai is not only the largest city in China but also a famous city of history, culture and tourism. It is the biggest economic center and the most important industrial base in China, a hub of trade, finance and culture as well.

Shanghai today has transport lines extending in all directions. It is the largest port in China, the largest transportation hub in East China, the starting point of Huning (Shanghai-Nanjing) and Huhang (Shanghai-Hangzhou) railways, an important aviation center of China, and one of the international aviation ports. With its advanced commerce, Shanghai is a super large comprehensive trading center of China, and one of the international economic, financial and trading centers.

20. 台湾岛

重点词语注释：

1. 第一大岛 the largest island

2. 大陆架 the continental shelf

3. 太平洋地区 the Pacific region

4. 作为交通枢纽 serve as the hub

5. 夏季炎热，雨量充沛 hot and rainy in summer（适当省略）
6. 盛产稻米 rich in rice
7. 经济作物 cash crop/industrial crop/commercial crop
8. 蔗糖 cane sugar
9. 水果王国 kingdom of fruits
10. 名贵木材 famous and precious wood
11. 四周是海 be encircled by seas
12. 渔业资源 fishing resources
13. 丰富的水力 abundant resources of waterpower
14. 经济发达 developed economy
15. 交通便利 convenient transportation
16. 美丽富饶 beautiful and richly endowed
17. 名胜古迹 scenic spots and historic sites
18. 阿里山 the Ali Mountains
19. 日月潭 Sun-Moon Lake
20. 乌来瀑布 Wulai Waterfall
21. 旅游胜地 tourist attraction（省略）

参考译文：

20. Taiwan Island

The largest island in China, Taiwan Island is situated on the continental shelf along the southeast coast of China. It serves as the hub connecting China and other countries in the Pacific region. Taiwan is warm in winter, and hot and rainy in summer. The island is rich in rice, and its major cash crops are cane sugar and tea. It is reputed to be the "kingdom of fruits". It also produces famous and precious wood. Since Taiwan Island is encircled by seas, it has rich fishing resources. It also has abundant resources of waterpower, forestry and fishery.

Taiwan has a developed economy and convenient transportation. It is a beautiful and richly endowed island. There are many scenic spots and historic sites, such as the Ali Mountains, Sun-Moon Lake, Wulai Waterfall, etc. Taiwan is indeed a "treasure island" of the motherland.

21. 杭州风光

重点词语注释：

1. 钱塘江北岸 the northern bank of Qiantang River
2. 大运河南端 the southern terminus of the Grand Canal
3. 古老的风景名城 ancient renowned city for its picturesque scenery
4. 蜿蜒曲折的 winding
5. 崇山峻岭 high mountain ridges
6. 江面开阔，景色壮丽 wide with majestic scenery（适当省略）
7. 中秋前后 round the Moon Festival
8. 钱塘江潮 the raging tidal billows
9. 怒涛奔腾，激流汹涌，蔚为天下大观 most spectacular natural phenomenon（适当省略）
10. 总面积 a total area of
11. 苏堤 Su causeway
12. 分成五个部分 fall into five sections
13. 外湖、里湖 Outer Lake, Inner Lake
14. 岳湖、西里湖 Yue Lake, West Inner Lake
15. 小南湖 Minor South Lake
16. 波光闪闪 glistening water
17. 茂林修竹 luxuriant trees and bamboo groves
18. 景色四季宜人 attractive landscape all the year round
19. 北宋 the Northern Song Dynasty (960—1127 AD)（适当增添）
20. 古代美女西施 ancient Chinese beauty named Xishi
21. 名扬四海 enjoy a high reputation in the whole country

附　录
各单元翻译练习参考译文及解析

参考译文：

21. Scenic Hangzhou

Hangzhou, an ancient renowned city for its picturesque scenery, is situated in northern part of Zhejiang Province, along the northern bank of Qiantang River and at the southern terminus of the Grand Canal. After winding through high mountain ridges of the western part of Zhejiang, Qiantang River becomes wider with majestic scenery. Especially round the Moon Festival every year, one can enjoy the raging tidal billows, which are a most spectacular natural phenomenon.

Lying in the west part of the city, the charming West Lake covers a total area of 5.6 square km. Divided by Su causeway and Bai causeway, the whole lake falls into five sections: Outer Lake, Inner Lake, Yue Lake, West Inner Lake and Minor South Lake. With glistening water and luxuriant trees and bamboo groves along its bank, the West Lake has attractive landscape all the year round. Su Dongpo, a celebrated poet of the Northern Song Dynasty (960—1127 AD), once in a poem compared the Lake to an ancient Chinese beauty named Xishi. Since then the West Lake has enjoyed a high reputation in the whole country.

22. 北京大学

重点词语注释：

1. 北京大学 Peking University
2. 成立 establish/found
3. 原名 originally known as
4. 京师大学堂 the Imperial University of Peking
5. 中国近代史 China's modem history
6. 高等教育 higher education
7. 进步思想的中心 center for progressive thought
8. 中国新文化运动 China's New Culture Movement

9. 五四运动 May Fourth Movement
10. 重要事件 significant events
11. 高校排行榜 domestic university ranking
12. 顶尖大学 the top universities
13. 重视 attach importance to/lay emphasis on
14. 提高本科生教育和研究生教育质量 improve the undergraduate and graduate education
15. 领先研究机构 leading research institution
16. 做出很大努力 make great efforts
17. 以……而闻名 renowned for...
18. 校园环境 campus environment
19. 中国传统建筑 traditional Chinese architecture

参考译文：

22. Peking University

Originally known as the Imperial University of Peking, Peking University was established in 1898. The establishment of the University marked the beginning of higher education in China's modem history. In modem history of China it was a center for progressive thought and was influential in the birth of China's New Culture Movement, May Fourth Movement and many other significant events. Today, Peking University is listed by many domestic university rankings as one of the top universities in China. The university lays emphasis on both teaching, and scientific research. It has made great efforts to improve the undergraduate and graduate education, and maintain its role as a leading research institution. In addition, the University is especially renowned for its campus environment and the beauty of its traditional Chinese architecture.

23. 清华大学

重点词语注释：

1. 高等学府 institutions of higher learning

附 录
各单元翻译练习参考译文及解析

2. 改革开放 reform and opening
3. 研究生院 Graduate School
4. 继续教育学院 Continuing/Adult Education School
5. 为了适应 keep abreast with
6. 兴起 the upsurge of
7. 新技术革命 technical renovation
8. 不同学科间交叉综合 cross-disciplines and comprehensive research
9. 新趋势 the new trend
10. 系科设置结构 the structure of the departments and disciplines
11. 不断进行调整 have been constantly readjusted
12. 高技术及新兴系科专业 departments of hi-technology and new specialties
13. 理科 disciplines of science
14. 文科 liberal arts
15. 恢复 rehabilitate
16. 理学院 School of Science
17. 法学院 School of Law
18. 经济管理学院 School of Economics and Management
19. 人文学院 School of Humanities and Social Sciences
20. 信息科学技术学院 Information Science and Technology
21. （被）并入 be merged into
22. 美术学院 Academy of Arts and Design

参考译文：

23. Tsinghua University

Tsinghua University is one of the renowned institutions of higher learning in China. Since reform and opening in 1978, it set up its Graduate School in 1984 and then Continuing Education School in 1985. The curricula and the structure of the departments and disciplines have been constantly readjusted so as to keep abreast with the upsurge of the worldwide technical renovation, the development of modern science, the new trend of cross-disciplines and comprehensive research which emerges as a result of social progress. A number of departments of hi-technology and new specialties have been set up, and in addition to the newly established disciplines of science, economics and management, liberal arts, the university has rehabilitated School of Science and School of Law, established School of Economics and Management, School of Humanities and Social Sciences and School of Information Science and Technology. At the same time Academy of Arts and Design was merged into the university and School of Medicine was founded.

24. 中国菜

重点词语注释：

1. 中国菜 Chinese cuisine
2. 各地区各民族 diverse regions and ethnic groups of China
3. 各种菜肴 all kinds of dishes
4. 统称 a general term
5. 烹饪方式 cooking styles
6. 流派众多 a number of different genres
7. "八大菜系" Eight Cuisines
8. 风格各异 distinctive from one another
9. 调料 seasoning
10. 丰富多样 a rich variety of
11. 地方特色菜 different local special dishes
12. 强调 lay emphasis on
13. 色、香、味俱佳 the perfect combination of color, flavor, and taste
14. 中国饮食文化 Chinese cuisine culture
15. 博大精深 extensive and profound
16. 海内外 both at home and abroad
17. 享有盛誉 enjoy a high reputation

参考译文：

24. Chinese Cuisine

Chinese cuisine is a general term for all kinds of dishes from diverse regions and ethnic groups of China. It also refers to cooking styles originating from China. With a long history, Chinese cuisine has a number of different genres, the main representatives of which are "Eight Cuisines". Every cuisine is distinctive from one another due to the differences in climate, geography, history, cooking techniques and lifestyle. Chinese cuisine contains a rich variety of seasonings, which is one of main factors contributing to different local special dishes. Chinese cuisine lays emphasis on the perfect combination of color, flavor, and taste, and the soul of the dishes is taste. Chinese cuisine culture is extensive and profound, and Chinese cuisine, one of the Three World Cuisines, enjoys a high reputation both at home and abroad.

25. 北京烤鸭

重点词语注释：

1. 北京烤鸭 Beijing (roast) duck
2. 封建帝王时代 the imperial era
3. 流行 be popular
4. 国菜 national food specialty
5. 以……著称 known for...
6. 薄而脆的酥皮 the thin, crisp skin
7. 片鸭子 the dish serving sliced
8. 真实情形 authentic vision
9. 专门用于制作烤鸭的鸭子 ducks bred specially for the dish
10. 屠宰 slaughter
11. 用调料腌制 season
12. 焖炉或者挂炉 a closed or hung oven
13. 葱 scallion/green onion

14. 黄瓜 cucumber

15. 甜面酱 sweet bean sauce

16. 用薄饼卷着食用 be eaten with pancake

参考译文：

25. Peking Duck

Peking duck is a famous duck dish that has been popular since the imperial era in Beijing, and is now considered a national food specialty of China. The dish is known for the thin, crisp skin with authentic vision of the dish serving sliced in front of the diners by the cook. Ducks bred specially for the dish are slaughtered after 65 days and seasoned before being roasted in a closed or hung oven. The meat is usually eaten with pancakes, green onion, cucumber and sweet bean sauce.

26. 春节

重点词语注释：

1. 农历 the Chinese lunar calendar

2. 正月初一 the first day of the first lunar month

3. 春节 Spring Festival

4. 最重要的传统佳节 the most important traditional festival

5. 神州大地,举国欢庆 celebrate grandly and extensively across the country（适当省略）

6. 除夕之夜 the New Year's Eve

7. 年夜饭 feast dinner

8. 必不可少的程序 a must for

9. 围坐一张桌子一同分享佳肴 sit at one table（适当省略）

10. 人多的话兴许不止一张桌子 or more tables（适当省略）

11. 为没能赶回家的亲人留些座位 seats will be arranged for the absent members

12. 仿佛他们也在一起吃似的 as if they were also joining the dinner

13. 中央电视台的春节特别节目 the CCTV special program for Spring Festival

14. 接近尾声 near the end of

15. 家家户户 every family/all families without exception

16. 放鞭炮 set off firecrackers

17. 驱妖除魔 drive evils away

参考译文：

26. Spring Festival

Spring Festival, widely known as Chinese New Year in the west, falls on the first day of the first lunar month according to the Chinese lunar calendar. It is the most important traditional festival in China and is celebrated grandly and extensively across the country.

Feast dinner is a must for the whole family on the New Year's Eve, when all the family members sit at one or more tables. Dinner seats will be arranged for the absent members as if they were also joining the dinner. After dinner, they sit together waiting for the coming of the New Year, usually by watching the CCTV special program for Spring Festival. At midnight when it is near the end of the program, every family goes out to set off firecrackers, which is said to drive evils away.

27. 端午节

重点词语注释：

1. 公元前 BC（Before Christ）
2. 汨罗江 the Miluo River
3. 攻破了楚国的国都 conquer the Chu's capital
4. 怀着悲痛的心情 overwhelmed with grief and despair
5. 抱一块石头 with a large stone in arms
6. 投江自杀 drown oneself in the river
7. 那天正好是 the day happened to be
8. 农历五月五日 the fifth day of the fifth month in the Chinese lunar calendar
9. 非常热爱 have a great esteem and love for

10. 被鱼虾吃掉 be eaten up by fish and shrimps

11. 包好的粽子 pyramid-shaped glutinous dumplings wrapped in reed leaves

12. 给鱼虾吃 divert the fish and shrimps

13. 以后 since then

14. 家家户户 each household in China

15. 都包粽子，吃粽子 would make and eat rice dumplings

16. 表示纪念 commemorate

17. 传统节日 the traditional Chinese festival

18. 端午节 the Double Fifth Festival/the Dragon Boat Festival

参考译文：

27. The Dragon Boat Festival

In the year of 278 BC, when he was 62 and staying at the side of the Miluo River, Qu Yuan heard that Qin troops had finally conquered the Chu's capital. Overwhelmed with grief and despair, he drowned himself in the river, with a large stone in his arms. That day happened to be the fifth day of the fifth month in the Chinese lunar calendar.

The people of Chu had a great esteem and love for Qu Yuan. Filled with a deep sense of loss and worried that his body might be eaten up by fish and shrimps, they threw into the water pyramid-shaped glutinous dumplings wrapped in reed leaves to divert them. Since then, on the fifth day of the fifth lunar month every year, each household in China would make and eat rice dumplings to commemorate the great poet Qu Yuan. This is the traditional Chinese festival known as the Dragon Boat Festival.

28. 月饼的传说

重点词语注释：

1. 月饼 moon cake

2. 唐朝的神话故事 Tang Dynasty myth

3. 说的是 a myth holds that

附 录
各单元翻译练习参考译文及解析

4. 美丽的嫦娥 Chang'e, the beautiful wife of Hou Yi（适当增添）

5. 忍受不了 no longer tolerate

6. 暴行 outrages

7. 长生不老药 elixir

8. 从此就有了……传说 and thus began the legend of...

9. 嫦娥奔月 the Moon Fairy

10. 元朝 the Yuan Dynasty

11. 朱元璋领导的起义军 an insurrectionary army led by Zhu Yuanzhang

12. 用起义的方式 by rising in revolt

13. 摆脱蒙古族的统治 rid the country of Mongolian dominance

14. 传递情报 deliver information

15. 掰开月饼 when the cake was opened

16. 读到密信 secret message could be read

17. 发动起义 unleash an uprising

18. 赶走了元朝的统治者 rout the Mongolians

19. 发生在8月15日 happen at the time of the full moon（采用意译）

参考译文：

28. Two Legends about Moon Cake

There are two legends which claim to explain the tradition of eating moon cakes. One Tang Dynasty myth holds that Chang'e, the beautiful wife of Hou Yi, could no longer tolerate her husband's outrages so she stole his elixir and fled to the moon. And thus began the legend of the beautiful woman in the moon, the Moon Fairy.

The second legend has it that during the Yuan Dynasty, an insurrectionary army led by Zhu Yuanzhang was determined to rid the country of Mongolian dominance by rising in revolt. The moon cake was created to deliver information. When the cake was opened, a secret message could be read. The insurrectionary army unleashed an uprising by this means and successfully routed the Mongolians. It happened at the time of the full moon, which explains why moon cakes are eaten at this time.

29. 十八大

重点词语注释：

1. 十八大 18th CPC National Congress
2. 全面建成 complete the building...in all respects
3. 小康社会 a moderately prosperous society
4. 决定性阶段 the decisive stage
5. 主题 underlying theme
6. 高举伟大旗帜 hold high the great banner
7. 中国特色社会主义 socialism with Chinese characteristics
8. 邓小平理论 Deng Xiaoping Theory
9. "三个代表" Three Represents
10. 科学发展观 the Scientific Outlook on Development
11. 以……为指导 follow the guidance of...
12. 解放思想 free up the mind
13. 改革开放 implement the policy of reform and opening up
14. 凝聚力量 pool the strength
15. 攻坚克难 overcome all difficulties
16. 坚定不移前进 firmly march
17. 沿着……道路 on the path of...
18. 为……而奋斗 strive to...

参考译文：

29. The Eighteenth National Congress

The Eighteenth National Congress of CPC is one of great importance being held when China has entered the decisive stage of completing the building of a moderately prosperous society in all respects. The underlying theme of the congress is to hold high the great banner of socialism with Chinese characteristics, follow the guidance of Deng Xiaoping Theory, the important thought of Three Represents and the Scientific Outlook on Development, free up the mind, implement the policy of reform and opening up, pool our strength, overcome all difficulties, firmly march on the path of socialism with Chinese characteristics, and strive to complete the building of a moderately prosperous society in all respects.

30. 文化实力和竞争力

重点词语注释：

1. 实力和竞争力 the strength and international competitiveness
2. 国家富强 China's power and prosperity
3. 民族振兴 the renewal of the Chinese nation
4. 重要标志 an important indicator
5. 把……放在首位 with priority on...
6. 社会效益和经济效益 both social effect and economic benefits
7. 全面繁荣 all-around flourishing
8. 新闻出版 the press and publishing
9. 广播影视 radio, television and films
10. 文学艺术事业 literature and art
11. 重大公共文化工程和文化项目建设 major public cultural projects and programs
12. 完善公共文化服务体系 improve the public cultural service system
13. 提高服务效能 make services more efficient
14. 文化和科技融合 integration of culture with science and technology
15. 新型文化业态 new forms of cultural operations
16. 规模化 large in size
17. 集约化 specialized
18. 现代传播体系 modern communications network
19. 传播能力 capacity for communications
20. 增强活力 invigorate
21. 国有公益性文化单位 state-owned non-profit cultural institutions

22. 经营性文化单位 profit-oriented cultural entities
23. 法人治理结构 corporate governance
24. 繁荣文化市场 create a thriving cultural market

参考译文：

30. The Strength and International Competitiveness of Chinese Culture

The strength and international competitiveness of Chinese culture are an important indicator of China's power and prosperity and the renewal of the Chinese nation. We should promote rapid development and all-around flourishing of the cultural industry and cultural services and ensure both social effect and economic benefits, with priority on the former. We should develop philosophy and the social sciences, the press and publishing, radio, television and films, and literature and art. We should launch more major public cultural projects and programs, improve the public cultural service system, and make such services more efficient. We should promote integration of culture with science and technology, develop new forms of cultural operations, and make cultural operations larger in size and more specialized. We should develop a modern communications network to improve our capacity for communications. We should invigorate state-owned non-profit cultural institutions, improve corporate governance of profit-oriented cultural entities, and create a thriving cultural market.